BOSS
The Mike Bossy Story

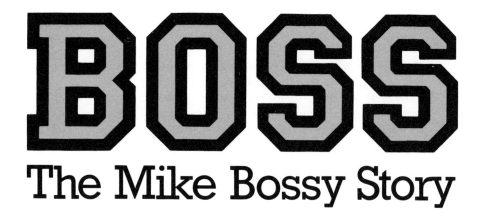

BOSS
The Mike Bossy Story

by Mike Bossy
and Barry Meisel

McGraw-Hill Ryerson
Toronto Montreal

BOSS: The Mike Bossy Story

First published in 1988 by
McGraw-Hill Ryerson Limited
330 Progress Avenue
Scarborough, Ontario, Canada M1P 2Z5

Care has been taken to trace the ownership of any
copyright material contained in this text. The publishers
welcome any information that will enable them to
rectify, in subsequent editions, any incorrect or omitted
reference or credit.

1 2 3 4 5 6 7 8 9 10 D 7 6 5 4 3 2 1 0 9 8

Canadian Cataloguing in Publication Data

Bossy, Mike.
  Boss

ISBN 0-07-549696-8

1. Bossy, Mike. 2. Hockey players — Canada —
Biography. I. Meisel, Barry. II. Title.

GV848.5.B6A3 1988   796.96′2′0924   C88-094883-3

Jacket and Book Design: Daniel Kewley

Jacket Photographs: Bruce Bennett

Printed and bound in Canada by John Deyell Company

To Dad: I wish you could have been here to see it all. To Mom: Thanks for all your help. To Lucie: I don't know what I would do without you.
To Josiane and Tanya: Daddy's almost home.

M.B.

For Mom, Dad and my favorite editor, Katy A.

B.P.M.

Contents

Foreword

I still can vividly recall the first time I saw Mike. It was in the fall of 1977, during the first week of training camp. Mike was stretched out on trainer Ron Waske's medical table at Racquet and Rink in Farmingdale, L.I., with one icepack on his eye and another on his shoulder. I walked into the room, introduced myself to him...and thought how our first-round draft choice looked pathetic just lying there.

Because his wife, Lucie, was back home in Montreal, I invited him home for dinner with my wife, Nickie, and me the next night. That meal sparked a bond that has grown and grown to what I like to call a great friendship.

I'm sure many people are aware of our togetherness on and off the ice. We've been roommates forever. We clicked immediately when we started playing together. We share many of the same interests —like money, how to save money, how to make more money.

We have the same sense of humor. Call it dry, witty, silly or weird, but our minds work exactly alike. There were hundreds of times when Mike or I cracked a joke nobody else even snickered at, and we'd look at each other and crack up. Mike has made a lot of people enjoy hockey because of his skill and his style. I'm one of those people and boy, has he made me laugh along the way.

Lighting my head on fire by striking a match too close to my head... turning himself loose in a country and western bar...the Ed Kea Exorcist play...Mike will tell you about all of them.

What can I say about the best goal scorer I've ever had the good fortune of playing with? I envy the way he sets goals and achieves them.

I envy how he stands up for himself and makes his points as diplomatically and frankly as possible.

He wanted to become the best offensive right wing in the league. He did. He wanted to become the first player in 36 years to score 50 goals in 50 games. He did. He wanted to speak out against fighting in the National Hockey League. He did. He thought he should have been the NHL's first-team All-Star right wing over Guy Lafleur in 1978–1979. He criticized the hockey writers for their sentimental selection.

Each time, he left himself vulnerable to criticism; but each time, he stood firmly behind his beliefs. No big deal, he said.

Scoring goals was what mattered to him most. He'd get mad at himself if he didn't produce in a game. Some teammates mistook him as an individual who didn't care about the team as long as he scored. But scoring was his motivator. He made me want to pass him the puck. He wanted the puck. I loved it because he mirrored me.

Often after games we'd lie awake in the dark and reflect. We'd analyze our performances, talk about stealing the good moves from the great opponents, make fun of bone-headed plays, second-guess Al Arbour and Bill Torrey. We must have traded everyone on the team at least once. We traded ourselves, too, when we weren't producing, but always in a "two-fer" deal. No sense breaking up a good thing, we thought.

It was great therapy.

If he doesn't play again, I'll miss knowing Boss is in prime scoring position. I'll miss knowing instinctively where to put the puck for him to finish a play and where to go for his passes. I'll miss his intentional humor and his unintentional humor. Most of all, I'll really miss the chemistry we've created, the energy we used to push and pull one another throughout our careers.

I want to thank Mike more than any one teammate for the role he's played in my career . . . on and off the ice. He's been responsible for a lot of the successes, the laughter, the fun and the memories we've shared as Islanders.

Thanks, Hawse. It's been an honor.

To the Bossy family, Mike, Lucie, Josiane and Tanya,

God Bless,

Bryan Trottier
June 1, 1988

Acknowledgements

We'd like to thank Islander publicity director Greg Bouris and publicity assistant Steve Blinn for their research assistance. Special thanks to Dorothy Bossy, Bob Shertzer and ten years of Bob's sixth-grade students at Dickinson Avenue School in East Northport, L.I., for compiling the scrapbooks that made our job so much easier. We'd also like to thank Denise Schon and Margaret Henderson of McGraw-Hill Ryerson. Thanks, too, to Frank Brown. We owe you one.

M.B. and B.P.M.

Chapter

1

The Beginning of the End

Figure-eights had always been an easy practice maneuver, so I was smiling, joking around, when the skating drill began. Three or four times around the Cantiague Park rink seemed effortless ... until I stopped and felt a burning sensation across the left side of my lower back. It was a stabbing pain I did not recognize.

What was that?

This was the first organized practice of training camp, the first day on ice of my tenth season as a New York Islander. September 13, 1986. We had a new head coach, Terry Simpson, who replaced Al Arbour, the only NHL coach I had ever played for. We had a new assistant coach, Bob Nystrom, who was my teammate since I broke into the league in 1977.

Moments into what I fully expected to by my tenth straight 50-goal season, this strange pain in my back reminded me of how much I dislike training camps, exhibition seasons, and everything prior to Opening Night.

"Wow," I thought to myself, trying to twist the kink out of my back without letting my teammates know I was in pain. "I'm a little rusty. A rest between drills and I'll be fine before we scrimmage."

I never was.

First they thought it was a muscle strain. Then they thought it was a degenerative disc. One doctor checked for nerve damage, another tested for cancer. The more they examined me, the less they claimed they knew. I still don't know exactly what's wrong with me and I don't know for sure if my back will ever get better. When I climb out of bed without feeling much pain, I call it a good day. I have days, though, when it's a chore just getting down the stairs.

My 1986–87 season was chiropractors and back surgeons, cross-checks I couldn't see and high sticks I couldn't avoid. It was acupuncture and magnetic resonancy imaging. It was X-rays and excruciating pain.

I wasn't healthy enough to take my place as the starting right wing for Team NHL at Rendez-Vous '87, the two-game series in Quebec City against the Soviet National Team that I had hoped would be my last international hockey competition.

It was a season of incredible frustration, the first time since my father laced my first pair of skates that my body refused to do what my head said I could. I was a 50-goal scorer in a five-goal scorer's body, and I couldn't handle that.

I hate being ordinary. I don't mean to sound brash, it's just that I've been fortunate throughout my career that my best had always been very good. This season it wasn't, and there was nothing I could do about it. That frustrated the hell out of me.

It was a season that prompted Bryan Trottier, my teammate, linemate, roommate, and close friend, to publicly speak out against the poor officiating that failed to protect the NHL's most talented players.

It was a season in which I missed being part of an incredible Stanley Cup playoff story, the Easter Epic, our four-overtime triumph in Washington that was the fifth-longest game in playoff history. I was forced to watch Pat LaFontaine win that game for us at 1:58 a.m. on April 19, 1987 — Easter Sunday morning — because earlier in the series I had suffered a sprained and slightly torn medial collateral ligament in my left knee.

Worst of all, it was a season in which I didn't score 50 goals, my personal gauge for success. It was a 38-goal season that snapped the NHL record I cherish most: nine consecutive 50-goal seasons.

It was a nightmare, the beginning of the end.

By sitting out the 1987–88 season in an attempt to rest and rehabilitate the back injury that a medical school of doctors have been unable to definitely diagnose, I realized I would have time to examine my career before it officially ended.

A few years ago, somebody asked me if I was interested in writing my autobiography. It was the first time I had thought about it. I decided that if I was going to write a book at all, I was going to write only one, and it would be after I retired. That book was supposed to have a happy ending. But reality got in the way.

Reality was my back: the aggravating 1986–87 season, the 1987–88 non-season.

I realized early last fall, three weeks after the October 5 press conference in which the Islanders announced that I would not play until my back was 100 percent, that not all stories have happy endings. I didn't know then if I was going to play again, but I knew the time was right to write, and I figured it would be an interesting way to keep busy since I couldn't play.

Frankly, I've had a lot to say over the years. I've never been afraid to tell the truth.

I love the game of hockey; always have, always will. It has made me famous and left my family financially secure for life. Because of hockey I have seen places I would not have otherwise seen, met people I would not have otherwise met, learned things I would not have otherwise learned.

I played with one of the greatest teams in the history of the National Hockey League: the 1980–83 Islanders. My name is on the Stanley Cup four times. I won the Calder Trophy in 1978, the Conn Smythe Trophy in 1982, the Lady Byng Trophy in 1983, 1984 and 1986. I was a first-team NHL all-star five times, a second-team all-star three times.

I'll be bitterly disappointed if I'm not inducted into the Hall of Fame in my first year of eligibility.

On March 10 of my lost season, the Islanders and their great fans choreographed one of the nicest moments of my life. I was touched by Mike Bossy Night because it showed me that people hadn't forgotten about me. I've always been touched by any positive fan reaction toward me. This year had been pretty lonely until then. It was nice to get out on the ice in front of the fans, even if I was in a tailored suit instead of my Number 22.

Because I'm a little insecure, I'm a perfectionist. I can't accept mediocrity from myself. I've always put pressure, often undue pressure, on myself to perform. When I was negotiating my first contract with the Islanders in 1977, I told general manager Bill Torrey that I deserved more money than he was offering because I was going to score a lot of goals for him that season.

"How many," he asked me.

"Fifty," I said.

The NHL record for a rookie was 44 ... until I scored 53.

Fifty goals, a career year for most players, became my measuring stick. I had to score 50 each season to satisfy my own demands. When I scored 53, 69 and 51 in my first three seasons I had to set my sights even higher. In 1980–81, I said I wanted to score 50 goals in our team's first 50 games because nobody had done that since Maurice 'Rocket' Richard for the Montreal Canadiens 36 years earlier.

The last ten games of that 50-in-50 run were torture: I received two anonymous death threats, was subjected to an incredible amount of media attention, and was the target of every opposing team.

I brought it all upon myself, I know. I never blamed anybody but myself. So I did what I had to do to keep from failing. I scored my 49th and 50th goals in the last five minutes of the third period of Game 50.

Being known as the National Hockey League's best player was a label I always wanted, but never got. I felt I was always one step from being recognized as the best. First there was Guy Lafleur, then Wayne Gretzky, even Trots. There were times, though, when I thought I was the best.

I never won the scoring title, something I wanted badly. I'm recognized as a great goal scorer, but I never felt I was recognized as a great player. That's bothered me for a long time. Maybe it's my fault, because I put such great emphasis on goals. But from the day I was drafted in 1977, 15th overall because the word from the scouts was I wasn't tough enough and I couldn't play defense, I vowed to prove that I was a complete player.

I'm satisfied that I did.

What is being tough? Is it not being afraid to punch somebody in the helmet? Is it hitting an opponent with your stick from behind? Or is it absorbing ten years of punishment in front of the net and answering only by scoring goals? I abhor violence in the NHL. Fighting is asinine. It just makes us look dumb. It's keeping the game from being taken seriously as another major sport in the United States. We are mocked by newspaper columnists, embarrassed by television sportscasters, ridiculed by fans.

And I can't say they're usually wrong.

My thoughts on violence have always been quite clear: Get rid of it.

Eliminate fighting and crack down on the illegal stickwork that has polluted the game. The men who run our sport naively believe that the fans want to see fights. Some do. In fact, many who fill our buildings do.

But most don't. And the ones who don't, stay home. They take their children to movies and baseball games instead of hockey games. They steer their kids to soccer and softball instead of hockey. There is a rich untapped resource in the United States, fans who think the game of ice hockey is neat. I saw the 1980 U.S. Olympic Hockey Team make potential fans out of people who didn't know a puck from a peanut.

And then they saw us.

I created quite a stir during my third pro season when I declared that I would not fight no matter how much physical abuse — legal and illegal — I took. "Each time you knock me down," I said to the game's goons, "I will get back up and score goals."

I was the first NHL player to publicly call for a ban on fighting, but I knew I didn't stand alone. While the stodgy traditionalists cried with outrage, a lot of players in the NHL who wanted to say what I said, but realized a shut mouth was safer than a fat lip, stood silently behind me.

I appreciated that, but I didn't care if I was the lone voice in the forest. It wasn't an easy decision to make, but rocking the boat never is. I just had to say what was on my mind.

Oh, did that cause me grief! You should have heard the disgusting taunts from the fans in Boston, Philadelphia, Detroit, not to mention intimidating sneers from the goons around the league.

Violence was worse in junior. During my four years playing major junior in Laval, Quebec, I realized that I would have to endure the punishment if I wanted to get to the NHL. Most of the time, I knew the price was one I wanted to pay. But if you had asked me that question after one of many nights on the road, after our team had been badly beaten and badly beaten up, I'm not sure how I would have answered.

You know what disappointed me the most? That after I finished my junior career with a broken nose, a lot of broken teeth and 309 goals, some scouts said I wasn't tough enough to play in the NHL. That sounded crazy to me, but I guess a lot of teams bought it. Twelve teams had the chance to select me in the first round of the 1977 draft. The New York Rangers and Toronto Maple Leafs passed on me twice before the Islanders chose me 15th overall.

They must have seen something the others didn't.

I'm very proud of the fact that as a junior I didn't join the zoo. I rarely got involved in the goonery, the raw violence that displayed a blatant lack of respect for another player. Sure there were times when I said enough was enough. Sure there were times I dropped my gloves, or raised my stick, or threw the odd elbow, but not without feeling sorry for it once the game was over.

I felt good about the way I played hockey and always thought that it may not be the way they wanted me to play, or it may not be the right way, but it was the way I was going to play.

I remember how many times my father said to me: "Don't put your head down near the boards." I remember how my times my mother left games scared, almost sick to her stomach, after watching another brawl in which I got physically abused on the ice.

You might want to say, "Come on, it wasn't that bad. Everybody goes through it."

You're right. Everybody goes through it.

But you're wrong: it was that bad.

My definition of violence in hockey is a hit with an intent to injure. I'm no dummy. I realize hockey is a physical sport and should be played that way. Some of the best games I've seen have been hard-hitting with body checks galore. Clean body checks.

One Montreal scout — I never did find out who he was — suggested the Canadiens not draft me because I never played well in Sherbrooke. Sherbrooke had a coach named Ghyslain Delage and a team that delighted in making sure I knew from the start that if I had too much success in their building, I'd regret it.

I heard threats regularly. "It's going to be a long night." "We're going to get you!" "You'd better keep your head up." "You're not going to finish the game!" And those threats were usually delivered face-to-face before a faceoff by an opponent whose only role was to make sure I either fought with him, became intimidated by him, or strayed from my game in order to keep an eye out for him.

That is my definition of a goon.

There were times I wondered: How come away from the rink people got arrested for what they were doing to me and others on the ice?

The only way the NHL can rid itself of violence is to severely punish players for their actions. And that's not being done. Take Dave Brown's horrible cross-check on Tomas Sandstrom at Madison Square Garden early last season. Obviously 15 games wasn't a heavy enough suspension because you still see those same fouls being committed. I don't know for certain, but I'd bet the Flyers paid his salary although the NHL suspended him without pay.

So did he learn anything? I doubt it.

I would have given Brown at least a 40-game suspension. And I would have incorporated some kind of severe team penalty or fine to ensure that the message was received.

I read in the newspaper recently that the Board of Governors will consider banning fighting soon. I'd love to see that happen, but if I had my choice, I'd like to see the intentional stick fouls, cross-checking and high-sticking dealt with first. I think they're more serious problems today. Players wear helmets and shields and think they're invincible. The ice has become a battlefield and they're all knights in heavy armor. Sticks come up more frequently than ever before, and it's no coincidence that facial injuries are on the rise.

I was talking to a referee last spring (I can't remember who it was) and he said to me, "Bryan's article helped, you know."

He was talking about Trots' guest column in *The Hockey News*. Trots, the president of the Players Association, caused quite a stir (and cost himself a $1,000 fine) by critiquing the state of officiating. The column forced the league to look at itself more closely. The officials were instructed to crack down on stick fouls, call games more closely, remain more consistent from period to period.

I'm happy to see the changes, but I was saying the same things for six years without writing an article about it and hardly anything was ever done. When Trots approached *The Hockey News* with the idea, it was after we had spent a lot of time talking about it. I helped him write the thing and many of the ideas were mine.

One of the biggest reasons I didn't want to get involved is because people would have said, "Oh, there goes Bossy again on violence." I was happy that Bryan decided to do it because I knew that Bryan saying and writing it would get more respect and prompt more action than if I had said it or written a column.

OK, Trots, I owe you $500.

If I was president of the NHL I would:

1. More closely police cross-checking, slashing, spearing and high-sticking by letting the linesmen call any stick infractions, deliberate or intentional. I don't think linesmen should be able to call all penalties, but it's too easy to get away with a cheap shot the way the game is played today. I would make *any* cross-checking, high-sticking or slashing penalty in which a player is hit from behind a major penalty. That would keep the sticks down.

2.   Ban fighting. If two guys fight, both are automatically out of the game. Give the instigator an extra major penalty. If one guy (usually a goon) starts with another (usually a more talented opponent), the guy being attacked can defend himself. He can grab his assailant, but he can't punch back. If he does, he's out. If he doesn't, no penalty on him.

3.   Stiffen suspensions. Three major stick fouls in a season earn a one-game suspension. Two games for the next one, four the next time, and so on. Ours is a league where a five-game suspension is a large one. Make ten games the minimum for a serious incident. Suspend the cheap-shot artists for 20, 40, 50 games.

If you started handing out penalties like these, the goons would get rid of themselves. There just wouldn't be a place for them anymore. NHL teams would have no reason to employ fighters, which means that junior-league teams would have no reason to encourage players to play that way. And that would trickle down to the midgets, bantams, pee-wees and mosquitos.

And one day, kids would grow up simply playing hockey.

Chapter

2

Skating Through Childhood

When I was two months old, Dad figured he had waited long enough. He reached into my crib without waking me and softly slipped a miniature plastic hockey stick into my hands. The stick wasn't a Titan, it wasn't taped and it wasn't curved. But it fit. And according to The Bossy Family Story, that was the day I became hooked.

Michael Dean Bossy, the sixth of ten children and the fifth of six boys, born January 22, 1957, in a north end neighborhood of Montreal called Ahuntsic, was going to be a professional hockey player. My father, Borden, who desperately wanted that for all of his sons, was sure of it. My mother, Dorothy, who still sends Gordie Howe a birthday card every year, heartily approved of it.

Being two months old, I didn't seem to mind.

At a very young age, before I turned ten years old, I envisioned playing in the NHL. This didn't just come to me one day when I had nothing else to think about. There was no frozen moment when I looked to the sky and saw myself in an NHL jersey. I simply grew up thinking that, ultimately, playing in the NHL was how I was going to make a living. To me it was just a natural progression. It felt right. There would be pee-wee, bantam, midget, junior and then I was going to be drafted into the NHL.

My parents never sat me down and said, "Michael, you're going to play in the NHL one day, so you had better start preparing for it now." It was just something I knew was going to happen. I know that sounds spooky and I can't explain how I was made to feel that way. I just did.

I guess the odds against me becoming a National Hockey League player weren't that great considering I had a rink in the backyard from the day I was born, skates on my feet from the time I was three, and a puck on my stick day and night.

My parents saw to that.

My mother, who rarely takes the gold and diamond-studded '22' off her neck and loves wearing Islander sweatshirts around the house, was born and raised in Ettington, England, six miles from William Shakespeare's birthplace in Stratford-on-Avon.

My father, who died two days after we beat the Minnesota North Stars in 1981 for our second straight Cup, was born in Russia, in the Ukraine.

They met in Ettington in January 1943, during World War II. He had enlisted in the Royal Air Force and was stationed in a little village called Wellebourne. They were married in August 1943, but they didn't settle in Montreal until after the war. Dad returned to Canada in 1945, but Mom, because she was a war bride, had to wait until May 1946. They settled in Grimsby, Ontario, on my grandparents' farm and soon after moved to Ahuntsic. My mother began raising a family and my father began a 30-year career as a draftsman, designing pulp and paper machinery.

Dad had emigrated to Saskatchewan as a young child with my grandparents, Walter and Marie Bossy. Our family name was originally Bosse, which means "barefoot" in Ukranian. My ancestors pronounced it Baw-SEE, much like the way my name is pronounced by those who think I'm French-Canadian.

I'm not. The Bossys were one of the only English-speaking families on Meunier St. in Ahuntsic, a middle class neighborhood of two- and three-family houses. Although my family lived on St. Urbain St. when I was born, I grew up at 10335 Meunier St., in the 4 1/2-room basement apartment of a three-family split-level: two bedrooms, a kitchen, a living room, a bathroom and an alcove that was more a large walk-in closet than a small bedroom.

How did two parents and ten kids share two bedrooms? We didn't. All 12 of us never lived together. Vivian, my oldest sister and my parents' only daughter for 15 years, was out of the house before my youngest brother Gordon (we call him Gordie) was born in 1965. Rodney and Patrick played junior hockey in Halifax for a farm team of the Montreal Jr. Canadiens coached by one of my uncles, so they were out of the house by the time they turned 16.

It's not easy having nine siblings. It strains the memory. Let's see: Vivian turns 44 in January. Rodney is 42, Donald turns 41 in February and Patrick will be 39 in March. Christopher is 36, I'll be 32 in January and Pamela will be 29 in March. The twins, Connie and Carol, are 26. Gordie, named after Mom's second favorite right wing, will be 23 in December.

I'm sorry to say we're not very close. I haven't spent very much time with any of my brothers or sisters since I left home to turn pro with the Islanders. I haven't seen Vivian, who lives in Halifax, since my Dad died. In fact, I've only seen her twice in 15 years.

When we lost touch in the late '70s, we started to forget who the other was. By 1981, we just didn't know each other anymore.

Playing in New York kept me distanced from them, and not just geographically. I don't believe any of my siblings was ever jealous of my success, but for a long time I felt they were intimidated by my fame. I believed that they thought that when I turned pro, I became another person, that I suddenly was above them.

That bothered me for a while, but we never discussed it openly until when we assembled to mourn my Dad's death. I think his death struck a nerve in all of us, taught us all how important family is. I know it made me realize how much I wanted and needed my family to be a major part of my life. Once I retire and move back to Montreal, I'm going to make sure my relationships with all my siblings improve. I'll have the time.

We really never got to know one another when I was young. By the time I was old enough to participate in an intelligent conversation at the dinner table or around the house, Vivian and Roddy were already in college and Don, Pat and Chris, who were born slightly more than four years apart, were five to nine years older than me.

I was the start of the second half of the family, and not just because I'm the sixth of ten. My parents had Vivian, Roddy, Don, Pat and Chris within 7 1/2 years, then waited 4 1/2 more years before they had me. They probably just took a break. Knowing my family, they needed a second wind.

My mother was always pro-kids. She was extremely protective of her children, very caring, very nervous, always taking our side of any story against whomever was trying to convince her we weren't telling the truth.

I was quite close to my father while I was growing up because he was always there to drive me to and from practices and games. But as far as sitting down and having deep conversations, we weren't close. He was not a complicated man.

Although I knew he wanted it for me more than anything in the world, not once did he ever say I *had* to become a hockey player. He wanted Roddy to become a hockey player, but Roddy's NHL career never got farther than a brief tryout with the California Golden Seals. He wanted Don to become a hockey player, but Don hurt his shoulder pretty badly in Junior B. Pat got as far as Junior A and Dad was always there for him, too.

He never had to tell me how much it meant to him. Everything he did for me, the ways that he reacted to whatever happened to me, told me how badly he wanted me to play in the National Hockey League.

In early June 1969, when I was 12 years old and in the seventh grade, I fractured my right kneecap during a track and field tournament called the Olympics. It happened just before Robert Kennedy was assassinated. I went to do a running broad jump, but as soon as I planted my two feet after my running approach, my knee gave out. I never got into the air. I just crumpled from my crouched position to the ground.

The kneecap didn't break through my skin, but I almost went into shock seeing the gap in my knee. I don't remember the pain, but I vividly recall being in the hospital, in a wheelchair, with my mother next to me.

"We're going to have to operate," the doctor said.

I nearly fainted. I grew hot and sweaty and nauseous.

But my reaction was nothing compared to my Dad's. When he first heard what had happened, he had a fit. Here I was, still playing pee-wee hockey, and he thought my NHL career was over. He was scared, frustrated and angry. He didn't know who to be mad at, so he yelled at us all summer, bickered with my older brothers like he never had before, and treated me like I was crippled for life.

"It's just a broken knee," I remember Pat screaming at him. "It'll heal. Stop babying him."

Not only wasn't it the end of my career, it wasn't even the end of my summer. This was probably one of the stupidest things I did as a kid, but I figured out a way to play a whole month of baseball with the cast and without my parents finding out.

I became a catcher. I used my ankle-to-thigh plaster cast to prop myself up in a semi-squatting position. I wasn't very mobile, but boy, did I block a lot of curveballs in the dirt! Batting wasn't too tough, except it was tough hitting for power with only one leg to stand on. At first somebody ran for me, but after a while I got pretty quick on my crutches. I developed a hop-step that forced me to put weight on my bad leg.

In a week, my cast was a mess.

I guess it's safe to say I didn't let my knee heal properly. To this day I don't know what the surgeons did, although it feels like they didn't do a very good job. My kneecap still floats around the joint, grinding bone on bone. And it's uneven. At least one doctor has wondered if the bad knee is the source of my back pain.

It's also safe to say now that, although I thought I was playing ball behind my parents' backs, they must have suspected what I was up to. How couldn't they, considering my cast looked like a wet newspaper wrapped around my leg? If that was why my Dad was so upset all summer, he never said anything to me.

Mom handled my injury well, and I never could blame Dad for getting so emotional over it. They were just so unbelievably supportive and unselfish when it came to my hockey. It meant so much to them. Whether it was practice at an outdoor rink at night or games in horrible weather, they were always there for me.

In our cramped quarters, everyone was always everywhere. Vivian slept in the living room on a sofabed. My parents shared the master bedroom. The other bedroom was the boys' room: Roddy, Don, Pat and Chris on two sets of bunkbeds. I started in a crib in my parents' room and didn't move into the boys' room until after Roddy moved out. The alcove, which was simply a slice of space cut into the wall off the hallway linking the living room to the bedrooms, was my first bedroom. It was big enough to fit a single bed and two dirty socks on the floor, provided the socks were one on top of the other.

By the time Connie and Carol were born, I was in the boys' room and their crib was wedged into the alcove. Pat was in junior by the time Gordie was ready for one of the bunkbeds.

Our kitchen fit one table with four chairs. In most households kids are taught that it isn't polite to leave the table until everyone is finished eating. At my house the first kid to leave the table was a hero, because he was making room for the next starving, screaming, eating machine. When we all sat down for dinner together, the meal was served in shifts. Some of us started in the kitchen, some of us started in the living room.

Sharing one bathroom? Don't ask.

We weren't poor. We ate sufficiently, but not extravagantly. We always wore clean clothes, we just never were able to afford anything special. It didn't bother me when I was young because I didn't know any differently.

I only went to two NHL games before I turned pro. Roger Bolduc, the father of one of my teammates, got us two tickets to see the Canadiens play the Rangers at the Forum during the 1970–71 season. I remember the year because I was playing Bantam AA hockey that season and I missed an outdoor practice to go to the game with my Mom.

Montreal vs. Boston a few years later was the only other NHL game I saw live. I don't know why I didn't go to more games, especially because Eddy Palchak, the Canadiens' longtime equipment manager, is my cousin. Eddy's parents owned a restaurant not too far from our house and Mom used to work there. They had this great five-cent pinball machine I loved playing. A baseball pinball game. That pinball machine and my aunt's french fries were why I rarely said no to a trip to the restaurant. I've always loved french fries. I still do.

Pinball, french fries and candy bars were all special treats growing up because I rarely had the money to buy them. I never bought hockey cards, either. Virtually every nickel I ever got went to candy bars or Fudgsicles, my favorite snack as a kid. Whenever I got a quarter around the house I went right to the corner five and dime store and bought five Fudgsicles.

Wednesday and Saturday nights were *Hockey Night in Canada.* From the time I was eight I bargained to stay up late to watch. Dad probably considered it part of my education, because he rarely waved me off to bed. Maybe he thought I'd have a better chance of becoming a National Leaguer by osmosis, as the TV's rays seeped into my skin.

If that was true, then I guess it's a good thing Tiger Williams wasn't playing then. I might have decided to become a truck driver.

We usually got to watch the Toronto Maple Leafs play on Wednesday and the Canadiens on Saturday. Pat was a big Maple Leafs fan, a big Bob Pulford fan. I never really had a favorite player. I never pretended I was anybody when I played and I never idolized anybody when I watched.

I always cheered against the Canadiens. I thought the 1970 Stanley Cup finals between Boston and St. Louis, the series that ended with

Bobby Orr's famous flying overtime goal, was boring because the Canadiens weren't in it and there was nobody to cheer against. Knowing how I am now, I probably rooted against them because they were so damn good. I root for the underdog all the time.

Well, most of the time. I never rooted against the Islanders in the 1980s.

We rooted for the Rangers or Bruins or Blackhawks when they played the Habs and Toronto when they played anybody but Detroit. Nobody ever rooted against the Red Wings, not with Mom and Gordie Howe on the same earth. If I had ever said a bad word about her idol, God knows if I would have ever seen a Fudgsicle or a french fry again.

Detroit, by default, was my favorite team. Howe, because my Mom loved him so, was my favorite player. But it's not like I ever tacked a poster of him to my wall. In our tiny apartment, none of us ever had his own wall.

I loved Christmas. I still do. Our tree took up half the living room and there were tons of gifts piled around it. When I was old enough to understand, I wondered how my parents got the money to make our holiday so special. That's when I learned what the words "borrow" and "owe" really meant.

It must have been well worth it for my parents, because they outdid themselves every year. The ritual was always the same. After putting us to bed at nine o'clock, Santa Claus (played by Dad or a friend of his named Mr. Messett) arrived at ten o'clock and knocked on our bedroom window. Out we spilled, piling into the living room.

Opening our gifts was a major production. Each kid had to unwrap his present, show it to everybody, and have his picture taken. As a kid it was torture. We just wanted to tear every gift open in five seconds.

Christmas was big, but our summers together at the Cartierville Boating Club, on the Riviere de Prairie, brought us closer than any holiday or any other family activity. My parents ran the private club's snack bar during the middle and late 1960s, and we kids were there virtually every day.

Although I never found it that exciting, the family loved to canoe. We didn't go white-water rafting or anything like that, just paddle canoeing. Don once competed at the Pan-American Games in the sport. My brothers were terrific canoeists. They were just as good in the water as they were on the ice.

I was always trouble around water, even when I was two years old. Dad used to cut our hair on the beach in Plattsburgh, N.Y. This one day everybody seemed to be preoccupied by the haircuts. I was bored. When it came to my turn, I wasn't around. Mom was petrified. It took Pat and Chris more than a half-hour to find me. I was just roaming around, unconcerned.

Summer weekends were great. I loved the ride to Plattsburgh because at the halfway point of the trip down, we stopped for what my folks called Grab Bag. Each of us got to spend 25 cents on sugar. When I was seven or eight, I got a heck of a lot of stuff for a quarter. Fudgsicles, bubble gum, candy bars, other junk. That was my favorite part of the trip.

On most Friday nights, we piled into the first family car I can remember, a green '57 Chevy. We drove until we reached Plattsburgh or Champlain, N.Y., for a night at the drive-in theater. We loved movies. The only movie I ever remember seeing out of the windshield of our '57 Chevy was *To Sir With Love*. I usually watch it whenever it's on TV because it rekindles fond memories.

Roddy and Don could tell you about an old station wagon we had. My Dad had to lay plywood boards on the floor to patch gaping holes and the doors didn't work. They had to be locked shut by chains roped inside the car. When we finally got a new car, a light blue '62 Chevy, it was a new old car.

Dad was such an excellent mechanic that he never felt he needed a new car. I guess he figured there were more important ways to spend the little money we had. His first new car was a 1980 or '81 AMC Spirit, which I helped him buy with my 1980 Stanley Cup winnings.

Another of Dad's hobbies was mice. He kept his mouse farm in a glass tank. He loved to play with them and pet them, but one day two of them wriggled free. When they broke loose, hell broke out. They crawled into the sofa and Dad had to cut away pieces of the sofa to retrieve them. The mice were eventually evicted.

My father wasn't just into cars and mice, he was into sports. He was a terrific baseball player and an excellent hockey player when he was young. He always believed that had he not enlisted in the Royal Air Force for World War II, he would have had a shot at playing professional baseball.

Once his dream died, ours was born.

Dad built our first backyard rink before I was born, behind the apartment on St. Urbain St. My mother has a picture dated January 1956 of Dad skating with Roddy, Don, Pat and Chris, all dressed in Canadiens sweaters.

When I was three years old, my father noticed that I was big for a toddler. So he figured he'd start training me immediately. He fitted me with a pair of skates and walked me up and down, up and down the hallway.

"We've got to develop his ankles," he told my mother.

"Just keep walking," he told me.

My family moved from St. Urbain St. during the summer of 1959. My Meunier St. backyard rink debut came during the winter of 1960. We have pictures of me on the ice in April 1960, handling a stick not much larger than a toothbrush, cradling a puck that, on my blade, looks like a spare tire. In one snapshot from the family album, Chris and I are preparing to face off. Pam, who was one month old, is between us sitting in a sled. Could we have been waiting for her to drop the puck? Who knows?

This rink was not Nassau Coliseum. Since our backyard was tiny, all Dad had to do once he laid the ice was line the chain-link fence with a mish-mash of slabs of wood. Those were our boards. Some were knee high, some were ankle high. One corner of the rink didn't even connect at a right angle.

Dad made pretty good ice. After the first significant snowstorm of the season, he packed down the snow and flooded the backyard. Our landlord occasionally complained of the mess Dad made of the grass, but that never stopped him. Dad flooded and flooded and flooded the backyard until he built a nice, thick sheet of ice. Some years it was even smooth. One of my most vivid memories as a very young kid was getting up in the morning during the winter and seeing Dad already up and watering the rink.

Dad even strung some lights out back so we were able to play after sundown. After one of my first few years with the Islanders, during one off-season, I drove back to Ahuntsic to take a look at the ol' pond. Only it was just another lawn-green backyard, a sliver of land. I couldn't believe how small that backyard was, that I once skated there fully convinced it was the Forum.

I ran into a neighbor who told me that he remembered hearing the incessant BOOM...BOOM...BOOM of the pucks smashing into the boards on a cold, clear night. When you're young you never think of those things, but my neighbor got me to stop and consider what I must have sounded like at night, when folks were trying to relax at home, eat dinner, or watch television.

I must have driven people crazy.

At the time, though, it was all I ever wanted to do. Every day was the same: I came home from school, dropped my books in the house, grabbed a stick, and — if there was nobody to play a game with — started shooting. Against the high boards, against the low boards. Shoot, shoot, shoot. It never felt like I was practicing and nobody ever had to push me outside to do it. I loved it.

When I shot by myself, I used real pucks. I hated losing pucks in the mounds of snow piled high behind the boards, because that would mean spending 20 minutes, or what seemed like 20 minutes, looking for a puck. All I did was waste my ice time.

I cherished my ice time. Even today that backyard rink stands out so clearly in my mind. Every bump in the ice, every rag-tag board, the time I broke our window. . . .

It was a Saturday. Mom was working at Aunt Sophie's restaurant, Dad was puttering around the apartment.

I went out like I often did, in boots, by myself, to shoot pucks against the tall boards. BOOM ... BOOM ... BOOM. It was nice out, but this was one of those chilly days. I'm sure they heard me shooting three streets over.

I got bored shooting at the tall boards. It wasn't hard enough. I needed a challenge. So I turned around and began shooting at one of the lowest boards, the six-inch barrier that separated the rink from the door leading down to our apartment. "This will be a challenge," I thought to myself. "Lift the puck off the ice just a little, but make sure it doesn't sail out of the rink and slam into the door. Make sure it hits the small boards."

I teed up my first shot. It was headed exactly where I wanted it to go ... until it hit a ripple on the ice. Now it was launched. It flew over the short boards and crashed into the window.

Oh, was that a horrible sound. Hearing it, I panicked. I did what any guilt-ridden 12-year-old kid would have done.

I threw my stick down and ran.

I raced out of the backyard, past the shrubs that separated our building from the next, and down the street. I saw nobody, so I figured that nobody had seen me.

That's when I stopped. "Why am I running? It's my house." So I marched back into the backyard and there was my father, standing silently. He knew I was the only one out there.

He didn't smack me. I wasn't even in trouble. What I had forgotten when I heard the glass break was the unwritten rule my Dad had set for Roddy, Don, Pat and Chris: If that window ever breaks, it had better be broken by a puck and not a rock or somebody's head.

Dad just disconnected the door from its hinges, grabbed one end of it, ordered me to grab the other end, and led me two or three blocks to the hardware store to have the window replaced. Once I realized I wasn't going to get punished, I felt a little like a folk hero, the bandit who knows he's done something wrong and gets away with it.

I got spanked here and there, but I didn't get punished too often. After Vivian, Rodney, Don, Pat and Chris, I guess my parents had just gotten tired of banging us around. Either that or I was a model kid. Take your pick.

I was, however, no angel in Pat's and Chris's eyes. They killed me all the time. If it wasn't shooting pucks at me outside or swatting tennis balls at me in the house, it was slamming me around simply because they believed older brothers are supposed to bully their younger brothers.

"We just want to make you tough," Pat would say whenever he beat on me.

"Mommeeeee," I'd scream. I'll never be able to forget crying for help because whenever I talk to Pat, he reminds me of the way I used to whine. Even today. *Especially* today.

We used to have games in the backyard all the time, Pat, Chris and I. That was the most fun I ever had growing up, playing a game in the backyard rink with my brothers. We weren't on skates, just in our boots. And I was usually the goalie.

Pat and Chris were sadistic. Even when I was just seven years old, they took me and stuck me in goal with no protective equipment anywhere (if you know what I mean). Even when we used pucks made of spongy rubber, in the freezing cold they hurt. My brothers didn't care. They just laughed. I must have vowed never to play again at least a thousand times. And every time they called my bluff, so I positioned myself in front of one of the boards and braced myself for another round of punishment. Pat and Chris were totally unlike Roddy, Don and I. They were pugnacious guys who loved to fight and stir up trouble. We tried to avoid it.

I loved playing goalie more than forward when I was six or seven. Whenever it was too cold to play outside, which wasn't too often, and during the spring and summer months when there was no rink out back, we played in the apartment. Our room was the rink. We played on our knees, using our hands as sticks. We swatted tennis balls at our desk, which was our net. The walls of our room were dotted with holes punched by flying tennis balls. Mom would yell at us whenever somebody took a particularly loud blast against the wall. It was a small rink, what with the size of the room and the bunk beds on either side. We used the desk as one goal and the doorway as the other.

We never had a net in the backyard, just the boards to shoot at. The only nets I ever saw growing up were the ones in organized games. Whenever we played in the street, two piles of snow made up each net. That's when I started taking my sharp-angle shots. And that's when I learned how to cheat. My shots never smacked through the snow as if they were hitting goalposts. They always grazed the snow as if to ricochet in. At least that's what I used to tell my brothers.

If my Mom wanted me home for dinner, she'd poke her head out back. If I wasn't there, she knew where to look next. Down at St. Andre Apostle Park on the far corner of my block. It was a full-sized rink open to the public, with lights. If I got home from school and didn't feel like shooting by myself, I flung my skates over my shoulder and ran to the park.

Tons of kids used to show up every day. Ten-year-olds, 20-year-olds, anyone with a stick and skates was welcome. We chose up sides, 20 to a side, and just played. These games didn't satisfy my need to shoot the puck because there were no goalies so you weren't allowed to lift the puck.

It was a great way to improve my skating, though, because after the sides were chosen, there was always a bunch of kids who either came too late to be included or didn't want to play. They stayed out on the ice during the games, shooting pucks against the boards and trying to stay out of the way.

It was complete bedlam.

The park had a full-sized rink for hockey and a full-sized rink for figure skating. Virtually every day in the middle of the winter, when it was brutally cold, I came home with frozen feet, probably one degree from frostbite, because I played too long. I cried to Mom as I soaked my feet in cold water, vowing never to play again.

And I was back out there the next afternoon, not quitting until my toes felt brittle and numb again.

During the winter I played as much soccer as I did hockey. We played soccer on the snow. It wasn't the soccer I liked, it was the competition. If it wasn't soccer, it was dodgeball. If it wasn't dodgeball, it was baseball.

As a boy, hockey was the only organized sport I was disciplined enough to stick to. I didn't mind canoeing for the heck of it, but once it became organized I didn't like it. Baseball, same thing. I loved playing baseball in the schoolyard after school and during recess. But although I was a very good player, I hated playing team baseball.

One summer I was on a team and I pitched. I had this side-armed curveball. For three innings I was great; they couldn't touch me. Then one inning they saw it coming and killed me. I quit pitching after that game.

I guess I was easily distracted because I knew I wasn't the best. If I couldn't be the best, or if I wasn't totally enamored with what I was doing, I didn't want to do it.

Although I quit school after tenth grade to concentrate on hockey, I liked going to class when I was young. My school, which was one block from my house, was called St. Rita's annex. There were enough English-speaking Quebecois in my neighborhood for them to build an annex to the French-speaking elementary school a few blocks away.

Oh, did I have fun at that little school on Meunier St. I remember my fourth-grade teacher Mrs. DiMichele, as well as Mrs. Martin in fifth grade, and Mrs. Sheasgreen in sixth. In seventh grade I had Mr. Simcoe, the biggest man I ever saw until I went into one of my first NHL corners and met Bob Dailey of the Philadelphia Flyers.

What a cast of characters we had. I was the jock. Johnny Mancini was my best friend. Peter Gerlick was the brain. Denis Simard and his sidekick Dennis Robitaille were the bullies. Donna Dextras was the best-looking girl in the class. Lisa Spino was the richest. Since we were the only class in our grade we stayed together for years.

Our dodgeball games were vicious. I once threw a ball that would have been chest-high had it not hit the smallest girl in our class, Virginia Paupelain. It hit her right in the head. TKO. For a while I was a hero with the boys and Public Enemy Number One with the girls.

I was an excellent student who maintained a high B average and didn't particularly dislike any subject. I loved math because adding and subtracting always came easy to me, but I lived for recess.

I hung out with two sets of friends: my schoolmates and my hockey teammates. Although I went to school a block from my house, I played youth hockey seven or eight miles away, for St. Alphonse parish. I joined St. Alphonse because my Dad, a few years earlier, had a falling out with the Ahuntsic team in the league he helped organize. St. Alphonse was the next closest team we could find.

I was the only English-speaking kid who played for St. Alphonse and I never saw any of these kids away from practice or games. I was perfectly happy, though. My parents drove me to every practice and game, the competition was excellent, and I kept scoring goals.

According to Mom, my first official statistician, I scored 23 goals and 0 assists in my first organized Tom Thumb game, when I was five years old. Years later, when she told this story at some party, I asked her why I didn't pick up any assists.

"Nobody else ever touched the puck," she said.

The Islanders' Quebec scout who coached me one season in Pee-Wee, the late Henry Saraceno, followed my entire amateur career very closely, and was instrumental in convincing the Islanders to draft me. He claimed I scored 170 goals one season. I laugh at the exaggeration, but that "fact" is in the Islanders' 1978-79 media guide.

My natural ability made it feel like I wasn't doing anything extraordinary. I never felt there was any reason for anybody to make a fuss over me. Mom remembers thinking that the other parents were a bit jealous, but what did I know? I was just a kid having fun with a lot of other kids, none of whom spoke a language I understood.

So I just kept speaking my favorite language. I just kept shooting and scoring goals.

I remember in pee-wees, when I was 11 or 12 years old, playing against this big guy, Michel Giguiere of St. Michel. He was always hitting everybody on our team. I skated across the ice early one game and absolutely nailed him. Pat and Chris weren't there, but if they were they would have either fainted from shock or gone wild with joy. I remember today how big a rush that hit was for me then.

That was my first bodycheck. If I thought long enough I probably could remember my other three.

My first taste of team discipline came in bantam, the day Mr. Bolduc gave me two tickets to see the Canadiens. I skipped St. Alphonse's outdoor practice to go to the game. Since we very rarely practiced outside, my teammates assumed that I skipped practice because I didn't like playing outside. Anyone from my neighborhood would have known that was ridiculous, but these kids who only saw me at games or indoor practices had no idea how many times I had crawled home numb.

Mr. Bolduc's son was no help. He was on the team and he knew that his father had given me two tickets, but he didn't say anything to my coach. When our next game began, I found out my coach was madder than my teammates. We played two 25-minute periods back then, and I was benched for the entire first period.

I was furious. So were Dad and Chris. They left their seats at least twice that period, walked right up behind our bench and vented their frustration. I'm sure our coach heard them, because when the second period began, I was on the ice.

I won a bunch of trophies during my minor hockey career, but I received my first major award on September 12, 1969. Twelve provincial youngsters (Real Cloutier and Andre Savard were two others who reached the NHL) were luncheon guests of the Canadiens as part of a program recognizing our induction to the Minor Hockey Hall of Fame. Jacques Lemaire presented us with plaques.

Three months later, just before my 13th birthday, I took my first trip away from home. St. Alphonse was one of two provincial finalists from the 1969–70 season (a team named Arvida was the other) and we were invited to a four-team tournament in France from December 18 to January 7.

Dad wasn't too keen on the idea of me going, but he lost the argument to Roddy, Don, Pat, Chris, Mom and myself. All of my expenses were paid, but I was expected to dress well for the three-week trip. I guess Dad was embarrassed that I needed clothes that I didn't own and we couldn't afford. With the help of my teammates' families, I managed to pack a presentable suitcase.

I had a great time. During the overseas flight each player was given an orange journal and told to record his thoughts and experiences. Here are mine, spelling mistakes and all:

December 19, 1969.
Visited radio station. Alain was sick the day before. We played that night and in total with Arvida we won 9-0. We got 5 goals and they got 4. I scored after about 4 minutes. After that I got hurt (my knee) and was unable to play the rest of the game.
Final score
Canada 9
France 0

December 20, 1969
We visited the Eifel tower. It took us along time to get there since it was on the other side of the city. I bought a small souvenir book worth 12 franks ($2.40). After that we had a reception at the arena with the mayor but we did nothing. By then we were starving and we couldn't find a place to eat. Finally we found one and ate chicken. We were supposed to play tonight, but Arvida played instead (the worst teams first). The final score
Arvida 5
France 3

December 21, 1969.

We had a good day, but we were all mixed up in the morning. After that we finally got settled we went skating and had a lot of fun. When we were finished skating we went swimming in a heated pool and we had lots of fun. After that we arranged our bags to please our coach. We played that night at 8:00 p.m. I was thinking of my friends at school. We won 14–1 and I scored 7 goals. We went to a restaurant after that and ate steak and french fries.

Final Score
St. Alphonse 14
France 1

December 22, 1969

We got up in the morning and headed for the train station where we were to take a train to Lyon. It was boring in the train. After we got to Lyon we were taken to a restaurant Midi-Minuit and the meal was good. Then we played against the French and tied 0–0. Then against Arvida and lost 3–1. I didn't score at all. Then we were placed in sort of a hotel and all my roommates were changed because they were fooling around.

December 23, 1969

We had fun today. We played a little exhibition game and won 2–1. I scored a goal.

Final score
St. Alphonse 2
C.P.L. 1

Christmas.

We had the morning and afternoon to ourselves until 4:00. I got up late in the morning because I was tired. After I got up I received a gift, a book. Then we went to the rink. We skated for about half-an-hour. Then we played and won 8–0. I scored four goals.

I guess I got bored of writing because I only completed one more day of my journal:

December 31, 1969

We had a lot of fun. We met a girl. She was nice. After that we played bowling. I finished 3rd. After that we watched Arvida play. They won 8–0.

The summer of 1970 was the idiotic stage of my adolescence. Puberty had arrived and I just acted like a punk. The family had switched from the Cartierville to the Lachine Boat Club, but we weren't nearly as involved together. I spent that entire summer hanging out with a kid named Brian Nimijean and trying to act cool. I walked around barefoot trying to act tough. I thought I was baaaaad, a bad dude. I didn't smoke or drink, but I was abusive to my friends. I remember pushing Johnny Mancini around.

Anyway, since I was now Bad Boss, Muscles Michael, nobody was going to push me around. So the next time the neighborhood bullies Simard and Robitaille started trouble, I was ready. It was after school, and those two jerks were up to their tricks, taunting and shoving people around.

Trying to be strategic, I waited until I was a half-block from my house until I made my move. After Simard shoved me from behind, I turned and punched him in the face.

Then I ran like a sonuvabitch. I was out of breath by the time I approached my house, but Mom happened to be standing outside the apartment. Simard and Robitaille couldn't do a thing. Eventually, the three of us became friends.

My first crush was on Donna Dextras. We became good friends, but I never had the guts to ask her out. Everyone in school assumed that we'd eventually start to date, but I never asked her out and I never found out if she knew I how much I liked her.

I never took out Donna Dextras, but I did date a little during my last winter in Ahuntsic, when I was 14. I don't remember my first date's name, but I remember exactly why she broke up with me one week after we first went out. It was because I didn't kiss her.

She was the only girl I went out with, other than Lucie.

Chapter

3

Lucie

The winter of 1970–71 was my family's last in Ahuntsic. Vivian, Roddy, Donald, Pat and Chris had moved out of the house. I had turned 14 and was no longer the barefoot punk of the previous summer. I was captain of St. Alphonse's Bantam AA championship team. Although I had a year of midget and a year of Junior B hockey in front of me, my family began thinking about my life in Junior A. The Quebec Major Junior Hockey League, the last step before the NHL, was fast approaching.

The QMJHL drafts its new players from the midget ranks, just as the NHL drafts its rookies from the junior leagues. Because I had drawn a fair share of attention the previous year by being inducted into the Minor Hockey Hall of Fame and leading St. Alphonse in scoring on its pee-wee expedition to France, and because I was the best player on our 1970–71 bantam championship team, I was going to be a closely watched midget in 1971–72 and a high midget draft choice in the summer of '72. That meant the possibility of me playing junior for any team in the province.

My parents didn't like that notion. Neither did I. I didn't want to play junior 300 miles away in Chicoutimi or 90 miles away in Sherbrooke. Hell, I didn't even want to play 30 miles away in Sorel. I liked playing and living at home, where my parents drove me to and from games, where I slept in my own bed and ate my Mom's home-cooked meals, and where I hung out with my own friends. I might have been prime QMJHL material, but I was still only 14 years old. Midget, Junior B and four years of Junior A was too long a time to spend living four or six hours away from home.

Enter Jean Rougeau, the head coach of the QMJHL's Laval Nationals.

Rougeau called early that summer. We had never spoken to him, but he had somehow learned that I didn't want to leave the Montreal area during my junior career. He called with an idea. He explained to my Dad that if I lived in Laval, I would be exempt from the draft because of the league's rules on territorial rights. As long as I played my 1971–72 season of midget hockey in Laval, I would automatically become property of Laval's junior program beginning in 1972–73.

Rougeau asked if we were interested in moving from Ahuntsic to Laval, a city just a few miles northwest of Montreal, just over the Riviere de Prairie.

He sweetened the offer to help us decide. Not only could I live and play at home, but the club would pay the difference in rent between our 4 1/2-room basement apartment in Ahuntsic and a 5 1/2-room duplex in Laval. We'd never see any money, we'd just live a little more comfortably.

That was the inducement. It was an under-the-table proposition, but it wasn't a big deal. We accepted. That fall the seven Bossys still living on Meunier St. — Mom, Dad, Gordie, the twins, Pam and I —moved to 1076 Mill Hill in a neighborhood of Laval called Chomedey. Because I was the oldest, and the reason we moved, I got my own room.

It was hard saying good-bye to friends I had known since first grade, but knowing that Laval's hockey program wanted me made the adjustment easier. The Minor Hockey Hall of Fame, an all-expense paid trip to France with St. Alphonse, a bigger apartment for my family in Laval, more and more press clippings: It started becoming clear that people considered me a special hockey player. I was growing old enough to understand that the NHL was a real possibility. It wasn't just Dad's dream.

I didn't realize this until a few years later, but they created a new midget league when I moved to Laval, a three-team elite league. The city had always had seven or eight district teams on the midget level, but the overall level of talent wasn't that good. And although the rules said I had to play one year of midget hockey before I could play for the

Junior B Laval Nationals, coach Camille Brind Amour invited me to attend Laval's Junior B training camp.

That's when I became a right wing.

Until then, ever since I scored those 23 goals in my first Tom Thumb game, I was a right-handed shooting centerman. That's where my Dad first put me, that's where I played for St. Alphonse, and that's what seemed natural to me. I never thought much about it until that first day of camp with Brind Amour. We got on the ice, skated to one end, and prepared to line up for basic three-man forward rushes.

"Centermen here, left wings there, right wings there," the coach barked.

I moved into the centermen's line ... along with just about every other forward. It seemed that every 14-, 15-, or 16-year-old kid good enough to be trying out for Junior B was a center in midget hockey. So Brind Amour began pointing.

"You, you, you and you," he ordered to a bunch of us. "Go on right wing."

See, it wasn't my accurate shot, my quick release, or any other part of my game that made me a right wing. Camille Brind Amour just had too many centers. He moved me because I was just a skinny newcomer a few months shy of my 15th birthday. I was going back to midget, anyhow, and he didn't want me in the middle of his practices.

I wonder if that's what Brind Amour tells people today.

It didn't make that much of a difference to me, but it did feel a little strange. I had played one position all my life, but now because there were too many players ahead of me I got thrown out on the wing for the first time.

I wanted to say, "Uh, coach. I'm sorry, but I play center, not right wing."

But I was so shy I didn't say a word. And when I returned to Chomedey, my Midget AA team, I automatically stayed on right wing because I was afraid of making trouble.

I reported to Chomedey with only one stick, and it was cracked. I had no tape for my shin pads. The Junior B training camp had provided us with all that stuff and I just assumed that when I went back to midget similar supplies would be available. Once I realized that you were supposed to bring your own sticks and tape, I began to feel stupid. I was too shy to dare ask for a new stick. I did ask for tape ... and got masking tape. I quietly taped my cracked stick, dressed, and joined my new team on the ice.

Chomedey Arena's manager was a short, pudgy, mean-looking fellow named Pierre Creamer. Does he sound familiar? Perhaps you remember him as coach of the 1987–88 Pittsburgh Penguins, or the American Hockey League's Sherbrooke Canadiens from 1984–87, or the QMJHL's Verdun and Montreal Jr. Canadiens from 1980–84.

I'll never forget him because I married his sister.

Lucie Creamer worked at the Chomedey Arena snack bar. I don't remember the first time I noticed her, but once I did I couldn't get her out of my mind. She was pretty. She was popular. She seemed interesting. And she was 15.

How was I going to ask her out? I was petrified.

Most of my teammates knew who she was, but because she spoke French, it wasn't easy for me to just casually start a conversation. Not that I would have had the guts to if she spoke fluent English.

I needed help.

She attended a French-speaking school and I attended an English-speaking school, so the rink was the only place I could meet her. That wasn't a problem, though, because she was always working and I was always practicing. Soon after I moved into Laval, I made friends with a bunch of the guys who worked at the pro shop, adjacent to the snack bar. I had an excuse to hang around the snack bar all the time.

After practices, a few of us would sit around the pro shop and play this silly flipping game. We flipped coins, heads or tails, and whoever lost owed the other guy some candy.

That's how I finally approached her. Summoning every ounce of courage, I walked up to the snack bar one day with the candy bar and box of gum I had won flipping and asked her if I could get my money back. She gave it to me, but not before she made sure I didn't slip a bite of candy out of the wrapper or a piece of gum out of the box.

She must not have heard my knees shaking and she probably didn't suspect that I couldn't have cared less about the candy, the gum or the money. I just wanted to talk to her. And that day I did.

So I guess you could say we met in January 1972, between the ketchup and the mustard, with a Hershey bar melting in my sweaty hands.

I felt an immediate emotional and physical attraction to Lucie. We started spending a lot of time together in late January, but it took me until March 1 before I finally kissed her. I never had the moves off the ice that I had on it, I guess.

Sometime in February, I found out that a teammate of mine,

Guimond Fortin, had asked her out. He had bought two tickets to the Ice Capades at the Forum. Oh, was I jealous.

First, I couldn't afford two tickets to a show like that. Second, I couldn't afford to take her out in Montreal. Third, what if she liked him more than she liked me?

When she told me she was going out with him, I didn't believe her. I thought that she might be making up this story just to get me jealous. That's what I wanted to believe, anyway.

She went all right. I checked. I went down to the rink that night and headed straight for the snack bar. When I saw her best friend behind the snack bar and she told me she was substituting for Lucie, I felt this awful pain in my stomach. That's when I knew I'd have to make my move.

Lucie knew she had angered me. For a few days after the Ice Capades escapade I didn't talk to her, didn't smile at her, and didn't spend much time around the snack bar. I was telling her in my own way that I didn't appreciate her going out with Guimond.

That was her last date with anybody but me. Years later she told me that she didn't think anything of going to the Ice Capades with Guimond because we weren't going steady.

Today we tell people that our first official date was on March 1, 1972, because it was the first date we ended with a kiss. We went bowling that night with a couple we knew from the rink. I walked Lucie home and kissed her in front of her house.

I knew right away that I really liked her, but I wasn't sure how serious she wanted us to become. It was difficult to search for hints because we didn't speak the same language. Once we kissed, though, we became a couple. From that day on we were virtually inseparable, an acknowledged twosome: Lucie and Mike. When I wasn't on the ice practicing or playing, I was at the snack bar flipping and trading in my candy bars. That's how I got the cash to take Lucie out. We didn't go out often because I didn't have much money and she gave her mother most of the money she made at the snack bar.

I don't think it was love at first sight, but when I got to know her, I knew there wouldn't be another. I had dated only one other girl, but I knew Lucie was what I wanted in a girlfriend. Tons of people over the years, her friends and family, my friends and family, have asked me how I knew.

I don't know how I knew. Although we stumbled through two languages, from the beginning I felt I could communicate with her and trust her. She made me feel comfortable. I didn't need to date anyone else to know that this relationship felt right. I'm not that kind of person. When I like someone or something, I see no reason to change.

For instance, I'm a very big steak eater. I could probably eat steak everyday of my life because I like it. Every once in a while Lucie would say, "Come on, let's try something different."

"Why?" I'd ask. "I love steak."

That spring, after an uneventful midget season, I realized I loved Lucie. As we grew closer, I became very possessive, very jealous. I wanted to see her all the time, so I often left my school and met her at hers. I wanted to see her every day, every minute. In my mind, there was no doubt I was going to spend the rest of my life with her.

One day that summer Lucie was talking about love and life and I vividly remember her saying: "Oh, I don't think I will ever get married."

I looked into her eyes and said, "Oh yes you will. You'll marry me."

We discussed love and marriage all the time that year, but she never took me seriously. She didn't know that I had mapped out my life in my head and expected her to be the biggest part of it. I was going to be a professional hockey player. I was going to play Junior B, Junior A, get drafted and join the pros. And I was going to be rich.

Unfortunately, one man speaking for an entire organization tried to break us up during the summer of '72.

Arthur Lessard was Laval's general manager. Now that I had completed my midget season in Chomedey, I was eligible to play Junior B for the Laval Satellites. It was going to be my preparatory season for his Junior A Nationals. Before that, however, the organization wanted to send me to an advanced hockey school at the University of Montreal for the summer.

Fine, I said.

Lessard began lecturing me about the sacrifices I would have to make in Junior A. He talked about how tough it was to make it to the NHL. He told me I'd have to dedicate myself to hockey for the next five years.

And then he said he didn't want Lucie visiting me while I was at hockey school.

"You shouldn't be worried now about girlfriends," Lessard said as I listened in stunned disbelief. "Now is the time to concentrate only on hockey. There'll be lots of time to have girlfriends when you turn professional. You'll have lots of time to meet blonde American girls."

I didn't say anything. I just nodded without expression and realized that he was trying to serve his own selfish purposes. He and I both knew that in a year or two I'd be playing for his team. His was the antiquated hockey mentality: If you had a girlfriend, you couldn't be serious enough, you couldn't devote all your energy to the game.

Lucie and I were nervous. It had been only three or four months since we had fallen in love and here was this selfish man, who just happened to be the GM of the team that would prepare me for my NHL career, trying to break us up because he thought I'd be more valuable to his team if I stayed away from girls.

We went out to some restaurant that night, crying in each other's french fries, wondering what would happen next. I guess Lessard noticed that he hadn't gotten through to me because he followed up his conversation with me by calling my Dad. With my Dad Lessard went one step further. He said he didn't want to see Lucie at my practices and games.

"Why don't you leave them alone?" Dad told Lessard. That was not what the GM expected to hear. Realizing that he had struck out on the Bossy side, the exasperated GM figured he'd try the Creamers. Lucie's Dad had passed away, so Lessard called her brother.

Pierre diplomatically told Lessard to mind his own business.

We weren't bothered after that.

I enrolled at the University of Montreal's summer hockey school, and I saw Lucie. To Lessard's astonishment, I also found time to improve my skating, stickhandling and shooting skills. All the while, Lucie and I grew closer.

In August, I received the following form letter:

August 2, 1972

Mr. Michael Bossy
1076, Mille Iles
Chomedey,
Laval.

We are happy to announce that the first practice of the Laval National Ice Hockey Club will be held Friday, September the 1st, at 7 p.m. (on the ice) which means we expect you in the Dressing Room at 6 p.m.

Hoping that your summer season was a very pleasant one and that you are in the best physical condition possible, we would like to bring to your attention that we have a lot of confidence in your talents and that the competition in the training camp will be very serious and we are hoping to know a great season next winter.

At your arrival, we will give you a list of the team's rules such as athletic hair cut, good behaviour, team work, the desire to win, etc.

So, counting on you Friday, September 1st, for the first practice, and you can contact us in the meantime, if you do have problem that we may solve for you.

Yours truly,

Jean Rougeau, Coach.
Arthur Lessard, General Manager.

P.S. Please find enclosed the schedule of our exhibition games.

Although this letter was my invitation to Laval's Junior A training camp, I knew I'd be spending the 1972–73 season playing for the Junior B Nationals. I was five months shy of 16. I was five-foot-nine and 150 pounds. I wasn't physically or mentally ready for Junior A.

I was able to handle Junior B. We had our share of fights there, but there weren't too many free-for-all brawls. I did notice that the more I scored, the more high-sticks and questionable checks I received. That was the first taste of what I'd have to cope with for the next 14 years.

It took me four or five games to adapt to Junior B, but after that I had a productive season. I played 43 of our 44 games, missing one after I crashed into a goalpost and hurt my leg. I scored 3 goals in my first five games and 12 in my next five. I scored at least one point in 39 of my last 40 games and I finished the season with a 27-game point-scoring streak. I won the scoring title with 58 goals and 64 assists.

How do I know? I still have my handwritten game-by-game stat sheet from that season in one of my scrapbooks, the one marked C–H–A–M–P–I–O–N across the columns.

I loved to count my goals almost as much as I loved to score them. I kept track of every season on a sheet of graph paper and at the end of the year stuck my records in one of my scrapbooks. Starting with my 1969–70 trip to France with St. Alphonse in pee-wees and ending with my final year of junior, Mom compiled a scrapbook each year of my amateur hockey career. Most of the books are filled with brittle yellow newspaper articles from the Montreal papers and an occasional program. I have no idea why my records from every minor season but one have disappeared; but I can tell you that in Junior B I had one five-goal game, three three-goal games and 16 two-goal games.

I also scored two goals in two games in one day that season. It was during the playoffs, when we played Rosemont in the semifinals. Prior to the series, representatives from both teams had to meet to structure the schedule of playoff dates. Pierre Creamer was our coach, but he couldn't make the pre-series meeting. So he sent my brother-in-law Bob Lagace, the team statistician, in his place.

Bob botched the assignment. He scheduled one of our home games on a night when our rink was unavailable. We ended up playing a Sunday double-header during that series. We played at Laval in the afternoon and at Rosemont that night. We swept the double-header to win the series, but that was Bob's first and last day as interim general manager. I still kid him about it.

The Junior A team called me up for one game late in the regular season. Although both teams played in the Laval Sports Centre, it was much more exciting playing in front of a few thousand fans than a few hundred. I scored my first Junior A goal in that game on a breakaway against Drummondville. The goalie was Andre Lepage, who was drafted by the Islanders in 1975, but never played for them. It was not one of my typical goals. As Al Arbour would have described it, I "rabidouxed" the defenseman, "rabidouxed" Lepage and slipped the puck behind him.

Rabidoux? Arbour invented that word to describe what happened when a player stickhandled through the defense and beat the goalie on a breakaway.

That goal meant a lot to me at the time.

I rejoined the Junior A Nationals for their playoff series against Sorel after we lost the Junior B finals to Montreal North. I didn't play much, but I still knew what to expect the following year. I had heard and read about enough Junior A games to know that 19- and 20-year-olds with no hockey skills loved to intimidate 16- and 17-year-old potential National Leaguers. I knew that players who had no business being on the ice in the exhibition season, not to mention the QMJHL playoffs, started ugly brawls for no reason. High-sticks, spears, cross-checks and sucker punches were as common as icings, offsides and face-offs.

Sorel was one of the league's toughest teams. I watched those guys play. Laval was one of the league's smallest and least physical teams. I watched our guys play. I was 16. I wasn't going to be eligible for the NHL draft until I was 20. I didn't like to fight, I didn't want to fight and I didn't know how to protect myself.

It was going to be a long four years.

Chapter

Survival

The Quebec Major Junior Hockey League was hell.

I scored 309 career goals, made the all-star team three times, led the league in goals once and had my green-and-white Laval Nationals jersey Number 17 retired. But that's not what I remember today. I remember the premeditated violence that sickened and frightened me.

Players deliberately attempted to injure their opponents every game. Coaches regularly encouraged bench-clearing brawls. Unruly fans made every road game dangerous. Goons constantly threatened to gouge out my eyes or break my neck after I scored because, as one newspaper headline put it, "Stop Bossy and you stop Laval."

I'm not exaggerating. I don't know how many times I sat on a silent bus after a road loss in the middle of the night wondering if a professional hockey career was worth this pain and punishment. I fought the desire to quit harder than I fought any of the junior-league thugs who tried to beat us and beat us up.

But deep down I knew I would never quit.

This "gutless coward," this "chicken," kept playing. I was a lot tougher than anyone ever suspected because whenever somebody knocked me down or jumped me from behind, I got up and scored goals: 70, 84, 79 and 75 in my four full seasons. I was Rookie of the Year in 1973–74, first-team all-star right wing in 1974–75, second-team all-star in 1975–76 and 1976–77 and the QMJHL's most gentlemanly player in 1976–77. My penalty minutes dropped from 45 to 42 to 25 to 12. I did not fight in my final year.

There was no doubt in my mind from the day I played my first Junior A game that I was good enough to play pro. I accepted the violence as the price I had to pay to get to the NHL. I had no choice. I sure wasn't playing junior for the $15 weekly expense checks.

But it was strange feeling that, in every game I played, there was a good chance I'd have to defend myself in a fight. I never skated away from a player who dropped his gloves and challenged me, but I steered clear of confrontations whenever I could. Five minutes for me in the penalty box, whether I won or lost the fight, was a victory for the other team.

I was too valuable to Laval on the ice.

August 1974. I reported to training camp at five-foot-ten and 160 pounds. I was average-sized, but I felt small. My whole junior career I felt small.

The lunacy began two weeks into my rookie season, when we played the Chicoutimi Sagueneens at home. Chicoutimi was the last-place team in the Eastern Division. We were winning big when a fight broke out with 5:06 left in the third period. I was on the ice when it started, so I grabbed the jersey of the first non-fighter I saw and held on.

The benches emptied. Ten fights broke out at once. Ten players from each team either got five-minute fighting majors or game misconducts. Seven of us who were on the ice when the mayhem began got double-minors for roughing. We played those final five minutes with only nine players on the ice, the only nine not ejected or sitting in the penalty boxes.

Our management suspended our coach, Claude LaBossiere, for two weeks for instigating the donnybrook. The front office asked our public relations director, Pierre Lacroix, to serve as interim coach. Little did I know that Lacroix would become my agent, financial adviser and lifelong friend.

Lacroix was still behind our bench when we traveled to Chicoutimi for a rematch with the Sagueneens later in October. Oh, were they ready. So were we. On the plane ride to the game, Richard Dutton, my best friend on the team, and I prepared for a long night. (Chicoutimi was one of the few trips we didn't make by bus.) I told Richard, who was another pacifist, that when this inevitable bench-clearer began I was going to search for the same guy I paired off with last time.

I wasn't kidding.

Warmup was unbelievably scary. Fans were lined up everywhere, leaning over the glass taunting and threatening us. Of course the benches emptied that game. Chicoutimi recruited one of their "finer" citizens, who was wearing a cast on his arm. Who knew if the arm was broken? When the fight started, this guy jumped on the ice and started hitting us with his cast. I can't remember his name, but I do remember that he was wearing glasses with lenses thicker than the rink's Plexiglas.

As the fight escalated, fans lined up in the rows of seats directly behind our bench. This wasn't an NHL building with protective glass behind the bench and security people. It was a tiny rink in a tiny French town with a rabid mob dying to see us get our asses kicked.

Pierre was frightened because some of the crazies confused him for LaBossiere. While the brawl was raging on the ice, people were threatening Pierre on the bench. "We're going to get you, LaBossiere," they screamed.

A motorcycle gang, complete with leather jackets and chains, pushed its way down to the first row of seats behind our bench and just waited for the fight to end. We stayed out on the ice fighting. It seemed safer. To top off the humiliation, we spent the rest of the game picking our spare sticks off the floor behind the bench because every time we'd stack them up and lean them in numerical order against the glass, some fan came by and knocked them down.

We lost the fights and we lost the game. We had trouble getting back to our dressing room when it ended. There were too many people lining the corridors leading from the ice. We had to pass through the Zamboni entrance. As we trudged off, the fans tossed a huge pail of garbage that hit one of our players on the head.

We were known as one of the teams you could intimidate, but we had a fairly good season. We finished fourth in the West Division with a 30–37–3 record and upset the first-place Cornwall Royals in the playoff quarterfinals. We were eliminated in a wild six-game semifinal series with the Quebec Remparts.

Bob Sauve was our goalie. He was a first-round draft choice of the Buffalo Sabres in 1975. Dave Logan was our best defenseman. He was a fourth-round draft choice of the Chicago Black Hawks in 1974. I played on the top scoring line with left wing Claude Dupuis and center Michel Hamel. Sauve, Logan and I played in the East–West

All-Star Game that season. Yvon Vautour, a sixth-round Islander draft pick in 1976, was another key member of our team.

Before Game 2 of our five-game first-round upset of Cornwall, I was honored as Laval's Player of the Year. In uniform, I climbed into a convertible and was chauffered around the rink. "I was surprised," I said to reporters that night after I was presented with the Molson Cup. "It's the first time something like that ever happened to me. I felt funny. When you see all the fans applauding you like that, you start to get a little scared. But I left it all aside once the game started."

"I thought the least they would do is give you the car," Logan joked.

Laval's Player of the Year was actually Michel Bossy. That's right, Michel. That's what the French-Canadians called me throughout my entire junior career. I quickly grew to learn that the Quebecois were extremely possessive. People who didn't know I was English called me Michel, but so did people who did know. I didn't really care. Michel, Michael, Mike, whatever.

With the spotlight directly on me that night, I had one of my best junior games. I took 16 shots on goal and scored two goals and four assists. We won 11–6 and grabbed a two games to none lead in a series we won four games to one.

Then came Quebec, an intimidating team loaded with talent: Real Cloutier, Guy Chouinard, Richard Nantais, Jacques Locas. The series was a mess.

In the first period of Game 1 at Quebec City, which we lost 5–3, a goon named Jamie Bateman started an incredible brawl. First he barrelled into Sauve and fought Logan. Then from the penalty box he threw his stick at our bench and nearly harpooned coach LaBossiere. Then he leaped out of the box and attacked LaBossiere. When he did, Quebec's entire team stormed our bench. Bateman and LaBossiere fought. Four Remparts jumped Logan and four others jumped Tony Peluso, a rookie defenseman who was pretty tough.

While I was paired off with Chouinard, I noticed why two of our players were badly outnumbered. Some of my teammates ran under the stands and hid when Quebec challenged us. I couldn't believe it.

Peluso quit the team the next morning. "My father won't let me play anymore," he was quoted as saying in the paper. "He didn't like what happened to me and he doesn't want it happening again. It's a good thing they picked on me instead of a smaller guy like Bossy, because they might have killed him."

Thanks, buddy.

We won Game 2 at home, 7–6, but lost the next game in Quebec,

7–3. That game started an hour and 15 minutes late because our bus got two flat tires — one at a time — on the two-hour ride from Laval. That night's crowd was in an absolute frenzy. They had come prepared and didn't want to be kept waiting. They greeted our arrival by showering us with bras and dead chickens.

Down two games to one, our entire team visited Peluso at home and apologized for abandoning him. After we promised him it would never happen again and pleaded with him to forgive us, he talked his father into letting him back on the team. And in Game 4 at Laval, Peluso gained his revenge. He jumped two of the four guys who had attacked him, beat them up one at a time, and keyed a 9–5 win.

"Sure I'm proud of Tony," LaBossiere beamed. "One-on-one he can take any of those guys."

We lost the next two games without major incident. Given the fact that I emerged from the season in one piece, I considered it a good year. I finished 20th in the scoring race with 118 points, received 91 out of 100 points in the coach's Rookie of the Year vote, and summoned the courage to publicly criticize violence.

A story was published late that season in the French-language Montreal daily *Le Journal* in which I said:

> **Hockey has become much too rough. It's obvious that the game isn't a game that you play in your living room. But there has to be a difference between rough play and sadistic attacks trying to decapitate your adversary. This side of hockey confuses me enormously.**

Although I told any reporter who asked about it that my workmanlike approach to goal-scoring didn't compare to Guy Lafleur's spectacular and flamboyant style, the papers in 1974 started comparing me to the Montreal Canadiens' third-year pro, the best right wing in QMJHL history.

I sensed a bit of jealousy from a few teammates my first year. There were a couple of 19- and 20-year-olds hoping to be drafted and here I was, a rookie, scoring 70 goals and commanding an awful lot of attention. I kept pretty much to myself on the road and spent most of my free time at home with Lucie or my family.

That summer I decided I wanted my own car. I didn't like relying on Richard Dutton or my parents for lifts to and from the rink every day. I had turned 17 in January, which meant I was old enough to apply for my first driver's license. I needed a car for hockey and I needed a car to take Lucie out.

All I needed was the money. I certainly didn't save anything on $15 a week from Laval. And my family didn't have enough. So somebody on the team suggested I see Come Lacroix, one of Laval's part-owners.

Lacroix (who wasn't related to Pierre) was happy to lend me the money. He told me to pick out a car and then see him. He said he'd take care of everything. So I shopped and shopped and finally chose a royal blue '74 Mercury Bobcat that cost $4,500.

And then Lacroix screwed me.

He loaned me the $4,500, all right. He drew up a contract that stipulated if I never turned professional, I could repay the $4,500 without interest. If I turned pro, however, I would owe him $7,500.

I knew that Lacroix was getting the best of the bargain. I might have gotten a better deal from a loan shark, but I didn't care. Richard Dutton was getting a new car, too. How would it look if I didn't get the car I had talked so much about?

I pleaded with my Dad. "I've got to have the car," I begged. "Don't worry about the money; $7,500 won't be anything three years from now. I'll use some of my bonus money when I sign my NHL contract. Please. I really want the car."

We signed the loan agreement. I signed it and Dad signed it. When the promissory note came due in 1977 we had already realized that Lacroix had taken advantage of us, so we considered suing him. But we didn't have much of a case. Dad and I had both signed the note. We didn't need the hassle, so I paid the loan.

I went to driving school in the spring of 1974. My first driving lesson ended because I got in an accident. It was my fault, but only because I was too cautious. I stopped at a yield sign. I was merging onto a road that was empty, but instead of yielding and proceeding, I came to a complete stop and got rear-ended.

I eventually passed that course and took my road test in Rosemere, a suburb north of Montreal where we live now. The Bobcat was delivered after I passed my test, but before my license was processed and mailed. There it was one beautiful summer day: a gorgeous blue Bobcat, which I wasn't supposed to drive yet, parked in front of my house. My parents were gone, Lucie and I were alone, and the ice cream parlor was only a few blocks away.

I grabbed the keys.

I felt so proud, so important, so mature sitting behind the wheel with Lucie at my side. The car looked great. Lucie looked great. I was living every kid's summertime dream. We bought our ice cream cones, climbed back into the front seat and headed home.

It was hot. My ice cream started dripping down the cone onto my hands and onto the steering wheel. I was too cool to pull over and clean myself. I was having so much fun being mature. I didn't notice how much of a mess I was making until my wet and sticky hands slid off the wheel while I was cooing to Lucie.

I barely missed sideswiping a parked car on the street. Just barely. My heart raced. Suddenly I didn't feel so old and proud anymore. I felt like a complete jerk. I pulled over, threw away the ice cream, cleaned my hands and the wheel, and sheepishly returned home. I parked the car in the driveway and didn't touch it again until my license arrived in the mail a few weeks later.

Once I got my license, I murdered that Bobcat. I gave it to my Dad when I turned pro, but there was nothing left of it. I had burned the engine out after one year so that, after a while, you could tell I had been on the road by the trail of blue smoke that belched from the tailpipe.

I got into another accident within a year. I was driving down a road heading toward an intersection. It was in the spring, but I was on ice when I tried to stop. I slid and rammed a car in front of me. I'll never forget that incident because when the driver got out of his car, he was wearing a cast on his arm.

I didn't want to tell Dad what had happened, but he came to practice that night and spotted my dented fender. The body shop repaired the damage, but it couldn't exactly match the royal blue paint. Less than a year after I had bought it, the car was never the same.

Late that summer, I reported to training camp a little taller, a few pounds heavier, and relatively certain that I would not have to endure a second season as crazy as the first.

Wrong.

Two Sorel Black Hawk monsters jumped me in one game. My nose was broken by a Three Rivers Draveurs, penalty-minute monster named Daniel Horne in another. LaBossiere was fired ten games into the season. All of Quebec shuddered when word of a Laval Nationals drug scandal hit the newspapers. We finished last in the West Division under coach Jacques St. Jean.

Believe it or not, though, I call 1974–75 a very good season. I led the league with 84 goals and finished fourth in scoring with 149 points. And although our record was 26–39–7, we made the playoffs with 59 points as a wildcard and surprised everybody by advancing to the finals. I scored another 18 goals in 16 playoff games, giving me 102 overall.

This was also the season in which everybody wondered if the NHL would declare the best 18-year-olds in the Quebec, Ontario and Western junior leagues eligible for its 1975 amateur draft. The year before, to combat the World Hockey Association's attempt to woo top underaged talent to its fledgling league, the NHL permitted each of its teams to select one 18- or 19-year-old player. In 1974, the Islanders used their second-round draft pick to choose an 18-year-old English-speaking center from Val Marie, Saskatchewan, named Bryan Trottier.

Before LaBossiere was fired, he placed me with a left wing named Richard Jarry and Jean Trottier, a French-speaking stickhandling centerman who could "rabidoux" past any defenseman in the league. We clicked immediately.

"Trottier and Bossy, the Laval Nationals' most potent weapon," one French newspaper wrote. "These two players play marvelously well together." In that story I was quoted as saying that one of the reasons we've been so successful is that there isn't any jealousy between us. Each of us uses the other's ability.

The year before, we had a forward on our team named Potvin. Gaetan Potvin. I didn't play much with Trottier that year, so I doubt that we ever scored a goal that looked like this: Laval, Bossy (Trottier, Potvin).

Strange though, isn't it? When Arbour first put Bryan and I together near the end of my rookie training camp with the Islanders, I wasn't struck by the irony. Now I am. Bryan, whose ancestors were North American Indians, and Jean, a French-Canadian, were completely unalike, but they both suited me. Jean, who was never drafted, used smooth finesse to get me the puck. Bryan used brute strength.

Trottier (Jean, that is) helped me gain an incredible amount of exposure in 1974–75. Scouts preparing for a possible 18-year-old draft began to watch me a little more closely. Twenty-three games into the season, after I had scored 19 goals in 17 games (I had missed six with a bruised knee), an interview with Saraceno appeared in print.

"Bossy has a pro shot," Saraceno said. "He probably has one of the best shots in the league. His only problem is his checking...he must learn how to cover his man better."

When asked if I was good enough to be drafted that June, Saraceno said the Islanders had too many right wings in their organization.

"But he could be drafted by some other pro club next season. But I'll tell you something. I would like to see him play another year of junior. His checking must improve, but that will all come, especially once he gets into a pro camp. But no doubt about it, Michel is pro material ... he's one of those natural-born hockey players."

A week later, this natural-born hockey player was subjected to some unnatural treatment by two Sorel Black Hawks named Francois Cadrin (three goals, 197 penalty minutes) and Gilles Bilodeau (six goals, 377 PIMs).

We won at home, 8–4. Trottier and I each scored three goals and three assists. Immediately after my second or third goal, Sorel coach Pierre Duguay sent Bilodeau out to line up next to me. Duguay called him back to the bench before the puck was dropped, whispered something in his ear, then sent him back out.

Think I wasn't shaking?

Once it became obvious that Bilodeau was out to get me, St. Jean yelled for me to back up. Our fighter, Tony Peluso, was on defense and my coach wanted to make sure that Peluso's path to Bilodeau wasn't blocked should trouble start. Trouble started seconds after the puck was dropped, but it wasn't Bilodeau who attacked me. While I was watching out for him, Cadrin jumped me from behind. While Cadrin threw me around, Bilodeau challenged Phil Bellemare, another of our tough fighters. Bilodeau and another goon named Roger Seguin eventually shook free and took a few shots at me, too. Incredibly, I wasn't hurt.

I wasn't so lucky when Daniel Horne (lifetime NHL goals, zero; lifetime NHL games, zero) attacked me later in the season at Three Rivers. They were the first-place team in the East, but I guess on this night they didn't want to just play hockey to beat us. Horne's punch splattered my nose from ear to ear. It's still crooked today because of the one-fisted knockout that appeared from nowhere except Horne's coach's game plan.

Horne's coach was Michel Bergeron, who coached the Quebec Nordiques after they joined the NHL and now coaches the New York Rangers. Bergeron was among the great majority of coaches who was always choreographing fights in junior. But remember how Bergeron cried when the Flyers' Dave Brown cracked Tomas Sandstrom from behind with that vicious cross check at Madison Square Garden?

I was watching that game when it happened and, like everybody else who witnessed that sickening attack, I was horrified by what

Brown had done. But the next day, when Bergeron called Brown's assault attempted murder and a million other things, I had to laugh.

"It was the cheapest shot I ever saw in my life," Bergeron said. "I've seen a couple, believe me."

Sure he's seen a couple. A couple of thousand that he planned, ordered and condoned. I guess he didn't like it when a goon beat on one of his best players. But he didn't mind his hit men dishing it out ten years earlier. Short memory, I guess.

But my broken nose seemed insignificant compared to the black eye Laval suffered in mid-March when a story broke claiming that several Nationals players used amphetamines during the playoffs the year before. Since LaBossiere had been fired, and since he was blamed for the incident, the league's investigation concluded that there was no narcotic epidemic to worry about.

Incidentally, the drug story was true. But the players who took the pills might have been innocent participants in one of LaBossiere's most idiotic schemes. Here's what happened:

On the bus to Cornwall for Game 1 of the quarterfinals, LaBossiere approached each player with a pill. He handed them out saying they were vitamins.

"Take them," he suggested.

They looked very much like the vitamin pills that sit on virtually every sports team's training room medical supplies table, so a couple of guys popped them into their mouths. I hated taking pills, so I threw mine under my seat. So did Richard Dutton, who was sitting next to me.

By the time we arrived in Cornwall, some of the guys were like caged animals. They almost broke doors down getting into the rink from the bus and onto the ice from the dressing room. We were hooting and hollering during warmup, acting ridiculous. I figured it was the pills, but I was too naive to even suspect that LaBossiere had served us uppers.

I have no idea if the players who continued using the pills during the playoffs knew what they were taking. But when the league concluded its investigation, it charged in a newspaper story that "several players" admitted taking pills. QMJHL president Raymond Lagace didn't name names.

That's when my usually quiet mother got involved.

"I'm not the type of woman who speaks out often or starts campaigns, but I feel that article was unfair to the team generally," she said in response to the first story. "If some players were taking pills, it should have named them. Not every player should come under suspicion."

Lagace responded by saying, "There's one thing I can tell you for certain. Mike Bossy never took any stimulants."

I had brought some pills home from the trainer's room earlier that season. My Mom thought those were pep pills, so she had our pharmacist analyze them. They were iron vitamins.

I've never used drugs. I've never had an inclination to try them. I've never been offered drugs and I've never been to a party where cocaine or marijuana was used. In fact, I've never seen a joint except on television or in the movies.

I was surprised to read the vague allegations in *Sports Illustrated* during the 1987 playoffs involving drug usage on the Edmonton Oilers. I always thought it was unfair to believe a story if it didn't contain all the facts, so I didn't believe it. I don't know if the story was true, but I hope it wasn't because our league goes through enough with the violence that it doesn't need to get a black eye because of drugs.

I'm proud of the fact that of baseball, football, hockey and basketball, our professional organization is considered the least involved with drugs. Why is that? I have one theory. It seems that a lot of drug usage starts in college. Not many of our players go through the college system. Also, most of our players grow up in small Canadian cities, where they don't have the exposure to drugs that a kid growing up in a major metropolitan area does. And a lot of small-town Canadian kids grow up without much money.

Even a tiny drug problem is a big problem. Right now, it looks like drugs are killing off people across the continent. The illegal drugs manufactured today are so dangerous. But on the other hand, alcohol is addictive, too. The NHL has more of an alcohol problem than a drug problem. In many cases, it could be an alcohol problem that guys aren't aware of because they don't think it's a problem.

Alcohol is legal, so the NHL can't police its usage like it can police drug usage. But when one's drinking starts hurting other people, then you have a legitimate problem. Take Bob Probert and the Detroit Red Wings, for example. Probert the last few years, has struggled with alcoholism and I sincerely hope he stays healthy. He's a terrific young player. But the truth is, his drinking problem is a black eye on the entire Red Wings organization and the entire NHL.

If you take the position that it's impossible to punish excessive drinkers because alcohol is legal, as president John Ziegler has, then you subject yourself to the problems that certain players will give you because of their drinking. Driving while intoxicated is a serious offense and the league has had too many players convicted of too many DWIs.

I don't want to sound lily-white here. I've gone out and had my binges in bars. I've had my parties. I'll tell you about them later. And just because I've talked about how much fun we had, I don't want you to think that what I did those nights was right. It wasn't.

I know Molson's owns the Montreal Canadiens. I know Carling O'Keefe owns the Quebec Nordiques. I know that Budweiser is a major NHL sponsor. I just strongly believe that the NHL ought to take a more serious look at its alcohol problem before it damages more players' careers and lives.

Chapter

This Man is an Islander

I was four months too young for the 1974 draft when the Islanders took Bryan Trottier. But if the NHL or WHA planned to draft 18-year-olds again in June 1975, I was ready to repay Come Lacroix 24 months early for the car I now hated. With the help of speculation, innuendo, rumor and a presumptuous uncle, I became convinced in March that I was ready to turn pro after my second season in junior.

My uncle Leo, Dad's brother, once coached the Montreal Jr. Canadiens. In the 1950s he played against Bill Torrey in a Montreal high school league. He claimed to have excellent hockey connections. Everyone believed him when he introduced himself as my representative.

"It's obvious that Maurice Filion (the general manager of the WHA's Quebec Nordiques) is interested in about five players who he would qualify as excellent acquisitions if the WHA decided to take 18-year-olds," Uncle Leo was quoted as saying in one French paper in March. "You can't keep an 18-year-old from voting, so (Bossy) should be able to play. I don't give a crap about the junior leagues. If a guy like Mike Bossy, whom I consider one of the best 18-year-olds, had an eye poked out today it's not the junior leagues who are going to pay for the rest of his life."

That churned the rumor mill. Would I challenge the NHL's 20-

year-old draft? Would I sign with the WHA? Had I signed with Quebec?

"I haven't signed anything, but I won't hide the fact that I'd like to," I said, more surprised by my uncle's comments than the reporters' questions. "I've proven myself in the junior league and I think that I'd be able to play professionally."

Uncle Leo never meant any harm, but I had never given him permission to identify himself as my representative and if Dad had, nobody ever told me. If Uncle Leo had talked to Filion or somebody from the Nordiques, I figured I had the right to know. I might have been only 18, but I had a sense that my life was reaching a crucial period.

It was time to hire an agent.

Uncle Leo realized that, too, because soon after the stories about Quebec's interest in me appeared he came to my house and told Mom and Dad — without me present — that if they would let him handle my negotiations, for a commission, he would get me a contract with the Nordiques.

My parents rejected Uncle Leo's offer and agreed with my decision to find an experienced professional. It was vital to Dad that I find the right agent to protect against one of his Three Big Concerns: Don't let anyone cheat you out of your money. (The other two were: (1) don't go into the corner with your head down; and (2) be careful when you're driving.)

As soon as I started looking for an agent, Dad said "be careful," a thousand times a week. "Always make sure that you know who you're dealing with and make sure you're comfortable with him."

By the end of the 1974–75 season Bob Sauve and I had become good friends. His goaltending was a major reason why we upset Three Rivers, four games to two, in the quarterfinals and Montreal, four games to one, in the semis before losing in the finals to Sherbrooke in five. Bob's playoff performance greatly improved his chances of being drafted in the first round, which he was two months later.

I knew he had hired Pierre Lacroix, Laval's part-time public relations and marketing director, but I didn't know until late that season how satisfied Bob was with the way Pierre was preparing him for his first professional contract negotiations.

I got to know Pierre Lacroix the year before, when he became Laval's interim coach during the LaBossiere suspension. I liked him then. Now I liked the fact that Sauve was his first and only client and that he was only 25. Once Sauve assured me that Pierre was spending a lot of time advising him on how to prepare for his NHL career, I didn't mind that Pierre held a full-time job as marketing director for Carling O'Keefe Breweries.

Sauve suggested I ask Pierre if he'd be interested in another client. After one late-season game at Laval (it may have been one of our playoff games), I found him in the Sports Centre lobby and quietly asked if I could speak to him alone.

"I've been approached by other agents and I've met with other agents," I explained. "I know you're not doing this full-time, that you have the job at the brewery and with the team. But I know you're doing a good job for Bob. Would you like to represent me?"

Pierre seemed surprised. He assumed I already had an agent, either my Uncle Leo or one of the full-time vultures who would sign an amateur player at birth if he could. Pierre told me he and his partner, a lawyer named Denis Gauthier, would consider it.

Lacroix and Gauthier had a career decision to make it. They had established a consulting firm, Jandec, Inc., to handle Sauve's negotiations. Jandec was short for January to December, which was how long Pierre figured he had to work seven days a week in order to keep pace at the brewery and as Laval's PR director while he represented Sauve.

I was sold on Pierre before Pierre was sold on me. But before I hired him, Mom, my brother Pat and I met with Alan Eagleson at Montreal's Dorval Airport. Eagleson, whose stable of clients at the time included Bobby Orr and Darryl Sittler, had called to arrange the meeting. I sat down with him, but I was turned off before I even met him. I didn't want to be just another stack of papers in a manila folder stuffed into one of a hundred file cabinets. I wanted to be better than the other players in junior and I planned to be better than the other players once I reached the NHL. I wanted an agent who really concentrated his time and energy on my affairs, not a big broker like Eagleson who had his fingers in so many pies.

Lacroix and Gauthier said yes to me before the 1975 draft. They told me they envisioned making Jandec, Inc. an exclusive firm that represented a small number of choice NHL players. Sauve figured to be a first-round pick that season. Once the NHL announced it would not permit 18- or 19-year-olds to be drafted, I prepared myself for two more years of punishment in the Quebec League and convinced myself I'd be a first-round choice in 1977.

Pierre and Denis might have lacked experience, but they sold themselves well. "We want you to be present whenever possible at any discussion we have with any team," was the first piece of advice they gave me. "We want you to take part in all the negotiations. We want you to know what's going on, so you never have the feeling that something was being held back."

That impressed me. I thought an agent's job was to talk money with the team that drafts you, negotiate a contract, give it to you to sign, lick the envelope and mail it back. I wasn't comfortable with that concept because it gave me no control. I realize now how preposterous my notion was; but as an 18-year-old who thought $100 was a fortune, I didn't have a clue until Lacroix and Gauthier sold me on Jandec.

In our meeting at Dorval, Eagleson hadn't led me to believe that if I hired him I would be his employer. An experienced agent should treat a prospective client like he's already a six-figure wage earner, not like he's an impressionable kid. Eagleson made me feel like I'd be lucky to be associated with him, not the other way around.

I've always wanted to know where my money was coming from and where it was ending up. When I was 15 years old earning a couple of bucks of expense money a week from Laval, I wasn't talking about much. But soon I'd be talking about hundreds of thousands of dollars.

Or so I thought.

Uncle Leo was talking about a contract in excess of $100,000 per year, so that figure stuck in my head from the time I was 18 until the Islanders drafted me in June 1977 and signed me about a month later.

Looking back at my career and looking at how the NHL has changed since 18-year-olds were declared permanently eligible in 1980, I'm glad I had to wait to join the NHL until I was 20. Although I believe now what my Uncle Leo believed then — that an 18-year-old adult has the right to earn a living in the NHL — I think the under-aged draft has hurt the game. It's the rare 18- or 19-year-old (Mario Lemieux in 1984–85 is the best example) who's physically and mentally mature enough for the NHL.

I don't disagree with the rules that permit an NHL team to draft a kid, sign him, and send him back to finish his junior career. Nobody has the right to prevent an 18-year-old from making the amount of money a first-rounder can earn these days. I just don't believe the average 18-year-old, first-rounder or 12th-rounder, is mature enough to handle the responsibilities and pressures of life in the NHL on or off the ice. Especially off the ice.

The underaged draft hurts the 21 teams, too. Scouts today are forced to assess players who are still growing, still maturing, still learning how to play the game. Ten years ago, every first-round draft choice was a potential blue-chipper. Now there usually aren't more than two or three certain NHLers in a given draft. I know I was a much better player and much smarter person at 20 than I was at 18. Although I said I could at the time, I don't think I could have handled the NHL or WHA at 18. Although the violence and scare tactics disgusted me, I know that a full four years in junior helped me have a better NHL career than if I had broken in at 18.

Now that I had hired Jandec, Inc. for the standard six percent commission fee, which included tax service, legal advice and financial planning, I wanted to make myself as marketable and valuable a commodity as possible. In 1975-76, I missed eight games with sprained ankle ligaments, but still finished fourth in the scoring race with 79 goals and 136 points in 64 games. Writers made the Lafleur vs. Bossy comparisons all season. Now that Lafleur was the NHL super-star everyone had predicted he would become, I can't say I minded.

But Laval had a horrible season. We finished last in the West with a 25-41-6 record and didn't make the playoffs. We staged a brief wildcat strike when St. Jean was fired as coach; and I started a fight with a forward from the Hull Festivals named Gilles Brunet.

Brunet wasn't a goon. He had only 31 penalty minutes in 71 games that season (I had 25). He was just an annoying player who always cross-checked and speared me in front of the net when the referee's back was turned. He was my size, not a Buffalo Bill-type that I knew I couldn't beat in a fight. I figured that if I went with him I'd have a chance to win. We were skating in the corner behind the net this one game and when the play turned up ice, he jabbed and cross-checked me like he usually did. Only this time I didn't take it.

I clicked.

I turned to him and said, "Do you wanna go?" Before he answered, I dropped my gloves and started punching. I knew if I wanted to have a chance to win this fight, I didn't have time to wait for an answer. My gloves were off by the time I said "Do you wanna." My first fist reached his head when I said "Go?" I got the first few punches in and wrestled his sweater over his head before I threw a few more rights. It was the typical hockey fight you see the good fighters winning. As soon as it was over, it was obvious that I had won. It felt good to beat the hell out of Brunet because he was one of so many players I had taken abuse from.

It's easier to accept abuse from a guy who's six-foot-three and 220 pounds than it is to take garbage from a pest like Brunet. That's probably why he was the guy who made me snap. I don't think it would have been wise for me to lose my cool against a Gilles Bilodeau or a Daniel Horne. As much as I disliked fighting, I disliked overnight hospital stays more.

After the game, a few reporters came into our dressing room and asked me if I was wearing a ring. I didn't know what they were talking about until they told me that the Hull trainer accused me of wearing rings because Brunet was cut in five places. The trainer told them that he couldn't imagine me doing that with one punch. I responded by saying anyone who watched the fight saw that it wasn't one punch. It was numerous punches.

"No, I was not wearing any rings," I said with some pride and some shame. I didn't like being the center of a postgame press gathering because of my pugilistic abilities.

That night Brunet symbolized every opponent who ever tried to hurt me for no reason. Once I started hitting him I couldn't stop. Word spread around the league that Bossy had picked and won a fight, but I wasn't about to defend any lightweight boxing crown and everybody knew it. One fight against a guy not known for his fighting ability wasn't going to earn me a reputation as someone to be reckoned with. I regretted the entire incident as soon as the delight in seeing Brunet crumble faded from my mind. Sitting in the penalty box for five minutes cost me ice time.

I read a lot of stories that season about how the Montreal Jr. Canadiens got beaten and beaten up by Sorel and Quebec, the two toughest teams in the league. Montreal's players must have grown two inches taller and 20 pounds heavier against us because whenever we played we were the ones getting clobbered. Every patsy likes to find another patsy, I guess.

We never found one.

Montreal's best player was defenseman Robert Picard, who is my age and was drafted 12 spots ahead of me in 1977, third overall by the Washington Capitals. It's interesting that in Picard's final two years of junior he amassed 282 and 267 penalty minutes, but in 11 NHL seasons he never collected more than 122 minutes and in only five of those seasons had more than 100.

Sorel's rink didn't have glass on the sideboards. One time, a gorilla by the name of Daniel St. Laurent (four goals, 364 penalty minutes) jumped me and had me pinned up against the boards long enough for the fans to come down and throw a few punches at me. None hurt me, but I could swear a few of those fans were wearing rings.

I remember one game, in Shawinigan, when Yvon Vautour and I combined for three shorthanded goals on one power play. I got one, he got one and I got another one. As soon as I scored that third shorthanded goal I began wondering if I was going to live to tell about it when I got home. Vautour and I probably could have scored at will that game, but we knew better. Whenever I scored a goal or two on the road, especially if it was in a game we were winning, I was afraid that I'd finish the game in a box. And I don't mean the penalty box.

We almost lost one game by forfeit that year, when coach St. Jean was fired and we struck in protest. We had three days off between games and we vowed not to show up unless he was reinstated. Our captain Vautour, Phil Bellemare, Richard Jarry and Yves Preston masterminded this plan, but it didn't get too far. The league stepped in and threatened to suspend us and expel the team if we didn't play our next game at Three Rivers. So we played. Vautour coached that night and we lost, 5–3. Then Andre Boivin was hired. That's how bad we were that season. We couldn't win anything.

Boivin didn't like me too much. He once said publicly that with me on the ice, it was like our team was playing shorthanded. I don't know what I ever did to displease him, but I must have done something.

I was never more anxious for a season to begin than I was in 1976–77. I was named Laval's captain. I was going to be eligible for the June 1977 draft. I was one step from the NHL. And Boivin was out as coach, replaced by former NHL goaltender Denis DeJordy.

I was generally regarded as the fourth- or fifth-best Quebec League player eligible for the draft. Picard and two wingers, Sherbrooke left wing Jere Gillis and Sorel right wing Lucien DeBlois, were rated ahead of me. Montreal left wing Normand Dupont and I were ranked below those three because we were considered one-way players, goal scorers who couldn't check and weren't physical. Gillis and DeBlois were physical checking forwards who scored a healthy amount of goals.

Naturally, I disagreed. Deep down, I knew I could check and be more physical. I knew I could and should spend more time in our defensive zone. Throughout my career with Laval I knew I had to score goals to be recognized as a great junior player. I also knew that if

I tried to play more physically, there was nobody to back me up and I'd get killed. So I sold myself to the NHL as a scorer.

Now that I had sold myself as a potential first-round pick, I wanted to prove to the scouts and to myself that I could do more than just put the puck in the net. At this point in the season it didn't matter to me where in the first round I was selected (Pierre eventually taught me to think differently). I just wanted to be a first-rounder.

Sherbrooke's Rick Vaive and I collided a few weeks into the season and I missed about three weeks with three broken ribs. It was an open-ice collision that was nobody's fault. He didn't see me and I didn't see him. I finished that game with a terrible headache and thought that I had just had my bell rung. But when I awoke the next morning in terrible pain and barely able to breathe, fractures showed up in the X-rays I had taken.

I scored 75 goals and 126 points playing in 61 of our 72 games that season. The time lost cost me a spot among the top ten scoring leaders, but I earned my second consecutive second-team all-star spot (behind DeBlois, who scored 56 goals, 134 points and was the league's MVP) and was named the league's most gentlemanly player. I had just 12 penalty minutes. Under DeJordy and Jacques St. Jean, who used up another of his nine lives to return as coach when DeJordy was fired, Laval finished third with a 26–35–11 record, then got knocked out in the first round of the playoffs.

Christmas 1976. I was selected to join a team of Quebec League All-Stars for a round-robin tournament against the Western Canadian Hockey League All-Stars, the Ontario Hockey Association All-Stars and the Soviet Junior Selects. The tournament was held in Alberta, at sites in Edmonton, Calgary, Lethbridge and Medicine Hat. This was my first time away from home since my 1969 trip to France with St. Alphonse.

Each team was scheduled to play six games, two against each opponent, from December 26 to January 2. I knew that every NHL and WHA team would be watching this tournament closely. It was very important that I play well. Scouts who comb the junior leagues find it difficult to compare the top players in the three Canadian junior leagues because they don't play against one another. This was their chance to assess just how good a scorer I was, just how poor my backchecking was, just how much of a chicken I was.

Of course it bothered me that the scouts were labeling me as a one-way player. I knew they were making a valid point, but I knew I could adjust. In my own mind, it was a matter of me adjusting and telling myself: "There are no Bilodeaus out there to jump you. Edmonton's fans aren't going to throw garbage cans at you if you score too many goals. Prove you can play a complete game. Check, defend, hit and score."

I did. Not only against the Soviets, but against the best from Ontario and the West. I led our team in scoring with six goals and three assists and finished third in the tournament overall, behind Ontario's Bobby Smith and the West's Brad Maxwell, who scored ten points apiece. The West won the tournament with a 6–0 record. We finished second at 4–2. Both of our losses were to the West, a team led by Maxwell, Barry Beck and Stan Smyl.

Gillis scored three goals and three assists. DeBlois scored three and two, Dupont one and three. Don't think I wasn't counting. My competitive fire burned from the start of this tournament hotter than at any time throughout my junior career. Here I was playing with the best, against the best. It was my opportunity to show the scouts that I was one of the best.

We won our opener in Edmonton, 7–4, against the USSR. I scored a goal and two assists and was voted the game's outstanding player. We lost 4–2 to the West at Lethbridge, but I scored once and assisted on our other goal. I had two goals in our 8–0 rout of the Soviets in Medicine Hat and a goal in our 4–0 win over Ontario at Edmonton. I didn't score in only one of our six games, the 4–2 loss that gave the tournament to the West.

I passed a critical test in that game. I doubt that any scout noticed that but I came to a personal crossroads when the puck was innocently dumped into our offensive right-wing corner and I got absolutely hammered by Beck, one of the West's defensive giants. My head was still ringing when the puck was shot out of their zone and we dumped it back into my corner.

"Do I have to go after it again?"

Any good player will tell you that hockey is played 99.9 percent of the time on instinct. There's no time to stop and think "What should I do now?" But for me, this was the 00.1 percent. In the seconds between the crunch I took from Beck and the second dump into my corner, I actually stopped reacting long enough to consider the consequences of this meaningless play.

I had to go after the puck again. I had to prove to myself that I wasn't afraid, that I could stand up to the physical game. It was something I didn't want to do, but I had to do it. So I stuck my neck back into the corner, got belted again, finished my shift and skated back to the bench in physical pain. But I felt great. My heart pumped. I wasn't afraid. I was tough enough. I could play with anybody. From that moment on, I knew what the scouts were saying about me was bullshit.

Soviet competition stirred me because I was competing against another select group of juniors. I didn't feel like I was competing against a Communist country. I never thought sports and politics mixed, not even during the Canada Cup tournaments. People compete against other people to see who's best. It's ridiculous for a country to feel politically superior because its hockey team beat another hockey team in a three-game series.

That tournament left one other lasting memory, although I'm embarrassed to admit it. Lucie to this day claims she first learned of my marriage proposal in the newspaper. Although I admit that we hadn't formally planned a wedding date, I assumed that when I turned pro, we'd get married. I thought she assumed that, too. So when a reporter asked me during the tournament, I told him I hoped to be drafted high in the first round so I could marry Lucie.

She read it the next day. She didn't know I planned to marry her after the draft. Neither did her family. Lucie's Mom didn't even know we were planning to marry at all, so it made big waves back in Quebec. To me it wasn't any revelation. I thought we had known for a few years that we'd end up married.

Lucie, Mom, Dad, Gordie and Lucie's sister Carol met me at Dorval Airport when I returned and I felt so proud. Lucie considered us officially engaged. I considered myself a sure-fire first-round draft pick. What a letdown it was returning to play for Laval. I knew I would be dead if I tried standing up for myself like I did in the tournament. If I even hinted that I would not take any more garbage, I'd get it double.

Trade rumors began floating across Quebec in January. Any good team that had a shot at winning the QMJHL championship and qualifying for the Memorial Cup had to figure acquiring me for the last couple of months was worth giving up a few prospects, a commodity Laval certainly needed.

I kept a low profile when the rumors surfaced, but I prayed I wouldn't be traded. That's right: Would Not. Yes, Laval was a bad team. Yes, I was tired of getting beaten up all the time. Yes, playing for a championship team might have lifted me above Gillis and DeBlois on the scouts' charts. Yes, a Memorial Cup tournament against the OHA and WCHL champions might have enhanced my overall first-round ranking.

But I didn't want to leave Lucie. I was very comfortable at home. Winning the Memorial Cup never meant that much to me, anyway. Playing for a contender might have helped my draft status, but I was confident enough then to believe I didn't need two months in Cornwall, Sherbrooke or Quebec City.

That was a tough few weeks. One day I heard I would be traded, then I heard I wouldn't be. I waited up until midnight on trade deadline day, listening to the radio and praying I wouldn't hear my name. It was one of the longest nights of my life, but what a relief it was to finally be able to sleep, knowing I'd be sleeping at home the rest of the season.

January 31, 1977, was a great day. The night before, the Canadiens beat the Islanders, 2–1, at the Forum. When I picked up one of the local French papers in the morning, the headline on the story of that game read: "Bossy could change a lot of things."

> **The Islanders desperately want to put their hands on Mike Bossy from the Laval Nationals. Their chief scout, Henry Saraceno, came out of the Forum after their 2–1 loss to the Canadiens with more arguments for his bosses.**
>
> **"We played well tonight, but you saw we need a scorer," Saraceno said. "A guy who could score with any little chance that he gets."**
>
> **Natural scorers are not running around in the streets these days. Where would a team get this pearl?**
>
> **"In the draft," Saraceno said. "Our guy's already found. Mike Bossy. He's the best scorer I've seen in junior hockey since Lafleur. He's as good as Lafleur was in front of the net. We've watched him a lot and he's definitely a natural."**

The article also said the Islanders, who figured to be selecting late in the opening round, were trying to trade for a higher first-round selection so they could use it to pick me.

The New York Islanders?

Other than that they had drafted Yvon Vautour in the sixth round of the 1976 draft and that he was in the minors, I knew very little about the Islanders. I knew that they were a pitiful expansion team a few years earlier and had built themselves into one of the better teams in the league.

I paid attention to their 1977 Stanley Cup semifinal series with Montreal. They lost to the eventual Cup-winning Canadiens in six games, but I rooted for them because they weren't the Canadiens. I was impressed. They had a few big forwards who were tough and could score, a tight defense and two good goalies. They also had this one guy who ran all over the ice hitting everybody. "Look at the little shit disturber," I said to Lucie, pointing to Number 19. "He's out there hitting everybody and he looks like a little runt."

And that's my first memory of Trots. He was Rookie of the Year in 1975–76, but I had not heard of him or seen him play until that series and when I finally did, I made fun of him because he looked 12 years old.

March 20, 1977, was a great day, too. Laval honored me on Mike Bossy Night. They sat me down in a plush leather recliner on the ice and presented me with a check for $1,700: one hundred dollars times my jersey Number 17. Honeymoon money.

It was the only day in my life that I wished I grew up wearing Number 99, but the first of many days over the next few months when the subject was money.

Seventeen hundred dollars was a wonderful present, but I had numbers with more zeros at the end on my mind that spring. The NHL amateur draft was scheduled for June 14, 1977, to be held at the league's Montreal office via conference call with the 18 teams. I couldn't wait.

I rented my own apartment for the months of June, July and August, a three-room apartment near my parent's in Laval that cost $300 a month. I borrowed the money from Pierre. I figured it wasn't going to be long before I could pay him back.

With the WHA grabbing headlines by signing 18-year-olds to huge contracts, I was thinking big bucks. I had very big bucks in my head that whole year. I was thinking I'd get a contract worth $100,000 per year. Now I just wanted to know from whom. Lucie and I wondered out loud all the time: Toronto, Montreal or St. Louis? The Rangers or the Islanders? Where would we be going?

Before the draft, reporters constantly asked me if I was rooting for the Canadiens to draft me. I said I wanted to be drafted onto a team that I could make. It was a cliche, but it was exactly what Lucie and I had been telling each other. What I didn't say publicly was that Lucie and I were terrified of the minor leagues. We didn't want to get stuck in some small town where we didn't know anything or anybody.

Pierre, Denis Gauthier and I assembled in Gauthier's office just before the draft began at 9 a.m. At 9:28 a.m. somebody from the Cleveland Barons called. They had the fifth pick of the first round and it was their turn. They asked Pierre how much it would take to sign me.

"We want $100,000 to sign and $100,000 a year for three years," Pierre replied firmly. "That's $400,000 for three years."

"Thank you," came the abrupt reply. "Maybe next time. We'll call you back." Click.

Pierre asked for that much because I didn't want to go to Cleveland. We knew the Barons' franchise was in serious financial trouble. We knew $400,000 for three years was too much above the going rate for a first-round draft pick. For a team on the brink of extinction, it was out of the question.

The Detroit Red Wings used the first pick of the draft to take Dale McCourt, a center from St. Catharines of the OHA. The Colorado Rockies chose second and took Beck. Washington selected Picard. Vancouver chose Gillis. Cleveland, needing a right wing but no longer interested in my rich blood, chose Mike Crombeen from the OHA's Kingston Canadians.

We weren't privy to the team-by-team selections because the draft was taking place on the telephone, so we were forced to watch the clock and guess how far into the first round they were. After approximately 45 minutes, I began to worry. I later learned that Chicago had chosen defenseman Doug Wilson from the Ottawa '67s of the OHA. Minnesota took Maxwell. The Rangers took DeBlois. St. Louis chose defenseman Scott Campbell from the OHA's London Knights. Montreal chose right wing Mark Napier, who had played his junior hockey for the OHA's Toronto Marlboros, but had signed with the WHA as an underager for the 1976–77 season and had scored 60 goals with the Birmingham Bulls.

Toronto had picks 11 and 12, but we weren't surprised that they ignored me twice. A reporter had told Pierre the day before the draft that the Maple Leafs were afraid that I might hold out for too much money and jump to Quebec of the WHA. Obviously they had been reading the papers over the last few years, too.

After the Maple Leafs selected two Marlies, right wing John Anderson and defenseman Trevor Johansen, the Rangers used their second pick of the first round for center Ron Duguay of the Sudbury Wolves. Buffalo was next and they took another right wing, Ric Seiling from St. Catharines.

It was the Islanders' turn. They called a timeout.

I later learned there was a difference of opinion up until the final moment. Saraceno implored Torrey to select me, but the timeout indicated that Saraceno's choice must not have been unanimous. Torrey, Saraceno, director of scouting Jimmy Devellano, Ontario scout Harry Boyd and Gerry "Tex" Ehman, the Western scout who is now the Isles' director of scouting and assistant GM, had to quickly decide between me and center Dwight Foster, who scored 60 goals for Kitchener and led the OHA with 143 points.

Foster, five-foot-eleven and 195 pounds, rugged, defensive-minded and possessed with a scoring touch, was a typical gritty Islander-type forward. I was not.

Saraceno won.

When the telephone on Denis' desk rang, Pierre, Denis and I leaped at once. It was Bill Torrey on the line. He wanted to congratulate me on becoming the Islanders' first-round draft choice, the 15th amateur selection in the 1977 draft. In that wildly exhilarating moment it didn't matter that 14 juniors, five right wings and three Quebec Leaguers had been taken ahead of me.

What I had waited so many years for had finally arrived.

It was great to hear coach Al Arbour welcome me to the Islanders. He told me there was a spot on the roster open for me and he looked forward to meeting me. Al passed his phone back to Bill and I handed mine to Pierre. A contract was next on the agenda. We scheduled our first meeting for two days later, June 16, at the Château Champlain hotel in Montreal.

When we hung up, I felt happy to be an Islander. They were an established hockey team playing just outside an exciting city. They had finished fourth overall the year before and had reached the semifinals against Montreal. They were a disciplined team capable of going places, but they needed some offensive help.

"Although I would've liked to have gone higher than 15th, I'm happy to be going to the Islanders," I told the press that day. "I'm known for my scoring talent and I believe I could earn a position on the team. I'm not saying I can score 75 goals, but I can score half that and maybe even more if I can adapt to the Islanders' style of play."

Lucie and I set our wedding for July 23. I told Pierre that I wanted to be signed before we were married and he assured me that a month was more than enough time to negotiate a contract. We booked the restaurant, planned our Bahamas honeymoon, reserved our flight and placed a deposit on our hotel room.

Pierre, Denis and I met the next day to plan our negotiating strategy for our first meeting with Bill. Pierre was terrific. He insisted that every one of our sessions with the Islanders be preceded by a get-together in which we discussed our game plan. Pierre wanted me to know exactly what he was going to say, what I should say and how I should say it. At times we actually rehearsed our lines.

"Look, it's going to be difficult," Pierre explained to Denis and me. "The WHA is struggling. We can't make many mistakes because we don't have much bargaining power. It's very important, Mike, that you act confident."

Pierre didn't want me to act shy. He wanted the Islanders to believe they had drafted a supremely confident, almost cocky, 20-year-old who was sure he could score regularly in the NHL. They drafted me because I scored goals, so I had to tell them I could score goals. Pierre thought Bill might ask me how many, so he suggested that if Bill did, I should tell them 50.

Fifty? I didn't believe I could, but I believed that if I said it, they would believe I believed it. The NHL rookie record was 44 and before the season began I would have been happy to beat that.

Pierre made me comfortable. Two years earlier he had negotiated Bob Sauve's first-round contract. Sauve was drafted 17th overall, so Pierre knew the going rate for a late first-rounder. He kept reminding me not to act surprised by anything Bill said. He wanted me to consider Bill a businessman when we met at the hotel, not a general manager.

I walked into the Château Champlain the next day wearing a white suit. Pierre and Lucie still tease me about that suit. After Bill, Pierre and I shared a little small talk, the two of them exchanged some very general ideas. Bill then turned to me and asked what I expected from myself.

"If I play regularly, I'm going to score a lot of goals for you, Bill," I said.

"How many?"

"Fifty."

Bill just looked at me and laughed softly, a friendly chuckle. He probably thought I was crazy, but I acted like I believed I could.

Making a statement like that didn't faze me. I didn't think scoring 50 goals was impossible and I didn't worry about the pressure a statement like that might put on me.

That first meeting didn't last very long. As we shook hands and prepared to leave, Bill said we would receive his first offer shortly. Pierre deliberately did not make a specific financial request. He felt we would maintain a better bargaining positioning by waiting until Bill made the first move.

That first move, a formal offer, was delivered to me by Henry about a week or two later. We met over coffee at the Mirage Diner. What an appropriate name. The dollar signs that danced in my head all summer vanished the moment I opened the envelope and unfolded that first contract in the front seat of my car.

I had tears in my eyes as I read it: bonuses of $20,000 to sign, $5,000 when I played my first NHL game and $5,000 when I played my 40th NHL game. Salaries of $40,000 in 1977–78, $40,000 for 1978–79 and $50,000 for my option year, 1979–80 ... if I made the team. If I was assigned to the minors my salary would be $20,000 the first year, $17,000 the second and $15,000 the third.

It was a three-year contract worth $160,000 U.S., but with only $72,000 guaranteed. After hearing how the WHA a year and two years ago threw money at 18- and 19-year-olds who weren't half as good as me, I was heartbroken by what the Islanders were saying I was worth.

I was ready to say "Screw them," but Pierre calmed me down. He wasn't upset. He knew from negotiating Sauve's contract that this was Bill's lowball offer. He also knew that Bill was going to have to do a lot better.

For nearly a month, Bill didn't do any better. Pierre told him that his offer was lower than Buffalo's to Sauve two years earlier. He told him he was being ridiculous. I was so disenchanted. After getting my hopes so high all year, not only did I get that terrible preliminary offer, but the offer stayed on the table for nearly a month.

The Indianapolis Racers had chosen me in the WHA's draft, but everybody knew they had no money to spend on quality players and no chance of getting me to play there. Bill knew it. We knew it. Bill knew we knew it. The WHA as a whole was sinking fast, too, so we never considered my jumping to that league as a way to threaten the Islanders.

I was growing very, very nervous. And then Maurice Filion, the WHA Nordiques' GM, called Pierre on July 19.

"Is Mike signed, yes or no?" Filion asked Pierre.

"He's not signed, we're negotiating," Pierre replied.

Filion had no idea where we were with the Islanders. But somehow he had convinced his WHA partners to let him take a shot at signing me. He knew that Quebec was one of the few WHA cities I'd consider. What he didn't know was that we desperately needed a card to play in our discussions with Bill.

"Maurice, you're right up against it," Pierre explained at two o'clock that Tuesday afternoon. "We're probably coming to an agreement within the next few days. Mike is getting married on Saturday and he's going to be signed before he's married. If you want to see us, be here tonight at seven o'clock."

"I'll be there," Filion replied.

While Filion and his chief scout, Yvan Prudhomme, scurried to make a flight from Quebec City to Montreal, Pierre called me. "Meet Denis and I at Denis' office at seven o'clock," he said. "We have to get together because Quebec is coming."

My golden goose was en route.

Filion wasted no time. He offered me a three-year deal worth approximately $300,000 Canadian: a signing bonus of $75,000, three years at $75,000 per year, and an automatic spot on the Nordiques. Every dollar was guaranteed.

"Give us 48 hours," Pierre said.

Pierre called Bill the next day, Wednesday the 20th. "Bill, why don't we get together tomorrow because Mike is getting married on Saturday," Pierre said. "Let's meet at noon at Dorval."

We met Bill the next day, Thursday the 21st at the airport's lounge. In our pre-meeting meeting, we were sure that he had no idea that Quebec had contacted us. His first offer was his current offer. We felt certain he thought we called this meeting to accept.

Pierre opened the session. "We've got an offer from Quebec and we're ready to sign with Quebec tomorrow. Here's what we need: $55,000 the first year, $65,000 the second and $70,000 for the option year. Since we know Mike's not going to play in the minors, we'll give you the minor-league clause at $22,000, $20,000 and $17,000. We want a $45,000 signing bonus, $15,000 when Mike plays his first NHL game and $10,000 for his 40th game. Bonuses of $2,500 if Mike scores 30 goals, another $5,000 if he scores 40 goals and another $7,500 if he scores 50."

Pierre caught his breath. Bill looked shocked. Pierre, Denis and I were unanimous that based on his expression, this was not what he expected to hear.

"Mr. Torrey, this is it," Pierre continued. "Take this or forget about it. We know that you haven't moved on your offer because the WHA is struggling. But I'm telling you that if Quebec is not in the WHA one day, then it'll be in the NHL. And I'm telling you we have a firm offer from the Nordiques."

As I listened, I felt better and better. For the first time we were in the driver's seat. I was prepared to accept the offer Pierre had just outlined, a contract that would earn me $125,000 (counting the signing bonus) if I spent my entire rookie season in New York. And if Bill didn't accept our proposal or make a legitimate counter-offer, I was prepared to instruct Pierre to call Filion in the morning and accept Quebec's offer.

"Can I phone my boss?" Bill asked Pierre.

"Sure." It was approximately 1:00 p.m.

Bill returned in a half-hour. "I can't reach him," he said. "He's in court. I don't know where he is and it's going to be to be hard for me to reach him. So it's going to be hard for me to give you an answer today."

We came to an agreement in principle, giving Bill until that night, Thursday night, to get us a definite answer. We couldn't give him more time because we had asked for only 48 hours from Filion and that clock was almost expired and my wedding was on Saturday, another 48 hours away.

Naturally, Bill asked for more time.

"Bill, we're going to be at this number all night, at Denis Gauthier's house," Pierre said. "Our deadline is midnight tonight. Tomorrow is Friday and the wedding is Saturday."

"Gee, you're not giving me much time," Bill said.

"Bill," Pierre responded, "I think we've been negotiating clean. Our negotiations were clean for the past month, but nothing happened. Now we're at the end. We need a decision.

So Bill said, "OK, I'll call you before midnight tonight."

We assembled at Denis' house for a night of ping-pong. We waited and played, played and waited, then waited some more. At about nine o'clock the phone rang. It was Bill.

"Pierre," he said. "I can't reach the guy. I don't know what's going to happen."

Pierre held firm: "You've got to reach him before midnight. Midnight's the deadline."

"Gee, goddamn, give me another day," Bill pleaded.

"I can't," Pierre said. "Bill, there are three hours to go. Don't worry. We're playing ping-pong. We'll be here all night. We're not going to move."

Pierre later told me I appeared unbelievably cool, but he must have known that inside I was shaking. My wedding was less than two days away and I still didn't have a professional contract.

At about 11:30 Bill called back. "We're willing to accept this," he told Pierre.

"OK," Pierre replied. "Give us 15 minutes. I want Mike to give his final approval."

I still wasn't totally convinced I should accept the Islanders' offer. The signing bonus was lower than Quebec's. The guaranteed money was $196,000 less. The minor-league provisions were still included. I wanted more time.

"Mike, now it's time you decide," Pierre said firmly. "Make up your mind, one or the other. Which do you want?"

I went outside for a walk by myself. I thought about the money, the WHA's watered-down talent and second-rate status. I thought about how I had dreamed of playing in the NHL, of the Stanley Cup. What kind of tradition did the Avco Cup have? I wanted to prove the scouts wrong by becoming an all-around great pro, a complete player. If I did that in the vastly inferior WHA, the skeptics would still raise doubts. I had to play against the best in the NHL.

I decided to become a New York Islander.

We called Bill back at 11:45 and I got on the phone. Bill repeated the offer and I verbally agreed. Pierre got back on the line and told Bill that we wanted a contract by noon tomorrow.

"But it's nearly midnight," Bill complained.

"We trust you," Pierre replied diplomatically, "but Mike's going on vacation for two weeks, on his honeymoon, so we want the contract by tomorrow noon and we want the check, the $45,000 signing bonus."

Bill wearily agreed. We hung up. I felt great.

Pierre still had work to do. He apologized for waking up Filion at home, then told him that I had made my decision.

"Maurice, Mike has decided he's going to play in New York. We have accepted their contract. Thank you for your offer."

We were back at Dorval on Friday the 22nd, but this time to meet the Islanders' publicity director, Hawley Chester, who had the contracts and my signing bonus. I'll never forget the moment he emerged from the airplane, and not because he was carrying my $45,000.

Chester arrived in a suit, wearing shoes without socks.

We stifled our laughs. Pierre and Denis examined the contract, I signed it and Chester returned it to New York. That afternoon I deposited my signing bonus check in the bank. The next day Lucie and I were married, and on Sunday we flew to the Bahamas.

Filion's mistake was giving us 48 hours to accept his offer. Ten years later, it's still bugging him. Last year he bumped into Pierre and asked how my back was. Then he told Pierre how badly he regretted not telling us to take it or leave it.

If he hadn't given us 48 hours to accept his offer, if he had put a contract on the table that night and given us until midnight to sign, we never would've been able to use the WHA as a bargaining tool with the Islanders.

I would have been forced to decide right there between the Islanders' initial offer: three years for $160,000 U.S., but only $72,000 guaranteed; and the Nordiques' offer: three years for $300,000 Canadian, all guaranteed.

I would have taken the $300,000 Canadian.

Goulet–Stastny–Bossy?

Chapter

Rookie of the Year

Everything had happened so fast: Quebec made its offer on Tuesday, we met with Bill on Thursday at noon, the Islanders showed me how much they wanted me by increasing their offer that night, I signed on Friday. Now it was Saturday, my wedding day. And on Sunday Lucie and I were flying to the Bahamas.

Bill asked us to not publicize the signing until after we returned from our honeymoon. He wanted to announce it and introduce me to the New York media at a press conference. Although Lucie and I knew it was going to be incredibly difficult not to share the good news with everybody, we agreed. Of course I told Mom and Dad, but we kept the news out of the papers, which is all Bill wanted.

Lucie and I invited 26 people to our wedding ceremony and reception at a restaurant in Laval named Le Vicompte. The next morning we flew to Nassau for a two-week honeymoon at the Ambassador Beach Hotel. The islands were beautiful, but we were bored. We were very close to Carol and Bob Lagace, Lucie's sister and brother-in-law, and we missed them terribly. Both of us would have preferred playing cards with Carol and Bob than sitting on a beach for two straight weeks, but we were too scared to admit it.

When I asked Lucie if she was enjoying herself, she said, "Oh, of course I am. Are you?" And I replied, "I'm having a great time."

The truth was, both of us wanted to leave. Honeymoon or not, we missed Laval. But our hotel room was paid for in advance and neither of us was secure enough to admit that we were having a lousy time; so we stayed the entire 14 days.

Having never traveled before, I thought $1,000 would be enough for three meals a day, entertainment and souvenirs. I wasn't close. Bacon and eggs cost $5 and a burger was $3.50 at our hotel, but we managed. We budgeted $15 for one trip to the casino, but that went incredibly fast. I was down to my final dollar when our chartered bus began boarding. As we walked toward the casino door, I passed the roulette table and tossed my last chip on 17, my jersey number.

"Excuse me, sir," I heard from behind the roulette wheel. "Two-dollar minimum."

I blushed and sheepishly went to retrieve my chip when Lucie plucked another dollar out of her purse. And guess what?

"Seventeen. The winner is 17."

We stood stunned as the gentleman in the tux and bowtie pushed $35 in my direction. We scooped up the chips, cashed them in and raced triumphantly to our bus, feeling like millionaires. We enjoyed a nice dinner and quick shopping spree that final night, leaving a few dollars for coffee before our flight home the next morning.

We arrived at the airport to learn that our 10 a.m. flight was delayed due to an air traffic controllers' strike in Canada. What? I was starved. I was counting on my airline breakfast. Twelve hours later, when the plane finally departed for Burlington, Vermont, breakfast was the last meal on my mind. We landed in Burlington, took a bus to Mirabel Airport in Montreal where Bob picked us up. We got home at 4 a.m.

It was some honeymoon.

A few days after we recuperated from our honeymoon voyage home, we flew to New York City for my introductory press conference at Gallagher's, a Manhattan steak house. We had never been to New York and we couldn't believe how big and crazy everything was; the highways were unbelievably wild. Hawley Chester picked us up at the airport for the 45-minute trip into Manhattan and I think it's safe to say he would have made a good New York cab driver.

Although the press conference was uneventful, the presence of one spectator spoke volumes for the organization. Coach Al Arbour's wife Claire, who rarely attended these events, was there that day. Claire, who spoke French, showed up to make sure that Lucie would have someone to talk to while I was with the media.

After the press conference we were taken from Manhattan to Long Island, where I got my first look at Nassau Coliseum. It looked so big without the ice on the concrete floor. Lucie and I stayed that night at the Island Inn, less than a mile from the Coliseum, and were driven to the airport the next day in a limousine. We were so impressed.

We spent August in my Laval apartment. Rookie camp was one month away, but I spent my time playing golf. I had made big plans to get into great shape before I reported to camp, but I just never got around to it.

I got around to my bonus money, though. I gave Dad $5,000 to help with the cost of a house he and Gordie planned to build 40 miles west of Laval in St. Lazarre. Throughout my last year of junior, Gordie, Mom and Dad had spent almost every weekend clearing that tract of land while living in a little shack that was for storing gardening tools.

It was a sharp, white Buick Le Sabre with light blue velour upholstery that put the Bobcat to shame. My signing bonus enabled me to finally rid myself of that lemon. I also had to pay Come Lacroix $7,500 for the loan on the Bobcat. Most of the money was gone when Lucie gently reminded me that she paid for her engagement ring, too. To this day she swears that she paid for her engagement ring and our wedding rings. I plead no contest.

August passed quickly. Too quickly. Lucie and I decided that she should stay with her mother in Laval while I reported to training camp. We agreed there was no sense in her coming to Long Island before we knew if I was going to make the team. We dreaded the possibility, but if I was assigned to the Islanders' Central Hockey League farm team in Fort Worth, Texas, she would join me there.

Lucie was fantastic all summer. She could have pressured me to sign with the WHA Nordiques so we could move to predominantly French-speaking Quebec City, but she didn't. In fact, she believed as strongly as I did that I had to prove myself in the NHL. She could have complained about the threat of us starting our lives in Fort Worth, Texas, or the Isles' International Hockey League farm club in Muskegon, Michigan, but she didn't. Well, not more than a little. She got incredibly nervous when she read the training camp roster I got in the mail and couldn't find a familiar French name, but she never made a big deal out of what was going to be a difficult transition for her, too.

We cried together on Sunday, September 11, the day I packed the LeSabre and left for camp. I hated to leave Lucie behind and she hated to see me go. I spoke confidently the whole summer about breaking into the NHL, but deep down I was just another scared-stiff rookie. I didn't know if I would be good enough to make the team. What if my weak defense convinced them to start me in the minors?

I didn't know what to expect.

Henry Saraceno and I made the ten-hour drive down the Adirondack Northway and New York State Thruway. Those ten hours felt like ten days and it had nothing to do with Saraceno. All of a sudden I was crossing the U.S.–Canada border to become an NHL right wing. This wasn't a trip to Plattsburgh to the drive-in or the beach with Mom and Dad.

This was it.

Rookie camp — one week of drills and exhibition games before the veterans reported — opened the next day at Racquet & Rink, the team's Farmingdale, L.I., training facility. Physicals were scheduled for Monday morning. On Sunday night I checked into the Pickwick Motor Inn and introduced myself to my roommate, Andre Lepage, the Drummondville goalie who gave up my first QMJHL goal five years earlier.

I passed my physical, then promptly bruised my left shoulder without getting hit during my third day of rookie camp. I took a pass from behind the net during a scrimmage and, as I shot, I rotated my shoulder awkwardly. I was examined by the Islanders' team physician, Dr. Jeffrey Minkoff, who told me that my bruised shoulder had been carrying a bone spur for a few years.

"That's just great," I said to myself. "The first-round pick is damaged goods." I remembered injuring my right shoulder during my first junior season, but Laval's doctors had diagnosed a simple bruise. Wrong. Dr. Minkoff guessed that the original injury might have been a chipped bone. He recommended I stay off the ice for a few days.

The bruise in camp had aggravated the spur. Whenever my arm was placed in a funny position, my shoulder bone clicked and my arm went numb. Minkoff said if it persisted, I'd eventually need an operation. He said I might avoid surgery as long as I kept the muscles around the joint strong by exercising with free weights.

At times that season I did use free weights, but not regularly. And that bone spur, which I can still feel today, has never bothered me again. Not once. The doctors have no idea why.

Injuring my shoulder turned out to be a blessing, because on Thursday and Friday of that first week we played home-and-home rookie preseason games against the Rangers. The fights in those two Islander–Ranger rookie games were as bad as the brawls in junior. Free agents out to earn minor-league contracts will do anything to attract attention. Nick Fotiu and Paul Stewart, who is now an NHL referee, were two of the Rangers who went crazy in that game. Duguay and DeBlois played, too.

Fortunately, my shoulder was well enough to scrimmage a couple of days later. But I was incredibly shy that first week. The only guy I knew was Yvan Vautour, who had already become part of the Fort Worth gang from the year before. I could sense the other rookies watching everything I did on the ice and off. I don't think I said 20 words in the dressing room that week.

Then the pros showed up. Denis Potvin and Dave Lewis, Glenn "Chico" Resch and Billy Smith, Jude Drouin and J.P. Parise, Clark Gillies and Billy Harris, Eddie Westfall and Bert Marshall, Bob Bourne, Bob Nystrom and Garry Howatt.

And that runt named Trottier.

I met Trots after the second day of workouts. In a scrimmage earlier that day, center Andre St. Laurent threw me a pass as I cut across the middle. The puck deflected off someone's stick or skate and dinged me in the eye. Off I went, less than a week after my shoulder problems, back into trainer Ron Waske's medical room. I could imagine what the guys where thinking: "What a fragile first-round draft pick. Touch him and he breaks."

I was slumped on the trainer's table with one icepack on my shoulder and another over my freshly bruised eye when Trots, in street clothes ready to leave after practice, walked by.

"Hi, Mike," Trots said. "How're you doing? I'm Bryan Trottier."

"Hi," I muttered. "Camp's been rough so far. I hurt my shoulder and I just got walloped in the eye."

"Ah, don't worry about it," Trots replied. "Hey, how about coming over to the house for dinner tonight?"

Perhaps he invited me because he felt sorry for me. Perhaps it was because he knew I was lonely. It could have been because some veteran had him over for dinner when he was a rookie. Whatever the reason was, once I met him and his wife, Nickie, I knew this was a guy I could get along with. And with the training camp I was having so far, I needed all the friends I could get. After ten days of hotel rooms, hotel food and nightly calls to Lucie, an evening at the Trottiers was a welcome change of pace.

I was a terrific pain in the coach's ass all camp long. I was so conscious of the rap on the defensive part of my game that I rarely let one workout go by without asking: "Al, is this where you want me to be?" "Al, is this what I should do?" "Al, where am I supposed to be when they do that?" "Al, I want to know everything there is to know about this game." "Al, I'm serious about playing good defensive hockey."

Al, Al, Al. . . . I was such a nag that one day Al finally looked at me and said: "Mike, shut up. Just play like you did in junior and if you do something wrong, I'll tell you."

I wasn't scoring very many goals and I didn't think I was having a great camp, but since I didn't hear too many criticisms from Al or the scouts, I took it as a good sign. Then, about two weeks into camp, Trots offered me the guest room in his house. He knew I wasn't going to bring Lucie down from Montreal until after I found out if I made the team and he knew I was sick of the Pickwick Motor Inn.

Sure, I'll move in, I told Trots. I took his offer as a good sign, too.

With about three of four games left in preseason, Al put Trots and I together for the first time. It was for a game at Vancouver. Gillies, a rugged six-foot-three, 220-pounder from Moose Jaw, Saskatchewan, was our left wing. Gillies was a gentle giant with a great sense of humor. Gillies and Trottier had played most of the previous season together with Harris, the Isles' first-ever first-round draft pick.

We clicked in our first game as a line. Bill and Al told me last year that they remembered one rush that first game where Trots and I passed the puck back and forth together ten times and I ended up with a good scoring chance. Al remembers rubbing his hands together and telling Bill, "I think we've got something here."

The line made sense: a strong cornerman on the left, a playmaker and excellent two-way man in the middle and a goal scorer on the right.

At the time, however, I wasn't thinking about becoming the team's number one right wing. I was worried about making the team. Do you know how much courage it took for me to ask Al if I should start looking for an apartment? Not only was I afraid of the answer, but I was afraid of him thinking I was being too cocky and pushy. It was about a week before the start of the season when I finally summoned the courage to ask him.

My heart was pounding. I could hardly breathe. I asked him after practice in a half-squeak, half-whisper. The moment between my question and his answer seemed like an hour. He looked at me like I had just asked the most obvious question in the world. "Yeah, go get a place," he said nonchalantly, not realizing he had just prevented a heart attack.

The Trottiers decided it would make sense for Lucie to move into the guest room with me while we looked for an apartment. So, from the last week of training camp until a few weeks into the 1977–78 NHL season, life in one East Northport ranch house was not unlike *The Honeymooners.*

Lucie arrived at Kennedy Airport with two suitcases and about a dozen of my Sherwood hockey sticks. I had provided the Islanders with my personal pattern, but when they ordered my sticks from their supplier, Koho, the shafts felt terrible and the lie of my blade wasn't quite right. I'm very picky about my sticks, so I spent my first three weeks of training camp using sticks that weren't mine while I waited for Koho to manufacture a new batch and for Lucie to bring a batch of my old sticks from junior that the Nationals still had lying around.

Lucie and I were happy to move in with the Trottiers. We were all roughly the same age and we hit it off. Our rooms were side by side and the headboards of our beds shared the common wall. We were so careful never to disturb them by talking or playing the television too loud that Trots started teasing us about being too quiet for newlyweds.

Nickie loves to talk (90 miles-per-hour, Trots says) and she loves to cook. Lucie, who was trying to learn the language, insisted upon carrying a share of the household load so one night she cooked dinner. She made a spaghetti and meat sauce dinner that was great. Trots loved it.

I wasn't the only rookie in camp. Stefan Persson and Bob Lorimer were competing for spots on defense. Mike Kaszycki was a center with slick moves. Richie Hansen played left wing. Alex McKendry and Dave Salvian were my competition for one opening at right wing.

The hardest part of that first camp was those first few nights alone, lying in bed staring at a motel room ceiling wondering what they thought of you. I was terrified of going to the minors. I thought of what Fort Worth, Texas, would mean to our lives, of what a demotion would do to my confidence. I wonder if I would have had the career I had if I started in the minors? I didn't have a great first training camp, but as I look back, I think they had decided from the day they drafted me that I was going to at least start the season with the Islanders.

I wish they had told me that in August. It would have saved Lucie and I more than a few sleepless nights that fall.

The greatest moment of my first NHL training camp wasn't when Al told me to start looking for a place to live. It was when Jim Pickard, our assistant trainer and equipment manager, asked me what number I wanted to wear. What a feeling. That made it official. My junior number 17 wasn't available because that was Drouin's number, so Pick offered me a choice between 7, 16 and 22. I didn't want a one-digit number and 16 meant nothing to me. I chose 22 because it was my birthdate.

My first NHL game was at Buffalo. Al knew that I was temporarily living with Trots at home, so he roomed us together on the road. We checked into our hotel, Trots grabbed our room key, and about a dozen of us piled into one elevator. Dumb rookie that I was, I didn't bother to ask Trots our room number. On the crowded elevator ride, Trots was nearest the door. He kept popping out to let others exit, then popping back in. Only one time he didn't get back in, something I didn't notice until a few floors later.

The other guys must have been howling to themselves.

I went back down to the lobby, asked what room I had (yes, I was embarrassed) and got my own key. When I opened the door, there was no sign of Trots ... until I opened the closet. There he was, hiding. He scared the hell out of me.

About an hour before my NHL debut, while I was fidgeting with my equipment and trying to keep busy, Trots asked me if I was nervous.

"No," I said. "I'm taking it as just another exhibition game."

"It's not just another exhibition game," Trots snarled.

In the span of 24 hours, I had seen the scope of Trots' personality. The fun-loving, light-hearted jokester had turned into the deadly serious professional. That first road trip made quite an impression on me. So did my first game. I scored my first NHL goal against rookie goalie Don Edwards, on assists from Gillies and Trots. I did a little jig and fetched the puck after Clarkie set me up in close.

Although I constantly feared being sent to the minors, my season started smoothly. I scored 20 goals in my first 22 games and became a leading Calder Trophy candidate for Rookie of the Year. Gillies, Trots and I became one of the highest-scoring lines in the NHL.

Lucie and I found a nice apartment in East Northport close to Trots' house, which made it easy for Lucie to spend the night with Nickie while we were on the road.

I probably developed what scouts called my quick hands and quick release more out of self-defense than anything else. The NHL was zoom, zoom, zoom compared to junior. Even compared to training camp and the exhibition season. I learned to make quick passes and take quick shots to avoid getting hammered every time I had the puck.

Fifty goals was in my mind from Opening Night. I scored once in our first game, once in our second. Our fourth game was a 0–0 tie with L.A. and I must have missed five or six great chances. That's when I angered some players — on my team and in other cities — by saying it was easier to play here than in junior. I meant that it was easier to play with a center like Trottier, with teammates like Gillies, Nystrom and Howatt, who allowed me to play my game without fear, without worrying about getting my head beat in every night.

I meant that the NHL was more skilled and more civilized. I wasn't misquoted, just misinterpreted.

I realized I might have spoken too soon after I made my first visit to Detroit's Olympia, the rink where Gordie Howe won my mother's heart. Gillies, Trots and I lined up for the opening faceoff against the Red Wings' starting line of Dan Maloney, Dennis Hextall and Dennis Polonich. As I glided to the outer rim of the center circle, I noticed Maloney sneering at me. He never said a word, but five seconds off the opening draw he jumped me.

It was junior all over again.

Gillies was already fighting Polonich. Maloney never punched me, he just dropped his gloves, grabbed my sweater and started swinging me around like a rag doll. It was the first time an NHL team had tried to intimidate me. You know what? It worked.

I spent the rest of the game looking over my shoulder, listening for footsteps, staying away from a late hit. Once Maloney attacked me, I just had it in the back of my mind that it was going to happen again later in the game. I wasn't afraid like I was in junior because I knew I had teammates who would stick up for me, but I had been intimidated. I played terribly and didn't score.

After the game, which we won 4–1, I told the press that I was ashamed of the way I had played. I said I was disappointed that I wasn't able to ignore the intimidation. I should have been able to shake it off, because junior had taught me how to handle it.

Trots and I didn't talk about the brawl that night. For a while I thought what Maloney did to me didn't bother Trots, who loved to throw his weight around and deliver stinging bodychecks. Trots always played with a dose of machismo, so it shocked me when I learned early in my career that he despises fighting as much as I do.

But he does. Trots hasn't fought in years. I never quite understood how a guy who despises violence in the form of fighting can hit the smallest or biggest opponent with the same reckless abandon. That's just the way Trots is.

I, on the other hand, learned how to stay away from trouble. I was called for only six penalty minutes all season. With Gillies and Trottier dominating the corners and boards, I was learning how to find the holes. People who were surprised at how frequently I was scoring as a rookie didn't stop to consider that my linemates were opening up the ice for a guy who knew how to put the puck in the net.

At the same time, I took pride in trying to keep the puck out of our net. Al stressed defense and I was determined to show him I wasn't a one-way player. It was frustrating, though. After Maloney danced with me at Detroit, we flew to Denver for a game against the Colorado Rockies. We had a 3–2 lead and the Rockies had their goalie out for a sixth attacker late in the game when Billy Smith stopped a shot and took two steps out of the net.

Smitty dropped the puck and shot for the empty net. Paul Gardner intercepted Smitty's shot and, bang, it was in our net. I was on the ice at the time, but it was the last time I saw an open-net opportunity that season. Al, who earlier in the season replaced me with more experienced forwards in the last minutes of periods and games, returned to that strategy after that game. It wasn't that I did anything wrong in Colorado. I guess it was just that I was on the ice.

Could I have been that atrocious a backchecker in junior? I think there was a hurdle for me to leap when I got to the NHL, a hurdle that was built by the media in Montreal and the scouts who talked to the media and fed them their information.

I never argued with the fact that I didn't play defensively in junior. I justified it in the sense that not one of my coaches ever taught me to play defense. Laval was a bad-to-mediocre team that needed a 75-goal scorer to keep it competitive. I was supposed to hang out at the red line a lot of times waiting to score goals. That's what Claude LaBossiere and Jacques St. Jean and Denis DeJordy wanted. Nobody ever instructed me to check the trailing defenseman or follow my opposing left wing to the net.

In junior I was always the first guy forechecking, so I usually was the last guy back. I played junior the way Wayne Gretzky and Mario Lemieux play in the NHL, although Gretzky the last few seasons has adapted better to checking assignments. I rarely read or hear anything about Gretzky's and Lemieux's defense. When I do, it's one offhanded comment or one line in a story. With me it was THE story.

And throughout my rookie season I took it to heart.

A few days after I scored my 44th goal to tie the NHL rookie record, which I broke a few days later, I read the Islander director of player personnel Ed Chadwick's explanation of how the Isles selected me over Foster in the draft. There was a quote from Al that made me feel a lot better.

"Henry Saraceno had coached Mike in midget and loved him," Chadwick said. "It was between him and Dwight Foster, a Kitchener kid, and Al said, 'Tell me the difference.'"

"So we told him Bossy's a good skater and can score but doesn't backcheck, and the other kid's a good mucker and tough enough but doesn't score. And Al says, 'Get me the scorer. I can teach him to check a little but nobody can teach anybody to put the puck in the net.'"

That was exactly my point. I admit I didn't push myself enough defensively in junior, but I knew if I had to I could. And I was determined to prove to Al that my defense could get better and better.

Playing defense is one of the easiest parts of the game, if you want to do it. Players are either too lazy, which I was in junior, or too stubborn. And because defensemen and defensive forwards don't get the big headlines or make the big money in the NHL, and because scoring goals is more fun, who wants to sacrifice offense for defense? The only players who do that are the ones who don't have good offensive skills or the ones who want to be known as solid two-way players, which I wanted badly.

Playing defense simply means that when the other team has the puck, you hustle back into your zone and follow your man, even if he skates to the net. For a right wing, it means I stay in good position along the boards in case one of my teammates needs to foil a forechecker by making a pass. Al always preached that "If you're in good position defensively, you're in good position offensively."

To a degree, he's right. Trots, Clarkie and I started many a rush by taking a crisp pass from a defenseman and making two quick passes through the neutral zone. The word you hear all the time is "system." Players are reminded to stick to the system.

Hockey coaches aren't like football coaches. Our game doesn't have too many systems. Basically, the first forechecker tries to force the defenseman with the puck towards the second forechecker, usually toward the boards. That limits the opponent's options. While the first forward is supposed to take out the man who released the puck (that's what coaches call finishing the check) and the second forward is playing the puck, the third forward is supposed to stay high in the defensive zone and read the play.

Early in our careers Trots, Clarkie and I forechecked at once. We created more chances, but found ourselves too often having to scramble back into defensive position in case "our" system failed.

Al taught us that if I'm forechecking with Clarkie and I force the puck carrier towards Clarkie, who steals, I can position myself offensively and Trots, the third guy high, can attack. If Clarkie and I miss, Trots retreats and joins our two defensemen in picking up their three attackers. If one of the defensemen tries to join the play (Paul Coffey and Ray Bourque are great at this), it's up to Gillies and I to make sure they're covered.

Simple? I think it is. Coaches can tinker with the basic plan, but in any system the idea is to have each attacker covered by a defender. You want a man-on-man situation. You can go to any library and read a hockey book on how you're supposed to forecheck, how you're supposed to set up in your end.

A coach's primary job is to get the best out of all his players while making sure each one is executing the system. Al was able to do this without stripping his star players of their individuality. He adjusted the basic system slightly to make better use of Clarkie's strength in the corners, Trots' passing skills, my shot. That's what made Al such a great coach.

The Islanders exhibited defensive discipline the year before I arrived by yielding the second-fewest goals in the league. This was a close-knit team with a lot of Western Canadians and a lot of defensive-minded players who I'm sure were happy that I could score goals, but who wanted to make sure I didn't cost them goals with my supposedly weak defense.

I had a lot of watchdogs around me those first few months. Guys like Howatt, Nystrom and Marshall, Gerry Hart and Billy MacMillan, whose spot on the team I eventually took, constantly reminded me of my defensive responsibilities and made sure I worked hard.

Bert and Billy never accepted me for the player I was. I know my name came up often when those Western guys got together. Most Westerners I knew then and know now think that their league is better than it was and their players are tougher than they are. I don't know how the game was played out West ten years ago or is played there today, but I couldn't think of anything tougher than what I went through in junior. That's why I said that the NHL seemed easier to me.

My dressing stall at Racquet & Rink that first year was between Bert's and Potvin's. Bert doubled as Al's assistant coach and ran some of the practices that year. He was especially hard on me.

I don't think Potvin resented me. I quickly found out, though, that he wanted the puck. We got into an argument after a power play in Los Angeles my first year because of that. I had the puck on the right side and Denny was open at the point. Instead of passing it back to Denny toward the middle, I turned and shot. It was the improper play and it didn't work. I was mad that I didn't score and I wondered if a pass to Denny was the better play. When I turned to look at him, he had a scowl that said: "Why didn't you pass?"

We skated to the bench. He sat down and I leaned against the boards, still on the ice, and said, "Sorry. Maybe I should have passed it."

And he said, "Yeah, you should have."

We both stated our cases so loud that Al had to come over and tell us both to shut up. If Al hadn't, who knows how long that argument would have lasted?

I remember times when Denny would sneer if he didn't receive a pass when he was open and there were times when I thought I was open and didn't get the puck from him. But I never felt that he didn't want to share the puck with me, or vice versa. Potvin and I were two supremely confident players on the ice who each felt that whatever he did at a particular time was the correct play.

Potvin and I both played on instinct. As my career progressed, if I was skating in the open I expected to receive the puck. I guess that's how Denny felt that night in L.A. After all, four years earlier he had been the Isles' number one amateur draft pick. As the first choice overall, he entered the NHL under much more outside pressure than I did. And he had already delivered. He won the Calder Trophy in 1974 and the Norris for best defenseman in 1976. He had become one of the team's cornerstones and, in my rookie year, he was one of the reasons why we were Stanley Cup contenders.

I was still making a name for myself.

I was leery of Potvin when I arrived in New York. I had heard that he wasn't very popular on the team. I remembered how in 1976 Denny was annoyed that he lost the Team Canada MVP award to Bobby Orr, and how he said that publicly and angered a lot of people.

That was all I could remember when I first met him. He intimidated me because he didn't look or talk like a hockey player. He sounded like a businessman. I was envious that whole first year of how well he spoke and conducted himself with the press and public. I also learned that Denny thinks very highly of himself. It angered a lot of people that he was so confident and unafraid to show it, but I never had a problem with that. Whenever I saw how he handled himself, I just chuckled and told myself, "That's Denny."

I guess the best way for me to put it is to say our relationship was never deep, but I have a profound amount of respect for his talent.

Who's better, Orr or Potvin? I never analyzed hockey when I was young, so it's hard for me to compare Denny to Orr. I never played with or against Orr, so I'll just say that Potvin was by far the best defensemen in the league for the first six or seven years that I played with him. Even if sometimes we got on each other's nerves.

Al ticked me off once my first season, too, just before that game in Los Angeles when Denny and I argued. We had played on December 23 at Montreal and weren't scheduled again until December 27 at Vancouver, so I assumed I'd be able to spend my first Christmas as an Islander at home in Laval. I got up my nerve a couple of weeks before Christmas and asked Al if I could stay behind in Montreal after the game. I promised to be back on Long Island by Christmas Day so there was no chance of me missing the flight to Vancouver on the 26th.

Al told me he'd check the schedule and let me know. A few days later, he said no. We were going to practice at home on Christmas Eve, he said, and he wanted me there. I was devastated. I was already homesick and now I was being told I would miss Christmas at home for the first time since 1969, when I was in France.

I was disappointed, but I didn't get really angry at him until Christmas Eve. On the flight home from Montreal on the 23rd, Al announced that practice the next morning would begin at 10:30. What he didn't say until we showed up the next morning was that this practice would be optional.

Oh, was I annoyed. I thought about racing to the airport and flying home that minute, since Christmas Day was an off-day. But then I stopped to consider that since Al hadn't given me permission, I would be in major trouble if anything went wrong and I missed the flight to Vancouver.

Lucie and I spent Christmas Eve out to dinner and barhopping with Nickie and Trots. We had a great time, but it couldn't compare to being home with my family. Lucie, in fact, flew home Christmas morning to be with her family that night.

The season was zipping along smoothly. I scored my 30th goal in our 45th game, when we killed the Flyers 6–1 at the Coliseum in late

January to move into a tie for first in the Patrick Division. I played in my first NHL All-Star Game three days later at Buffalo (Campbell Conference coach Fred Shero didn't recognize me when I checked in for the game) and notched my first NHL hat trick two weeks after that at home against Washington. That gave me 39 goals in 51 games.

I scored my 40th two games later in Chicago, but it was a nightmarish day. Snowstorms turned our 3-hour flight into a 12-hour odyssey. We made it to Chicago three hours before gametime and lost 5–4. Blackhawks defenseman Phil Russell creamed me with a check in the third period, bruising my left shoulder. Waske initially feared a fracture, but the X-rays were negative.

I missed four games, scored a goal in each of my first two games back, and then in Game 60 scored twice against Dan Bouchard at Atlanta to tie the NHL record for goals by a rookie — 44 set by Buffalo's Richard Martin in 1971–72.

When the reporters who had been bugging me about the record brought it up again, I said, "Why don't you ask me something new?"

"What color shirts do you wear?" somebody asked.

"Red," I responded. "It reminds me of the goal light."

"What kind of shirts do you wear?"

"Cheap ones."

One not-so-red and not-so-cheap one, my Laval Nationals jersey Number 17, was retired on March 15. It was the night after I had scored my 49th goal. With 11 games left, I was certain of 50, so I was in a great mood as I flew up that night. Laval's pregame ceremony made me feel even better.

Pierre Lacroix, who played for Laval in the late '60s and also wore Number 17, got choked up when the pregame festivities ended. "It's so great of them to retire my jersey," he said with a straight face.

I returned to Long Island. Eleven games and one goal to go: I failed to score against Atlanta, Philadelphia, Toronto, Cleveland, Minnesota, or against the Rangers at Madison Square Garden. With five games left, I started to get nervous. We were in a 2–3–2 slump and our first-place lead over Philadelphia had dwindled from nine points to three. We wanted to finish first because it meant a first-round bye in the playoffs. I wanted that 50th.

I got it in our next game and I remember it like I scored it last night. It was in Game 76, on April 1 at home against Washington. Bernie Wolfe was the goalie. My brother Roddy had come down from Halifax to see me play pro for the first time. We were losing 2–1 with ten minutes left when I scored on a power play from the left side of the net, on assists from Trots and Potvin.

When I saw the puck slip behind Wolfe, I circled towards the boards and did a neat little two-step. No rookie had ever scored 50 goals and I was damn proud. I capped the night by scoring my 51st on a power play with five seconds left to break a 2–2 tie and keep us three points ahead of the Flyers.

We beat Detroit, 5–2. Then we tied the Flyers, 3–3, in a game they had to win. And on April 8, I scored my 53rd goal and we crushed the Rangers at home, 7–2, to clinch the title.

About a million people crammed in our dressing room after the game: players, wives, friends, fans who had snuck in. Champagne was everywhere. Two rookies who had escaped hockey's most barbaric ritual all season, Stefan Persson and I, got shaved by a few drunk veterans. I was drunk, too, and I have no idea who took the razor to me. They ignored the hair on my head, but shaved my, ahem, groin area. Then they threw me naked into the runway outside the dressing room.

Who did I see when I hit the floor? Lucie, Roddy and his wife Barbara. They were waiting outside, celebrating, and they cracked up when I came flying out the door. I started pounding on it to get back in. I wanted to celebrate, too.

First place meant a best-of-seven quarterfinal series against Toronto. Mike Bossy meet Tiger Williams.

Al shocked the Leafs (it surprised me, too) by taking me off Trots' line prior to the first game and fitting me with Bob Bourne and Mike Kaszycki. I scored a goal and we won Game 1, 4–1. I was reunited with Trots and Gillies in Game 2 and I scored in overtime to win it, 3–2.

Then the series turned from ugly to brutal. Not because Toronto beat us 2–0 and 3–1 at Maple Leaf Gardens, but because guys like Williams and Jerry Butler and Dan Maloney (who had been traded during the season) started running around trying to injure us and then bragging about how we were running scared.

"You know the Islanders are crying," Williams said. "They know that if we hit them, we'll beat them. I don't go around crying about getting hit or getting stuck. The only guys who don't cry on their team are their best players, Bryan Trottier and Clark Gillies. The rest of them are a bunch of fairies, yelling it's tough and rough and things like that."

Williams was talking about me and as I look back, he was right. I wasn't complaining, but I was intimidated. I always was afraid of playing against people who had a total disregard for others. Williams couldn't have cared less if he broke my neck. In Game 6 at Toronto, with us leading the series three games to two, Butler nearly did.

It was in the second period. I was fishing for a loose puck around my feet and I had my head straight down. My Dad had warned me never to do that and in a series as vicious as this one, I certainly should have known better. I never heard or saw Butler coming. He charged into me, rammed my neck with his stick and knocked me headfirst into the boards.

I dropped to the ice. I felt a crack in the back of my neck and a lot of pain. I didn't lose consciousness, but I was frightened. I didn't feel numb, but Waske told me not to move while we waited for Dr. Minkoff, who fitted me with a surgical collar. I was removed from the game by a stretcher, but X-rays taken at a nearby hospital confirmed that I had only suffered a sprained neck. I was back at the rink, in civilian clothes, when the game ended. I had time before the bus left for the airport to tell Lucie I was fine.

My biggest regret was the scare I gave my family and friends. Dad threw me his best "How many times have I told you?" look when I got home that summer.

The series had turned into a bloodbath. Toronto was nowhere near as talented as we were, but we were totally disorganized. The Gillies–Trottier–Bossy line had been dubbed The BTG Line (Best Thing Going) by our PR department during the season and The Trio Grande by some clever reporter.

But we were doing nothing. Clarkie wasn't hitting back, Trots wasn't grinding and I was looking over my shoulder. We lost Game 7 at the Coliseum, 2–1, on Lanny McDonald's overtime goal past Chico.

It was a sickening feeling, a horrible end to such a promising season. After winning the division and finishing third overall, we had such high expectations. The Islanders had reached the finals in '75, '76 and '77, and we were expected to win in '78. Losing in the first round to Toronto was stunning.

Clarkie, Trots and I were terribly disappointed because we felt we had let the team down. I finished with two goals and two assists. Trots had three assists. Clarkie had two goals.

But it was truly a despicable series, another black mark on hockey. The hoodlums had won. I didn't waste my money on the book Tiger wrote a few years ago, but I hope he and Butler read this. If they do, they'll probably laugh. I can laugh about that series now, too.

The team held a meeting two days after the series, and I arrived for it with the LeSabre packed. Lucie had already returned to Laval and there was no reason to stay on Long Island another day. So when I left to collect my belongings at the Coliseum a month earlier than anticipated, I locked the doors to the apartment, attended the meeting, and pointed the car toward Montreal. There wasn't anything keeping me in New York.

I finished that season with 53 goals and 91 points, four points shy of the NHL rookie record Trots set two years earlier. I finished sixth among NHL scorers behind Lafleur, Trots, Darryl Sittler, Jacques Lemaire and Denny. I was voted the second-team all-star right wing and I won the Calder Trophy with 232 points out of a possible 270. Beck finished second with 113. Edwards was third with 91 and McCourt, who was chosen first overall 12 months earlier, got 28.

Picard, Gillis and DeBlois didn't get a vote.

Chapter

7

Trots

Bryan John Trottier was my link to that close-knit band of New York Islanders in 1977. He was my security blanket.

I felt peer pressure as a rookie, the need to show the veterans that I could be one of the guys. But because I rarely drank and didn't enjoy hanging out in bars after games, and I liked keeping to myself, I ran the risk of being labeled aloof or snobby and alienating myself from my teammates.

My relationship with Trots prevented that. Howatt started calling us "bread and butter" that first year once Trots and I began rooming together, eating together, laughing together, playing together. Although Trots was only 21 years old with two NHL seasons under his belt, he already was one of the most respected guys on the team. The vets must have thought that if he was hanging with me, I was OK.

Not that they didn't get on my case. Drouin loved to frighten me into thinking I was going to get shaved. When I'd pass him or he'd pass me at practice, he'd start singing the old theme song from the Gillette razor commercial. And with Westfall and Parise it was always, "Come on, come out with us. C'mon, we'll buy you a Coke. Or how about a glass of milk?" I hate beer, but a few of the vets had me chugging one night in Colorado, when Trots was off visiting relatives. Trots almost always had family come down from Saskatchewan when we went west. It's one of the reasons I never liked our long road trips.

Most of my teammates were good guys, but only Trots and I clicked. I liked Harris quite a bit. I appreciated the fact that he wasn't bitter about me talking his spot on Trots' and Clarkie's line, but Harry and I had nothing in common off the ice. He was single, I was married. He went out a lot, I rarely did.

A bunch of guys in those early years did go out a lot. I felt sorry for Westfall every Sunday morning because at practice he looked like he had spent Saturday night on a clothesline. But there he'd be, every Sunday morning, with a big smile on his face. Eddie would dare Al to skate him. Eddie would skate up and down, up and down, up and down. Al knew that Eddie had been out, but Eddie never got sick after a practice, no matter how hard Al tried to turn his guts up.

In a business where you spend so much time wasting time — waiting for buses, bus rides, waiting in airports, plane trips — you need to be able to have fun. For Trots and I, it meant laughing at ourselves, each other, the world. Trots and I have the exact same sense of humor, silly as it may seem. We could laugh at something funny in the street, a terrible joke, or the "rooster tail" sticking up from Al's scalp while he kicked garbage cans and chewed us out after a bad loss.

It got the point where Trots and I could pick up our heads during one of Al's tirades, just look at each other, and have to bow our heads and grit our teeth to keep from cracking up.

Two years ago, Trots and I were on the bench during a game with the Minnesota North Stars when Frantisek Musil, the Czech defenseman, skated past us.

"Boy, are you ugly," I said. I know it was a mean thing to say, but I said it only to get a laugh out of Trots. I didn't mean for Musil to hear it. But he turned to me while the game was going on and sheepishly shrugged his shoulders as if to say: "It's not my fault. What can I do about it?"

When Musil skated away, Trots reminded me of how lucky I was not to be a tough guy. "If you were," he said, "you'd be in big trouble."

One of Trots' favorite Boss stories took place a few years ago in Los Angeles. Ron Hoggarth was the referee, but from the start of the game I called him Bob. It turned out that this was one of those games when I was complaining about being hooked and held all night.

"Hey, Bob, watch that guy!" "Geez, Bob, he's holding me." "Bob, dammit, that's a penalty!"

I grew more and more frustrated as the game wore on because

Hoggarth wasn't acknowledging me. I thought he was being stubborn and arrogant. Trots, who must have been cackling inside all night, waited until the end of the game before he said, "Boss, who were you yelling at all night?"

"That ass Hoggarth," I said.

"His name is Ron, Boss," Trots said. "Not Bob."

Trots is easy. I can tell him the same old story ten times a year and he'll laugh every time like he's never heard it before. Sometimes we're like the old joke about the comedians' convention; all I need to do is blurt a punch line to crack Trots up: "Gee, it's crowded in here."

See? I can hear him laughing now.

My favorite story involves Billy Smith and it happened two years ago. Smitty was amazing when it came to falling asleep. He could plop into his reserved window seat on a bus or airplane and be asleep before the last guy boarded. It didn't matter what time of day it was, how long the trip was, or what Smitty had been doing five minutes earlier.

That guy could sleep.

We were flying back from the West Coast on this particular trip and, as usual, Smitty was in the window seat out cold. Trots was sitting in the middle seat and I was on the aisle. Smitty must have slept for four hours, then woke up a few minutes before we were due to land. He rang the stewardess' buzzer and when she walked over, he asked for some aspirin and a glass of water.

Having just woken up, his face was all red, his eyes were blurred and his hairpiece was all over the place. Trots and I were blabbing away mindlessly, but we stopped when we heard Smitty wrestling with his package of aspirin. He was cursing under his breath, crumpling the package and having a very difficult time.

"What's the matter, Smitty?" Trots asked.

"You won't believe this," Smitty mumbled in dazed astonishment. "This package says Anacin 3 and I can only find two of these damn aspirins."

Then there was the time that Al called us dogs after one game on the road and to make his point put a plate of dog biscuits on the buffet table at our next pregame meal.

A few of us laughed at the prank, but Persson bit into one, thinking they were cookies.

"Hmm," Stefan said. "This tastes different. Pretty tasty."

Trots and I loved Al for being so damned funny, and he often made jokes at our expense. We played with Anders Kallur as our left wing one season, and for a while Trots and I virtually ignored Anders. We didn't do it purposely, but Trots and I tended to hog the puck too much because we were so comfortable with each other.

Al didn't like it. We played one night in Minnesota or Calgary and landed in Winnipeg for a game two nights later against the Jets. After practice in Winnipeg, Al scolded us in front of everybody.

"You two guys never use your left winger," he yelled. "You might as well have a vacuum cleaner on the left side for all you guys care."

Trots and I bit our tongues. So did most of the guys. The next morning, at the pregame skate, Kallur was greeted at his locker by an upright vacuum cleaner wearing his jersey, his helmet and his pants.

Trots and I each tell one story that the other does not find funny. I still can't believe he was stupid enough to burn the upholstery on my LeSabre. Trots can't believe I was stupid enough to burn his hair.

No, two of Al's children didn't always behave.

During my rookie year, Jean Potvin's wife, Lorraine, had a baby. At practice that day, Potsy passed out cigars. I was still smoking cigarettes back then, so I accepted one. Trots never smoked, except this time he said, "Yeah, let's smoke cigars."

But instead of depositing the ashes in the ashtray of my car like a normal human being, Trots decided he was going to flick them out the open window. At first I didn't know what was happening because I was driving, but when I glanced through the rear view mirror I saw ashes blowing out the window, back into the car and onto my back seat.

Something smelled strange. It was the velour seat, smoldering, dotted with six or seven fresh burn marks.

I stopped the car, jumped into the back and frantically started putting out the tiny fires. Trots was still in the front seat laughing. Ask him now and he'll tell you how sorry he was, but back then he thought it was a scream. I sold that car a few years later in perfect condition except for that damn, polka-dotted back seat.

Trots also put two fresh footprints onto the side of another of my cars, a black Audi. Twice one winter he kicked it. He didn't dent it, but he left two marks that were hard to wax out the following spring.

"Look what you did?" I said one day after I washed the car.

He spotted the outline of a shoe sole. "I didn't do that," he insisted. "Are you crazy?"

If Trots didn't kick my car, then I didn't light his hair on fire six or seven years ago on a bus trip from the airport to our hotel in Detroit.

When we bus, each player gets two seats unless the bus is too full.

Then the rookies double up. I always sat behind Trots, usually toward the front, behind the coaches and trainers. At first we sat farther back, but we loved listening to Al tell stories. Al was a riot even when he was trying to be serious.

In those days Trots had longer, frizzy hair. Whenever he woke up or got off a plane, his hair would stand up in a million different directions and everyone would ask him if he combed his hair with a brick. I guess I was bored on this trip in Detroit because I remember looking at that same old frazzled head and saying to myself, "Boy, Trots' hair is so dry. It looks like straw."

I lit a match, lit myself a cigarette, then held the match in front of my face. Without Trots knowing, I inched it closer and closer to the back of his neck. It became my own little game, seeing how close I could move the match before Trots felt the heat.

WHOOOOOSH.

You've heard about summer brushfires? That's what happened. Trots' hair just erupted in flames. I dropped the match and started beating on his head before he even knew he was on fire. Guys were laughing, straining their necks to check out all the commotion. Trots was too stunned at first to be mad. He just kind of looked at me and said, "Are you nuts?"

From the beginning, a healthy rivalry bubbled under the surface. We never talked about it, but we knew it was there. I was never jealous of Trots' skill and I don't think he was ever jealous of mine. But early in my career I was envious of how Trots was labeled this great two-way center who could do no wrong, although I have to admit he did very little wrong.

I was struggling just to be considered a decent defensive player and Trots was seen as the perfect defensive center, no matter what happened. If our line was scored upon, I was labeled the culprit because I was the defensive liability. Trots used to think it was funny that I thought that, but I was very self-conscious of my defensive play.

In the late '70s and early '80s, we both wanted to be labeled the NHL's best player. I felt I was always one step from being recognized as the best. First there was Lafleur, then Gretzky, even Trots. There were times, though, when I thought I was the best. I wanted to lead the league in goals and points and so did he. When he won the scoring championship in 1978–79 with 134 points, I finished fourth with 126. I was happy for him, but I was disappointed that I received little recognition for finishing so close.

I hope Trots and I will land in the Hall of Fame, but I think history will remember Trots as a great hockey player and me as a great goal scorer, not a great hockey player. That bothers me, because I think he and I are comparable. I can't say who's better because we were so different. Any team that needed a strong and determined center who could score and check and win face-offs would naturally choose him over me. Any team that needed somebody to score goals would choose me over him.

We wanted to keep pace, but we rarely tried to outdo one another. The times we did made us better players. I pushed him, he pushed me and we relished the success we enjoyed as linemates. Gillies, Kallur, John Tonelli, Bob Bourne, Greg Gilbert all played left wing with us for substantial periods of time and must have been frustrated by our relationship. I don't blame any of them, but we weren't about to change anything.

I'm sure those guys sometimes felt that we were selfish. But our game was instinct. Trots, a left-handed shooter, was instinctively a better passer to his right wing, his forehand side, before I ever met him. Once we jelled, Trots to me or me to Trots was the proper play because we just read each other, knew each other's moves.

The chemistry was eerie. At times we felt like we were the only two skaters on the ice, attacking a helpless goalie.

That chemistry extended off the ice. On road trips, Trots was responsible for the tube of toothpaste we shared. People find that strange, but it was as simple as this: Trots carried a nice shaving kit and it was easier for me to throw my toothbrush in there and not worry about lugging my own kit. On the road the trainers provided shaving cream, razors, hair dryers and brushes for the dressing rooms, so what else did I need? I didn't start carrying a hair brush of my own until a few years ago, although Trots needed one for his mop. I just borrowed his until we got to the rink.

Over the course of ten years rooming together, we reversed roles. When I was a rookie, Trots loved to fall asleep with the hotel room freezing cold and the television on well into the night. He used to lay low in his bed, ducking under my cigarette smoke to watch TV. It would be 3 a.m., he'd be snoring like an animal, and I'd get out of bed to turn down the air conditioner and shut off the TV.

"I'm not sleeping," he'd growl.

Years later, I became the TV hound and he was the one turning up the heat.

I can remember a lot of great plays Trots made and a lot of great goals I scored, but the Ed Kea Exorcist Play stands out as one of our most memorable. Kea was a tall and lanky defenseman for the Atlanta Flames and St. Louis Blues, a solid player whose career ended sadly a few years ago when a check in a minor-league game left him permanently injured.

Kea was with the Blues this particular night in St. Louis when Trots and I attacked. I had the puck deep in the zone along the right boards. Trots circled from the bottom of the slot to behind the net. Kea was watching me, trying to force me to the corner, so I passed to Trots behind the net.

Kea was between Trots and I, but he didn't know if he should stay with me or pressure Trots. He knew if he left me, I was going to walk in front of the net. But he knew that if he stayed with me, Trots was going to walk out from behind the net for a wraparound. Before he decided what to do, I skated toward the net from the boards, but backed up to the lower rim of the right circle to put more space between Trots and me.

Kea skated toward Trots, so Trots passed back to me. I couldn't have been more than six feet from Kea, who bumped Trots, but still managed to turn his head to follow the puck onto my stick. I saw the back of Kea's jersey and his face. Trots saw the crest of his jersey and the back of his head. It was incredible. It was as if Kea's neck spun his head completely around, like Linda Blair in *The Exorcist*.

Trots was checked by Kea, who still managed to watch me pull the puck in front of me and score. Trots and I rushed to the hotel after that game to watch the replay on the news.

Trots and I have another story that's so bizarre, so embarrassing, that I'm going to name names without mentioning each character's exact role. It took place in Los Angeles in 1983 after we had played the Kings. We weren't scheduled to play again until three days later, so Al gave us the next day off. Consequently, nobody, not even Trots or I, was in the mood to get back to the hotel early.

The night started at a place called Tequila Willie's. There must have been a dozen of the guys there, laughing at Trots and I as we downed who knows how many shots of tequila. Any appearance by Trots and I at a bar fired up the guys, so we remained the center of attention for a few hours. When it was time to depart, Trots told us there was no need to call for cabs. He had a friend who was willing to drive us back to the hotel.

Trots' friend was Tom Klimasz. Tom was a guy from Connecticut who made a trip or two to California each year. He was driving a Dodge Colt hatchback. The car obviously wasn't big enough for nine circus clowns. Nevertheless, I piled in with Trots, Denis Potvin, Jean Potvin (who had played with us during our first two Cup years and was now one of our radio announcers), Gord Dineen, Mats Hallin, Tomas Jonsson, John Tonelli and Dave Langevin.

Two of us were up front with Tom, four of us were in the back and three of us were hanging out of the hatchback, with our feet dragging on the road. Trots to this day swears he saw sparks coming from some of our shoes.

Tom headed for our hotel, the Airport Marriott. We were singing like children, having a great time being drunk until we heard a police siren. Luckily, Tom wasn't drinking. Our sober savior quickly jumped out of the car. He told one cop who we were, explained how we were trying to get back to the hotel before curfew, and how we had implored him to drive us because we couldn't find cabs.

Tom was beautiful.

After he finished his chat with the cops, he walked back to the car and they drove off. "OK," Tom said. "Everything's fine, only a few of you are going to have to wait here. I can't take all of you at once."

That was a reasonable enough suggestion for nine sober men to accept, especially nine who were dangerously close to a trip to the local precinct. But on this night Tom's suggestion didn't seem right. He did manage to get four of us back into the Colt while leaving five of us waiting on Sepulveda Boulevard, but when he arrived at the hotel about five minutes later, only Langevin and Hallin said good-night. (OK, they're totally innocent. That still leaves seven of us nuts.)

"My buddy's stranded on Sepulveda and I've got to see if he's OK," slurred Trots or I (take your pick).

"Your buddy? What about my brother? He may be in trouble, too," one of the Potvins rambled in reply.

This went on for a few seconds. Tom tried to explain that if two of us went back, there wouldn't be room for the five guys waiting a few miles up the road.

Trots/Boss: "I can't leave my roomie."

A Potvin: "I can't leave my bro."

Somehow, one exasperated hockey fan from Connecticut was convinced that there would be room for eight the second time around.

"We've got to stick up for our buddies," we yelled.

"Yeah," we echoed.

Tom just shook his head, praying that this evening would go away.

Sepulveda Boulevard is a huge street. Three or four lanes in each direction are separated by a concrete divider, an island that's large enough for five guys to stand and wait on. We knew where we had left the guys, but we weren't sure we'd spot them because not everybody was thinking very rationally.

We spotted one of them ... in the middle of the road, mooning Southern California.

But that's not the end of it. Everybody sardined themselves back into Tom's hatchback and off we went. This time Tom closed the hatchback. You should have seen Dineen, the rookie, with his nose mashed up against the glass.

We hadn't even pulled away from the curb when a second patrol car with two cops pulled alongside us. Tom squirted out of the car again and explained again to one cop how we were trying to beat Al's curfew. In the meantime, the other cop slowly paced around our car, billy club in hand, observing. Two of us were uncontrollable.

"What'd this cop do, have a fight with his wife?"

"C'mon, what's the big deal? Let's get home."

"Hurry up, Tom, I'm tired."

Policemen with billy clubs sober me up in a hurry. I started screaming, trying to shut these two guys up, praying I wasn't going to be the next morning's headlines. All I could imagine was the bunch of us thrown in jail overnight and Al having to come bail us out. Everybody else was laughing, keeping relatively calm. I was telling everybody to act cool and I was panicking.

As if this wasn't enough of a circus, Mike McEwen and Kallur pulled up alongside us in McEwen's car. Q-Ball had been traded by us to the Kings a month earlier and he wanted to know if he could help. A few of us who had gotten out of the Colt by now figured we'd catch a ride with Q-Ball, except the cop sensed that Q was drunk and asked him to step out of the car.

Q was sober, but he was nervous. He had trouble walking that straight line. His legs were shaking. Those of us in the car who had figured out what was happening were roaring. Q-Ball got off, probably cursed the entire organization, but took Dineen, Kallur and Jonsson back to the hotel.

That left the gladiators: the Potvins, Trots, me and our trusty driver Tom. It must have been nearly 4 a.m., but Potsy said: "Let's go to this place that's open late. I know the guy." So we went. We sat there drinking for two or three hours when Tom decided to call his buddies in New York, where it was nearly 10 a.m. After all the trouble he had narrowly avoided he wanted to make sure his friends believed his story, so he made each one of us get on the phone and swear we were out with him all night.

Trots and I were too blurry to think anymore. We finally convinced Tom, we pleaded with him, to take us to the hotel. Trots and I stumbled to our room. I reached into my pocket for my card key, slipped it into the lock, opened the door and turned the card key like it was a regular key.

It snapped off in the lock. We couldn't lock the door.

I locked the door with the inside chain, threw off my clothes, crawled into bed, picked up the phone and called the front desk.

"Look," I said. "Don't ask me how or why, but I just broke my card key off in the lock. Can you send someone up to fix it so we can close our door and go to sleep?"

Most of the guys awoke early that morning (probably not long after I fell asleep) and spent the day playing golf. Trots and I woke up sometime in the early afternoon and just wandered around. That night we visited Jamie Farr, a big hockey fan, on the set of *M*A*S*H*.

Al never said a word about our escapade until we returned home, when he told us he had found out about it that night. Someone had called him to tip him off to the fact that a couple of his prized possessions were frolicking like morons around the city. I felt like such an idiot.

Trots and I made drunken fools of ourselves a couple of other times. Once was in Chicago, after we kayoed the Blackhawks four straight in the 1979 quarterfinals.

The other was in St. Louis in 1983. It was just before the March trading deadline, we had been blown out 6-0 and there was no curfew that night. Most of us had congregated in the hotel bar, but Trots and I allowed Tonelli and Denny to talk us into joining them at this place in Illinois, right over the Mississippi River. It was a country and western honky-tonk, and since Trots loved to play guitar, he fell in love with the place the minute we walked through the door.

Denny couldn't get over the fact that he had talked us into coming out. We got a kick out of how Denny was acting like the ringleader, so Trots and I started bugging him: "Where are we going, Dad?" "How much longer till we get there, Dad?" "Are you going to let us stay out late, Dad?"

It didn't take long before I was drunk. Trots must have been hammered, too, because when I pushed him up to the stage and begged him to strum a few strings, he didn't even hesitate. And so I started dancing to my roomie's beat.

Tonelli and Potvin were stunned. Shy Boss kicking up his heels?

Quiet Trots wailing some sad song in front of 50 or 100 midwestern cowboys? We had a great time. We closed the joint.

Lorne Henning, who retired after our second Cup in 1981 to become Al's assistant coach, ran practice the next morning. I was incredibly hung over and every move I made was a painful chore. It didn't take the boys long to figure out that I hadn't gone right to bed. Al (who always found out everything) soon learned that Denny had been our host for the evening. Instead of being mad at us, he was mad at Denny.

We laughed and laughed. And from then on Denny was nicknamed Dad.

Trots and I rarely socialize away from the rink now. Lucie and I and Nickie and Trots haven't spent much time together in years. We never spent time together during the off-season because Lucie and I returned to Montreal and we rarely spoke to them.

Why? Our relationship was dictated by hockey. The game brought us together and kept us together. I've always looked at myself as two different people. I'm one person when I walk into the dressing room and another when I come home and greet Lucie and my daughters, Josiane and Tanya, at the door.

Nobody knows both people, because nobody sees both people. Around the ice I carry myself with an aggressive attitude, a confidence that Trots tells me people often mistake for arrogance. Away from hockey I question myself all the time. Lucie seems to have more confidence in me than I do in myself.

At times the two personalities take turns. Lucie and I speak almost every night that I'm on the road. Trots and I could be laughing and giggling, but when the phone rings and it's Lucie, I'm her husband, not the hockey player. If Lucie ever got a glimpse of Trots and I acting ridiculous, or took a peek inside our dressing room after a practice, she'd probably laugh at how comical we were, but she'd probably be disappointed at the language we use and embarrassed by the stupid things we do.

But that's why Trots and I were so good for each other. Think of the mindless routine we have, then think of trudging through 180 days of that same mindless routine for ten years.

Consider the day of a game: we wake up, shower, dress, eat breakfast, wait for a bus that takes us to the rink. We get to the rink, undress, put on our equipment, skate through a light workout, take off our equipment, shower, dress. We climb back onto the bus, return to the hotel, eat lunch, go back to our rooms, undress, take an afternoon nap. Three or four hours before the game we wake up, dress, get back on the bus for the ride to the rink, undress, put our equipment on, play the game, take our equipment off, shower, dress, eat a light dinner or snack, go back to the hotel. We undress, go to sleep, wake up the next morning, shower, dress, and catch the bus that will take us to the plane for the next game that might be that night or the next.

Isn't it ridiculous? A road trip that ends in Vancouver might mean a ten-hour flight the next day. So we wait an hour in the morning for the flight, two hours in Toronto for the connecting flight. Then we land at LaGuardia, hop in the bus that takes us to the rink. I hop in my car, get home. All I want to do is sit and relax for the night and have a home-cooked meal with the kids. But Lucie has been home alone with the kids all week and all she'd like is a nice, quiet meal at a restaurant.

Bryan Trottier is special to me because he made those ten years of bus rides, plane rides and morning skates bearable.

No, he made them more than bearable. He made them memorable and fun.

Chapter

Those Damned Rangers

Training camp 1978. Although our seven-game loss to Toronto in my first Stanley Cup playoff series was a disaster, it was five months old and part of my past. Too many good things had happened in my rookie season. I couldn't let one disappointing playoff carry into the start of my second NHL season.

"What's over is over," I repeated to myself all summer. "There's nothing the Islanders can do about the Leafs, but there's plenty we can do about this season." I knew we had a team that could win the Patrick Division and the Stanley Cup. I knew I could better my 53-goal, 91-point, Rookie of the Year, all-star season.

Not only did I feel the pressure of repeating my rookie year, but I kept hearing about the sophomore jinx. Everybody expected me to have a bad season so they could justify the sophomore jinx. I couldn't understand that because I didn't know what the jinx meant. Why would anyone expect me to have a worse season? In junior, my second season was better than my first. And heading into my second NHL training camp I felt much more relaxed. I was older, stronger, smarter and a better player.

I was going to make less money, though. Not counting my $45,000 signing bonus, but counting my $55,000 salary and bonuses for first NHL game ($15,000), 40th NHL game ($10,000), 30 goals ($2,500), 40 goals ($5,000) and 50 goals ($7,500) I made $95,000 my first year.

My second year salary was $65,000. I had the opportunity for $15,000 in bonuses if I scored 50 goals again. So even if had a better year I was certain to take a pay cut because I was no longer eligible for those games played bonuses.

It didn't matter to me. Pierre and Denis constantly advised me that the better I played, the more I'd earn down the road; if not this year, then next year. "We'll worry about the future," they told me. "You worry about 1978-79."

What, me worry? I set an NHL record for goals by a right wing, 69. It was the second-highest total in NHL history at the time and it missed Phil Esposito's record by seven. I finished fourth in scoring with 126 points, the highest total ever by a sophomore. (Jinx? What jinx?) For the second straight season, I was the NHL's second-team all-star right wing.

The Professional Hockey Writers Association selected Guy Lafleur to the first team, although I scored 69 goals to his 52 and finished with 126 points to his 129. I deserved to make the first team, but I wasn't upset. Lafleur was such a classy superstar over the years that I assumed the writers were showing a measure of respect for his past performance. That was OK with me. I just told myself that if I had the type of career Lafleur was having, I'd probably earn that same respect when it came to postseason awards.

We opened the season with a 25-4-7 record, lost two games in a row only once, never went more than three without a win, and finished first overall in the NHL with a 51-15-14 record. I tied a modern NHL mark by scoring at least one goal in ten consecutive games and joined Trots, Clarkie and Denny on Team NHL, the all-stars who played the Soviets in the 1979 Challenge Cup. I finished fourth in the voting for the Lady Byng Trophy. I might have won the NHL's most gentlemanly player award, had I not gotten into my first (and only) NHL fight.

I fought a Flyer.

It was at the Coliseum, during one of what seemed like a thousand grudge matches with Philly. It started when a beaut of a winger named Dave Hoyda (lifetime NHL games, 132; lifetime NHL goals, 6; lifetime NHL penalty minutes, 299) tried to take my head off along the boards with a cross-check.

I ducked. He missed. And before he bounced off the boards to get back into the play, Clarkie had pounced. Clarkie's gloves were off and his fists were in fifth gear before Hoyda had time to cower. While Clarkie destroyed him, the rest of us on the ice paired off. In those days, during a fight the noncombatants didn't have to separate and skate to a neutral area. Everybody dropped their gloves and selected dance partners.

Mine was Behn Wilson, a young, tough defenseman who liked to fight but could play the game, too. Wilson was a rookie, but he must have known I was no fighter. I just grabbed onto him and tried to kill time until the linesman got over to us, but Wilson began shoving me and tugging at my jersey while the officials wrestled with Gillies–Hoyda and a blossoming side bout, Gerry Hart–Mel Bridgman.

When Wilson finally let go of me, he did so by shoving me in the chest as he pushed off. Determined not to show I was intimidated, I pushed back.

Mistake.

My push was Wilson's invitation to start beating on me. That's when I said, "Uh, oh. I'm in trouble now." I tried to cover up, but got thrown to the ice. Players from both sides tumbled on top of us and I tried to poke my scared little head out of this massive pile of angry bodies.

With my nose pressed to the ice, I saw the brawl escalate into a bench-clearer. I watched Nystrom hop the boards. I watched Smitty hammer Bob Kelly. Chico piled on, too. It felt like the entire National Hockey League was sitting on me.

Wilson and I got five-minute fighting majors (is there such a thing as a five-minute "getting-the-shit-kicked-out-of-you" major?) and ten-minute misconducts. Those were 15 of the 25 penalty minutes I had all season. And there went the Lady Byng.

Wilson was one lucky macho man. There were a lot of bozos who wanted a piece of me: Tiger Williams; the Rangers' two goons, Ed Hospodar and Nick Fotiu; the Flyers' Paul Holmgren. Fotiu and Hospodar always aimed at my face with their elbows whenever they had me lined up against the boards or in the corners. Holmgren raced all over the rink to hit me when I had the puck. We were in Philly once and I was straddling the blue line. Trots hit me with a pass a moment before Holmgren approached. I spotted him, so I made a quick stop and ducked. When I stopped, I inadvertently stuck one of my legs out, and Holmgren went flying over it. He landed on the ice with a twisted knee.

Trots was no help. "You're in trouble now, Boss," he whispered as Holmgren was helped off. "Look what you did to him."

Bridgman, who had a pair of the meanest eyes in the league, loved to try and intimidate me by sneering. Like most of the Flyers, he thought nothing of throwing cheap shots, too. Montreal's Bob Gainey was one of the hardest hitters back then, but his checks were almost always clean. I had no problem with Gainey.

Believe it or not, I ran into problems the few times I threw my six-foot, 185-pound body around. Getting hit by me jeopardized one's manhood, I guess. When Hartford's Dave Babych was with Winnipeg, he creamed me good one game. It was a marginally legal check, but I remembered I owed him one. A few years later, after he had been traded to the Whalers, I lined him up in our building and repaid him with a crunch from behind.

He bounced off the boards, saw it was me, and started running off his mouth. "What's the matter?" I asked. "You don't like it when you get hit?"

I didn't have to worry about getting a stick rammed down my throat those first few years, because whenever some thug threatened me he'd eventually have to answer to Clarkie. Now, Clarkie wasn't just my bodyguard. He was one of the best left wings in the NHL in the late '70s, definitely the best tough guy in the league. If you wanted to fight him, he'd fight. If you wanted to grind with him, he'd grind. If you left him alone to play, he could skate and shoot as well as any physical winger.

The word around the league was, "Don't wake Gillies up," because Clarkie tended to be lackadaisical when he wasn't riled. He was not naturally mean. As he got older, his pleasant personality hurt him because he didn't command the respect he would have had he played tough and mean all the time. Clarkie was intimidating when he wanted to be. He never had to hit anybody. Whenever he let an opponent know that he was in an ornery mood, he, Trots and I automatically found a lot more open ice.

Clarkie had such mean eyes. When he got mad, he would look down at guys (remember, he was six-foot-three) as if he was looking right through them. He was one guy I wouldn't have messed with if I played against him. He never liked fighting, but he completely lost the urge a few years ago. I don't blame him. But once his offensive skills diminished, his unwillingness to play physically cost him his spot on the team. If he didn't want to play physically there was no room for him at age 31. That's why Bill let him go to Buffalo on waivers in 1986.

Clarkie was one of the greatest joke-tellers I ever met, great with the one-liners. He reminded me of an emcee and I always thought that if

Clarkie didn't play hockey, he'd be a comedian or an actor. Clarkie and I rarely hung out together, but in my rookie year *Sports Illustrated* did a story on our line from Colorado, and we had to stay behind at McNichols Arena for a picture session after the game. We were driven from the rink to the hotel by limousine afterwards and Clarkie had Trots and I in pain from laughing so hard the entire trip.

Almost everything was funny that second season. We didn't lose many games. Whenever we did lose, it gave Al license to try another motivational tactic. After one particularly feeble effort, he marched into the room while we were undressing and announced he was pissed off.

"You played like a bunch of pansies," he hissed. "If I put an egg in each of your pants before the game, none of you would have broken any."

At practice the next day, he came around the room with one of those large cartons of eggs, 36 or 48 of them. And he handed each guy one. I started to giggle, but Al wasn't in a joking mood. He was trying to reiterate his point. As I looked around the room, guys were biting their tongues. I took my egg, put it on the shelf of my stall, and walked out of the room.

A few seconds later, I heard Al explode. Pat Price, a defenseman who sat two stalls from me, was pinned into his stall by Al, who was screaming. "If it was up to me you'd be gone tomorrow."

I got a closer look at what was going on. Al had egg dripping all over him. Price had taken his egg and smashed it over Al's head. Do you know how painful it is not to laugh at the sight of your coach looking so angry and so foolish at the same time? My eyes were watering. I didn't know whether to run out of the room so I could crack up or hang around to see what happened next.

And there was no way I was going to look at Trots.

Some of the guys ran out and peeked from around a corner. Others tucked their heads between their legs. It was hysterical, seeing Al so furious with pieces of egg shell in his hair and egg yoke dripping down his face.

By the way, Price, who was never an integral part of the club, was claimed by Edmonton in the expansion draft the following fall.

Price was just one of four new Islanders who improved our club in 1978–79. On defense we added Bob Lorimer, who had failed to make it the year before. At center all year we had a solid defensive player in Wayne Merrick, who was acquired in the middle of my rookie year for Jean Potvin (who was later reacquired) and J.P. Parise. And on left wing we added John Tonelli, a workaholic who had played three seasons for Houston of the WHA.

When Tonelli and I played together throughout most of 1984–85, he became the answer to a tough trivia question: Name the only player in pro hockey history to play with the top two goal-scoring right wings (that's Howe and me). J.T. centered for Howe when Gordie played with his son Mark at Houston.

The highlight of my regular season was the Challenge Cup, the three-game All-Star series at Madison Square Garden in February between Team NHL and the Soviet National Team. I nearly missed it, though. I got whacked on the back of my left hand in our last game before the tournament. I missed one day of practice while I went for X-rays, but rejoined the team when the X-rays showed no break. My hand was sore and it hurt when I shot, but I was determined to play.

The team pitched camp at the Waldorf-Astoria in midtown Manhattan. Lucie, who was two months pregnant with Josiane, stayed with me at the Waldorf. Here we were, two hicks from Laval, in one of the world's most famous hotels. This was only our third visit to New York City. The first was my introductory press conference in 1977; the second was when Roddy came down from Halifax to see my 50th goal in 1978 and we took him to see a Mets game at Shea Stadium and *Grease* on Broadway.

We were so impressed to be staying at the Waldorf, but Lucie didn't want to roam around the big city without me. I was at practice one afternoon and she got hungry, so she ordered room service. She ordered a club sandwich and coffee. The bill came to $12. This was ten years ago. She was so stunned and embarrassed that when she gave the bellboy $20 and he asked if she wanted change, she said no.

When I got back, she told me what had happened. She was embarrassed then, but we laugh now: an $8 tip for a $12 club sandwich. Welcome to the Big Apple, Mr. and Mrs. Bossy.

The Challenge Cup was my first international competition as a pro and it was a great thrill, much better than my first NHL All-Star Game the year before. I played on a team with so many great players who I had watched on TV: Lafleur, Marcel Dionne, Gilbert Perreault, Steve Shutt, Marcel Dionne, Serge Savard, Ken Dryden, Phil and Tony Esposito, Gerry Cheevers. I played on a line with Trots and Clarkie, who was named our team's MVP.

We won Game 1, 4–2, and I scored a goal and an assist. The Russians took the series, though, beating us 5–4 in Game 2 and blowing us out in Game 3, 6–0. That 6–0 game was unreal. They toyed with us. It could have been 60–0. I remember Helmut Balderis doing these Denis Savard–type spinarama moves and I remember when they scored their sixth goal, one of their guys came by and laughed at us at our bench.

I thought it was pretty funny, but it had our players steaming.

I never understood the hate for the Russians that I witnessed as a hockey player, in that Challenge Cup or in so many of our other exhibition games and Canada Cup tournaments against them. I don't understand it in everyday life, either, but maybe that's because I've gone through life without hating anybody — even Tiger Williams. I've disliked people, but hate is too strong a word for my vocabulary when it comes to describing my relationship with people. But when that Russian mocked us, our team went nuts. It's a good thing he skated away. Our guys were ready to jump him.

Vladimir Myshkin replaced Vladislav Tretiak in goal for that third game, but it didn't matter. We were walloped. Steve Shutt, one of the best left wings in the NHL, cried before the game because he was told by Team NHL coach Scotty Bowman that he wasn't going to be in the lineup. That surprised all of us because Shutt was a Canadian and Bowman was his coach. Dionne was scratched from Game 3, too.

Although we lost, that tournament left me feeling great about myself. Team NHL had scored eight goals in that series and I led our team with two goals and two assists. It was a huge confidence builder before an important playoff season. We approached the 1979 playoffs planning to erase the ugly memory of Toronto in 1978. In finishing first overall during the regular season we proved to ourselves that last spring's failure hadn't bothered us. Now it was time to do something about it.

We had a bye in the first round, then met Chicago in the quarter-finals. We bombed the Blackhawks four straight: 6–2, 1–0 in over-time, 4–0 and 3–1. I was flying. I led the team with five goals and two assists and I scored the overtime winner in Game 2, my second overtime goal in two seasons. Unlike last spring, these Stanley Cup playoffs were fun. Off the ice, Trots and I couldn't stop laughing.

During the afternoon prior to Game 3 in Chicago we couldn't nap, so we decided to do something we rarely did. We took a cab ahead of the team bus. It was a 15-minute ride from our downtown hotel to the rink and we figured it would give us a chance to relax in the room before everybody got there.

"Chicago Stadium, please," I told the driver who pulled up at the hotel.

He looked confused.

"You know, where the Blackhawks play. The hockey team."

He looked confused.

"The basketball team plays there, too. The um, um, Bulls."

He nodded slightly, so we relaxed ... until Trots and I agreed that we didn't recognize this route to Chicago Stadium. After a brief backseat discussion in which we convinced ourselves that we weren't wrong, we told the driver we'd never gone this way before.

He told us not to worry. So we didn't worry for 45 minutes, until the cabbie stopped in front of the main entrance to Comiskey Park.

"This isn't it," I said. "This is where the White Sox play baseball."

He looked confused. Then he kicked us out of the cab.

We didn't pay him, of course, but we were left standing on some deserted street corner in a section of Chicago we didn't know. Luckily, we spotted another cab stopped for a light across the street. We ran into the street, hailed the cab and made the cabbie swear he knew how to get to the Stadium.

He did. We pulled up to the players' entrance of the rink just as the guys were filing out of the bus. Trots and I have made every team bus since.

Other than that cab ride to nowhere, the most dramatic part of this series was the celebration after Game 4. Call it Bournie's revenge.

On a road trip early in the season, Kaszycki coaxed Trots, Tonelli and I into playing a trick on Bournie. We were in the lobby of our hotel when Kaz told us that Bournie, his roommate, was sleeping.

Each of us filled a small garbage pail with water. Kaz unlocked the door and flicked on the lights. We barged in and dumped the water on Bournie, who was sleeping on the bed nearest the door. Then we ran out.

Bournie was so cool. He dragged his soaking wet mattress off the boxspring, dumped it on the floor, pulled Kaszycki's pillow and blanket off his bed, threw it on his boxspring and went back to sleep. He was out again in 30 seconds.

At breakfast the next morning Bournie vowed to retaliate, but by April we had all forgotten about it. Almost all of us.

After we won Game 4 to complete the sweep, Al lifted curfew. He knew we'd have at least three days off before we started our semifinal series, and asking guys to be in by 1:00 a.m. in Chicago was cruel and unusual punishment. Trots and I spent the night on Rush Street. And I mean the night. If you've ever been to Chicago, you know it's not hard to find something to do on Rush Street. We went from club, to after-hours club, to after-after-hours club. The sun rose sometime between our fourth and fifth stop. We finally stumbled into the hotel at about 7:30 a.m., 30 minutes before our bus was to leave for the airport.

I was polluted, but I was alert enough to sense that something in our room wasn't right. It didn't look like a room that hadn't been slept in. Our bedspreads were on the floor, our mattresses were drenched, our clothes weren't in our suitcases.

They were in the bathtub, soaking. That's when Trots and I connected the crime to Bournie. I was too drunk to do anything but laugh. We wrung out our clothes, stuffed them soaking wet into our suitcases, dragged the mattresses off the bed and went to sleep in the only dry garments we owned, the ones we had worn through the night.

I slept for about 20 minutes. Trots got about ten minutes sleep before our wake-up call came. We brushed our teeth, slapped a few handfuls of cold water on our faces, hid behind dark sunglasses and marched onto the bus, drops of water from our suitcases forming puddles at our feet.

"Good morning, Al," I said.

"Good morning, Al," Trots said.

We dried out at home that day (Lucie couldn't believe what I looked like when I walked through the door), then learned the next night that our semifinal opponent would be the New York Rangers.

The Ranger–Islander rivalry officially began when the Isles were born in 1972, but it didn't heat up until April 1975, when the three-year-old underdogs from Long Island shocked the Rangers in Game 3 of a best-of-three preliminary series and earned a piece of New York's sports pages.

A piece, but not our fair share. The Islanders had become the better team by 1976, but in 1979 we still hadn't replaced the Rangers in New York's hockey hearts. To be honest, we still haven't and we probably never will. We're from the suburbs. New York City belongs to the Rangers.

In 1979, a game at the Garden was definitely a Ranger home game. A game at the Coliseum gave us only a slight home-ice advantage because of the Ranger loyalists on the Island. We weren't too worried about playing the Rangers, though. We won the regular-season series, five games to three, and split the four games at the Garden. We weren't thinking about the excitement of a New York–New York semifinal, we were thinking Stanley Cup.

We knew that to win the Cup we'd eventually have to play the Canadiens. That was in the back of my mind because the Canadiens symbolized the Cup. They had won in '76, '77 and '78. They had won more Cups than any NHL team. When I was a kid, if the Canadiens were eliminated from the playoffs the playoffs stopped being real.

And then we lost Game 1 to the Rangers at home, 4–1. That jolted us back to reality and automatically put a lot of pressure on us because the media was pro-Ranger. The Rangers always got more ink than us throughout my career. In a way it bothered me because we deserved more than we got. We had accomplished more than they had. The pressure was automatically on when we lost Game 1.

The first game didn't bother me. The fact that I didn't score had no effect on me. It just made me eager for Game 2, which we won 3–2 on Denny's overtime goal. I didn't score in that game, either.

Our line was checked by the Steve Vickers–Walt Tkaczuk–Anders Hedberg line. Vickers was on me. I've watched films of that series and seen that while the Tkaczuk line played hard and clean, it didn't do anything special. We were awful. We were skating in cement.

When the series moved to the Garden for Games 3 and 4, the city went nuts. Scalpers were asking $500 for top tickets. The series was front page news: "THE BATTLE FOR NEW YORK." And after Game 3, which we lost 3–1, I got psyched right out. I stopped talking to the media after failing to score a point for the third straight game.

This was the year I signed to represent Titan and use their sticks. I liked the feel of their sticks, but the batch they sent me during the playoffs weren't right. They kept breaking when I took slap shots. Before Game 3, I had the company fly a new batch directly from Montreal to the Garden. It didn't help. After one of my first shifts that game, I crossed the blue line, shot, and watched as the blade of my stick snapped off. It went flying in one direction as the puck slithered embarrassingly into the corner.

That's when Clarkie looked at me and said: "Get rid of those goddamned sticks."

I just shrugged. What could I do?

After Game 3, I started to panic. I sensed that the team was headed for a second straight playoff debacle and that I was going to be smack in the middle of this one. The year before I was a rookie, less was expected of me, and I was getting cruelly mugged by Toronto. This year the Rangers were just beating us and silencing me.

I stopped talking to the press partly because I felt I was being unfairly singled out for criticism. Trots and Clarkie were playing as badly as I was, but because I had no goals and our power play was ineffective, everyone was blaming me.

We won Game 4 at the Garden, 3–2, on Nystrom's overtime goal, but I didn't do a thing for the fourth straight game.

We lost Game 5 at home, 4–3, and I did even less.

Before Game 6, I realized how stupid I was being with the media. I had grown tired of trying to avoid them after games and practices. I was trying to beat the Rangers and shake a terribly mistimed slump, but here I was worrying myself sick over being blamed by the press. I was sneaking out back doors, dressing and showering quickly after games in order to dash out of the locker room before the media arrived. I was acting ridiculous.

It reminded me of the time I shot a puck through our basement window from our rink on Meunier St. and started running away. I finally stopped and said: "What am I running from?" The press was going to write about my slump whether they talked to me or not. I figured I might as well try to say something in my defense.

I scored a power-play goal early in Game 6 at the Garden to give us a 1–0 lead. I hoped my first point of the series would do something for us. As I sat on the bench after that goal, I prayed it would be one of my five in the game. I was trying to lift the earth off of me, because all series long I had been buried and it was getting hard to breathe.

But nothing happened. The Rangers won, 2–1. I was heartbroken. For the second straight season we had lost to a team we should have beaten. Did we choke?

The team didn't, but I did. To me, choking is being unable to do something in a pressure situation that you're accustomed to doing under normal circumstances. The Islanders had never gotten to the Stanley Cup finals. We just weren't ready. We weren't mature enough. That became obvious over the next few years, when we did everything we had to do to win.

I choked, though, and our whole line choked, because we had been able to score all season, on the road and at home, against the best scoring lines and the best checking lines and the best goalies. Trottier, one goal and one assist; Bossy, one goal; Gillies, one assist. We let the team down. We failed. Had our line contributed, we would have won the series.

Think about how I handled it: I worried about my sticks. I stopped talking to reporters. For the first time that I could remember, I made my problems worse. By acting like a fugitive, I stopped being me. I stopped having fun. I made hockey a chore that whole series and it ate away at my insides.

That's when I learned that there's a big difference between working hard and accomplishing something. Especially in my case. If I was scoring, I was playing well. If I wasn't scoring, I wasn't playing well. It was that simple. The Ranger series was the first time in my career, maybe in my life, that I wasn't able to grab hold of a pressure situation and thrive on it.

The drive back home that spring was terrible, but I didn't lose confidence in us that summer. I felt Bill would make some changes before we won the Cup, but I didn't believe that the team that had lost to Toronto and the Rangers wasn't good enough to win it all. Hell, I was 22, Trots was 22, Clarkie was 25, Denny was 25, Smitty at 28 had started playing his best goal.

In the disappointing postgame locker room scene after Game 6, I heard Bournie tell the press that we had a monkey on our back. There was no doubt that the loss to the Rangers haunted us as we went into next season, but we were prepared to exorcise that demon.

Chapter

The First Time

What's going to happen?

I asked myself that question all summer for a variety of reasons. Lucie and I were anxiously awaiting the birth of our first child, who was due in September. I was sure Bill was going to somehow shake up our roster in an attempt to avoid a third consecutive playoff failure. And Pierre was ready to negotiate my new contract.

Pierre and I agreed that the playoff upsets of 1978 and 1979 did not deserve to lessen my value to the Islanders, so we planned to be aggressive. Pierre asked me to weigh the benefits of a long-term deal (immediate financial security with a baby on the way) against a second short-term deal.

"The collective bargaining agreement between the NHL and the players' association expires in 1981, Mike," Pierre explained. "If you sign for only two years, play like you played these first two years, and put up more of the numbers you've put up, you'll be in the best position of your life to secure your future. And if you guys win the Cup, who knows?"

We knew it was risky, but we felt it was a good gamble. Bill had offered us a six-year deal worth $2 million. Do you know how difficult it was for me to refuse? At the age of 21 I had made $80,000. But I trusted Pierre. What he said made sense.

We considered Bill's $2 million offer all summer. Pierre wanted to see how much more Bill would be willing to pay if he thought we were serious about me playing out my option, so we waited until just before the September 10 option deadline before rejecting the offer.

It didn't pay to play out my option. Under the terms of my first contract and the collective bargaining agreement, it meant I would earn $70,000 with a chance to collect another $15,000 in goal bonuses. It also meant that after the 1979–80 season, I would become a free agent with compensation. But true free agency doesn't exist in the NHL because of the strict compensation guidelines, so playing out my option wasn't going to increase my bargaining position.

What we wanted was a new short-term contract.

At a meeting on September 7 at Denis and Pierre's new office in Laval, we officially rejected Bill's six-year, $2 million offer and asked for a three-year pact (two plus option) worth $300,000 per year. Bill initially refused, made a quick call to his office, and then officially refused.

So we bargained. We agreed that day to a contract that included a $75,000 signing bonus, a salary of $200,000 for the current season and $225,000 for 1980–81. I accepted two bonus clauses: $25,000 for 50 goals and $25,000 if the Islanders won the Stanley Cup.

A week later, on September 15, 1979, Josiane was born in Montreal. Camp started that day at Cantiague Park, our new training facility in Hicksville, but I had permission to report late. I flew from Montreal to Long Island the day after Josiane was born, attended the press conference in which my new contract was announced, skated that afternoon and the next day, flew back to Montreal, brought Lucie and Josiane home from the hospital, and drove back alone to Long Island.

Lucie and Josiane moved back into our East Northport apartment about a month later. Josiane rarely cried at night and I remember thinking, "Boy, parenthood is easy." When I said that to Lucie, she reminded me of the four previous weeks, when Josiane was acting very much like a newborn.

The season was a few weeks away and I was on Cloud Nine: a new daughter, a new contract, and a new Afro hairdo.

Not all was so wonderful with the Islanders. Two days before our opener Clarkie resigned as captain. He said his responsibilities to the team were affecting his own game. Denny became the team's third captain, succeeding Eddie Westfall and Clarkie.

I would have enjoyed being captain at some point in my NHL career, but I don't think I could have put up with all the stupid moaning and groaning by the players. A captain is supposed to be the liaison between players and the coaching staff and I'm just not a great sounding board. Trots is a great sounding board and I think he would have made a great captain. He served as acting captain when Denny was injured, but he never became captain of the Islanders. He'll never admit this, but he was deeply disappointed when Denny resigned the captaincy in 1987 and the players chose Brent Sutter over him in a two-man election.

That was last year, the year I sat out. The election was on the afternoon of our opener in Los Angeles. I voted by telephone...for Trots, of course.

When Clarkie handed the "C" to Denny, Trots and I felt that was only the first shoe to drop. Everyone on the team feared shakeup. Trots and I conjured a million different trades involving everybody but us. I'm sure everybody else was planning to trade their teammates, too.

Bill and Al did reshape the team. Westfall and Marshall retired. Hart was lost to Quebec and Price went to Edmonton in the expansion draft that stocked the four teams joining the NHL from the WHA (Hartford and Winnipeg were the others). In their place came Kallur, a rookie left wing from Sweden, center Steve Tambellini, defenseman Dave Langevin, an Islander draft pick in 1974 who was acquired from Edmonton, and Jean Potvin, reacquired from Minnesota, which had merged with Cleveland the year before.

Bill wasn't finished. In November he permanently promoted Duane Sutter, a scrappy 19-year-old right wing who was our first-round draft pick in June. And in December he traded Kaszycki to Washington for physical defenseman Gord Lane.

The maneuvers added depth. None of these new players were superstars, although management was hoping Duane would be, but they were excellent role players. Kallur and Tambellini added speed, Langevin and Lane added size, Sutter added grit.

By Christmas we were 12–14–6. We were playing without life, without intelligence, without heart. We were terrible. We had meetings with Al, meetings without Al. We talked among ourselves formally, we talked among ourselves informally. I remember one players-only meeting when Langevin stood up and blasted us. It was after practice one day at Cantiague Park and that meeting, more than any other, made a lasting impression on me.

"I had heard so many great things about this team before I got here," Langevin said. "I thought we all had more pride than we're showing."

Al stormed in as we were dressing after one practice and screamed at Clarkie, Trots and I. He cut us up for being the last guys on the ice every practice and the first guys off.

I was concerned. We were in Colorado during a dismal 1–4–1 road trip in November when I asked Bill if I could meet with him in the hotel lobby. We were 6–9–4 going into this game and although I had 14 goals in the 19 games, I was more concerned with our team's inability to win consistently. I did most of the talking. I told Bill that I felt more responsible for the team's performance now that I had signed my new contract and was making big money, and I wanted him to know I planned on taking on more of a leadership role. I wanted him to know that I took it personally that the team wasn't playing well.

We lost that night in Colorado, 7–4, but we made NHL history. Actually, Smitty did. He became the first goalie in history to be credited with a goal when the Rockies' Rob Ramage accidentally shot the puck down the ice and into his own empty net while the Rockies were attacking during a delayed penalty. Smitty got the goal because he was the last guy on our team to touch the puck.

Smitty and I had our share of arguments. One happened midway through the season at Cantiague Park. We were playing a game of Showdown when I whistled a shot just under the crossbar for a goal. Smitty, who hated when anybody lifted the puck above his ankles during practice, yelled at me to keep my shot down.

I heard him, but I felt he was being ridiculous. If I'm trying to score, why can't I aim for the top half of the net? The next time I came down on him, I shot high again and tucked a second goal under the crossbar.

Smitty went crazy. He skated out after me, swung at me with his stick, and didn't calm down until after I skated away. Smitty's beef was that it was wrong for shooters to attempt plays that we wouldn't attempt in games. I agreed, then told him that I often tried to shoot for the top of the net in games. It was exasperating trying to argue with the guy. Sometimes I wonder why I ever tried.

The funniest moment of this aggravating first half-season came in Winnipeg, during our first visit to Winnipeg Arena. I wiped out nearly half their team at one time ... in warmup.

Both teams were skating through their basic shooting drills before a game: line up near the red line, take a pass, skate over the blue line, slap. You do this for five or seven minutes just to get your goalies loosened. The teams line up with their backs to each other, left wings on the left, centers in the middle, right wings on the right. It's a good time to gab with familiar opponents that you don't get to see too often.

My turns were notorious among the team for not being the best. I didn't chop the ice into cubes, but let's just say I wasn't the most fluid skater changing directions. Anyway, I went to take a shot on Smitty, then I figured I'd stretch my legs with a little dash. I hustled from the right side of the ice to the middle, then went to turn from the middle back toward the right boards. As soon as I hit the right wing edge of the center circle, I lost my balance and skidded over the red line.

WHOA! Like a bowling ball, I headed straight for the Jets' center line. Guys went down one-by-one, like bowling pins. Some scrambled to get out of the way, others toppled teammates. Five Jets ended up on top of me. I looked for Trots, who was doubled over laughing.

There was nothing funny about our 8–2 loss to the Rangers on February 24, 1980, at the Garden. That was the day the U.S. Olympic Hockey Team completed its gold-medal Miracle at Lake Placid; it was also the night I vowed not to fight and threatened to quit.

The hockey world was buzzing that afternoon. Forty-eight hours after the U.S. beat the Russians, 4–3, they defeated Finland to clinch their improbable championship. It was a great moment for hockey in America, a great moment for our sport. At the Garden before our game, the thunderous chorus of U!S!A! ... U!S!A! ... filled me with chills.

And then the Rangers and Islanders played. Both teams were despicable. We clutched and grabbed, hooked and held, slashed and speared. Fist fights and stick jousts, hair pulling and name-calling. It was sickening.

"If this is what hockey is going to be, then I'm going to get out of it," I told Larry Brooks of *The New York Post*, whose column marked my first announcement that I wouldn't fight.

> **This isn't the way hockey is supposed to be played. It's ridiculous. People who watched the American team saw freewheeling hockey that's fast, exciting and good to watch. Tonight, those people who might have turned this game on TV because of what they saw in the Olympics, well, I don't even have to say the obvious ... it's not the same game.**

> I'm not talking about taking a check, that's part of the game. I'm talking about all the cheap shots guys have to take in this league, especially guys who won't drop their gloves and fight. I'm not going to fight. I'm not going to let this game turn me into a person I'm not.

Those weren't the comments of some hothead who had taken one too many cross-checks from behind. Sure I was frustrated by our lopsided loss, but I was more annoyed at how ugly the average NHL game had become. That this New York gang war occurred 12 hours after the Olympic team's victory served to highlight just how stupid we were.

OK, OK, I did get carried away when I said I was going to quit. But I meant it when I said I wouldn't fight. And boy, did that cause me grief in the playoffs two months later.

The loss to the Rangers left us 28–25–8. We went 3–3–1 in our next seven games when the bombshell everybody was expecting to fall, fell on March 10, 1980: Bill announced he had sent Harris and defenseman Dave Lewis to Los Angeles for center Butch Goring.

I walked into the Coliseum for practice that day and before anybody said a word, I sensed that something big had happened. The building was too quiet, the faces too stunned. Before I could ask what happened, I knew. There were Lewie and Harry in the dressing room, both red-eyed from crying, both shocked beyond belief. These were two of the best-liked guys on the team. Harry had been an Islander since Day One, the first draft choice in the team's history.

Traded?

No matter how sure you are that something's going to happen, it's a shock when it finally does happen. We were stunned to see Lewie and Harry go, but with that drastic move came a feeling of relief. Once Harry and Lewie left and the trading deadline passed, nobody had to worry about being the guy dealt. I think that's one of the biggest reasons why we had played so badly all season. Trade rumors had run rampant from the start of training camp and as we floundered through the season, they never let up.

By acquiring Goring, Bill added a little spunk to the lineup. Goring was one of those digging little centers, a buzzsaw who worked all the time, could play the power play and kill penalties. People said that Butchie took a little pressure off Trots and I, but we never bought that. We felt just as much pressure after Butchie arrived as we did before the trade. Trots still took all the defensive face-offs and he and I still anchored the power play, but there was no doubt that Goring was a great addition to the team.

So was Ken Morrow, a lanky, defensive defenseman who looked more like Abe Lincoln than a hockey player. Morrow didn't have to prove himself to us, however. He was drafted out of Bowling Green University in 1976 and he arrived on March 1, 1980, straight from the gold medal-winning U.S. Olympic Team.

It's important to note, too, that Denny had missed more than half the season with a serious thumb injury. He returned about two weeks before we traded for Goring. So with a healthy and rested Denny, two new quality players in Morrow and Goring, and no threat of trades (until next year), Bill had built the team he thought could win the 1980 Stanley Cup.

Now it was time to go about our business. We were 31–28–9 when the trade was made. With Goring, Morrow and Potvin in the lineup we went 8–0–4 in our final 12 games to finish fifth overall and second in the division behind Philadelphia.

I had 47 goals when we got Butchie. I cashed my $25,000 bonus clause by scoring 48, 49 and 50 in successive games. I finished the season with 51 goals, 92 points and 12 penalty minutes.

And then the Run for One began ... with a best-of-five preliminary round series against Harry, Lewie and the Los Angeles Kings. We were confident. Our failures against Toronto and the Rangers had taught us lessons we wanted to prove we had learned. We'd been thinking for three years now that we had the team to win the Cup. Our strong finish helped us believe this was our year.

Al did something very interesting before the series started. He fit Clarkie on a grinding line with Goring and Sutter and placed the speedy Bourne with Trots and I. We blasted the Kings in Game 1 at home, 8–1, then lost Game 2 at home, 6–3. And I got hurt. I jammed my right thumb into the boards near our bench as I absorbed a check. At first we thought it was only a bruise, and the negative X-rays confirmed that optimistic diagnosis. But I couldn't play Games 3 and 4 when we eliminated the Kings by winning 4–3 in overtime (Morrow scored the goal) and 6–0.

That 4–3 win might have been one of our biggest. After losing the home-ice advantage by losing Game 2, we had set ourselves up for another disaster. Although I couldn't play, I joined the team in the dressing room prior to the game and between periods, and we were as uptight as we'd been for any game. Morrow's goal took a million pounds of pressure off everybody. The 6–0 shutout proved it.

September 1959. I'm in Dad's right arm, my sister
Pamela is in his left.

April 1960. The earliest
photograph we have of me on
skates with a stick and a puck.
That's the St. Urbain St. rink.

Same day. Chris is waiting for Pam to drop
the puck. I'm waiting for Mom to call us
for lunch.

Winter 1971. St. Alphonse wins the Bantam AA championship. I was the team's captain.

Dad, Mom, Gordie, Lucie, Lucie's sister Carol and her daughter, Annick, greet me at Dorval Airport on January 3, 1977, after the Junior All-Star tournament out west.

Photo by Normand Pichette, Journal de Montreal

Photo by Denis Brodeur

Maurice Richard and I.

A moment to relax during the 1981 Canada Cup. *Left to right,* Scotty Bowman, Guy Lafleur, Wayne Gretzky, Alan Eagleson, someone I don't know, Larry Robinson and me.

Photo by James Lipa

Celebrating our third straight Cup at Pacific Coliseum, the only Cup we won away from home. I'm on the left of Stefan Persson and Trots.

The sweetest taste in the world, no matter what's in the goblet. That's in Vancouver after our third Cup.

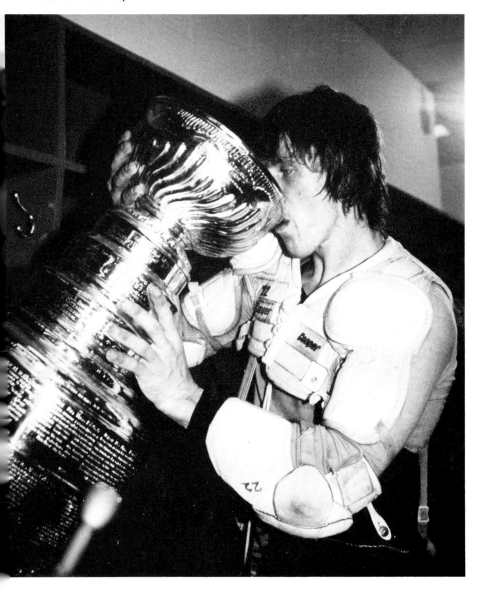

Our third Stanley Cup parade down Hempstead Turnpike. I'm sharing the fun with two of my favorite ladies—my daughter Josiane on my arm and Mom to my right.

Showing off the team colors during the 1981 Canada Cup. *Left to right*, Guy Lafleur, me and Wayne Gretzky.

Team Canada, 3, USSR, 2 (OT). In one of the greatest international games ever played, my overtime tip-in of Paul Coffey's shot knocked the Soviets out of the 1984 Canada Cup semifinals and set up our two-game series sweep of Sweden. The goalie is Vladimir Myshkin. The defenseman is Vladimir Kovin. Mike Noeth is the referee.

What a clutch goal-scorer that Morrow was. Wolfman, we called him, because he was so hairy. He was the textbook defensive defenseman, but he had an uncanny knack of scoring huge playoff goals. In 516 regular-season NHL games including 1987–88 he scored 15 goals. But in 127 playoff games he scored 11. And of those 11, three were in overtime. In the history of Stanley Cup play, Morrow trails only Maurice Richard (6), Bobby Nystrom (4) and Dale Hunter (4) in overtime goals. He's tied with me and 11 others for fourth place all-time, and he's the only defenseman in the batch.

You figure that out.

Our next obstacle was Boston, where overtime settled three of the first four games in a grueling, physical series. We knew the Bruins were going to be difficult. Boston Garden and its small ice surface is a hard place for a visitor to play at any time. These Bruins had finished fourth overall during the season. With Terry O'Reilly, Wayne Cashman, Al Secord and Stan Jonathan, they were one of the strongest teams in the league.

I had hoped my bruised thumb would heal in time for Game 1, but it didn't. I badly wanted to play, but I couldn't grip my stick or shoot the puck. Waske started me on a program of heat, ice and therapy after the injury, but when the thumb didn't respond, he ordered another set of X-rays.

That's when they detected a slight fracture.

I watched the first three games from the stands, Games 1 and 2 in Boston and Game 3 at home. It was a very strange experience, knowing that the game was going to be filled with fights and wanting to be out there to join my teammates. In junior, I wished I wasn't out there whenever a fight started. Now, I wished I was. Not to fight, but to support guys like Clarkie, Howatt, Lane and Sutter; guys who were standing up to the Bruins and telling them that the Islanders would not be intimidated.

Clarkie pummeled O'Reilly all series. We won most of the brawls in Boston and we won the first two games, 2–1 on an overtime goal by Clarkie, and 5–4 on an overtime goal by Bournie. We were learning what it was like to win in the playoffs. When a team goes through an experience like that, when it's forced to stick up to a favored foe and does so, it forms a bond that's so important in the playoffs. I sensed the guys coming together. We were standing behind one another and standing up for each other like we hadn't all year.

We won Game 3 at home, 5–3, and I came back for Game 4. I scored two goals, but we lost 4–3 in overtime on O'Reilly's goal. Was I a jinx, or what?

No, I wasn't. I picked up two assists in Game 5 and we eliminated the Bruins with a 4–2 win at Boston, giving us a sweep of the three games at the Garden. We sensed something special. But we were determined not to look too far ahead.

Our semifinal opponent was the Buffalo Sabres, who had finished 47–17–16 during the regular season. They were second overall behind the Flyers and had allowed the fewest goals in the league, but the pressure we had felt in '78, '79 and through the first two rounds of this season were gone. We knew that we weren't going to have to play the Rangers, who were knocked out early. We knew we weren't going to have to play Montreal either. It was Isles–Sabres and Flyers–North Stars in the semifinals.

This was going to be a tough series for Pierre to watch, because his first two clients were after the Stanley Cup: Sauve was the NHL's leading goalie during the regular season for Buffalo. It was my job to beat him.

Sauve played in four of the six games. I didn't play much at all. Al tried to match lines with Buffalo coach Scotty Bowman, so he played Nystrom on right wing whenever Bowman played The French Connection, the line of Rick Martin–Gil Perreault–Rene Robert. Martin was their sniper, but Ny did a fabulous job on the left wing, holding him to no goals and three assists.

I was mad at Al, selfishly I admit, because I played well in the final two games against Boston after recuperating from my thumb injury. But I was not about to rock the boat. With the Rangers out of the playoffs we were gaining confidence every game: we won 4–1 in Game 1 and 2–1 in Game 2 on Ny's goal in double overtime. We took a three-game lead with a 7–4 win at home, then lost two straight. But we won Game 6 at home, 5–2, to reach the finals.

The Stanley Cup finals. We had beaten the intimidators from Boston. We had beaten the favorites from Buffalo. Now we were asking ourselves to defeat the intimidating favorites from Philly. The Flyers had won the regular-season championship with a record of 48–12–20. They had set an NHL record by going 35 games without a loss, 25–0–10. Few experts gave us a chance, which worked to our advantage.

And then, on the eve of Game 1, *Inside Sports* magazine published a story penned by yours truly. The timing couldn't have been worse. The article, which I had written two months earlier, was spawned by statements I had made in late February, when I threatened to quit and vowed I would not fight.

"Each time you knock me down," I said to the game's goons in this article, "I'll get back up and score more goals."

I had no idea the article was going to appear two days before the finals. Suddenly, with the Stanley Cup four wins away, I was a target under the spotlight. That article set me up for a ton of abuse, especially from the Philly fans in the Spectrum for Games 1 and 2. They leaned over the glass and called me "faggot," during warmup. They asked if I was wearing pantyhose. I wasn't intimidated, but I expected at least one Flyer to test my declaration.

The test came in Game 1. We were on a power play and we accidentally iced the puck. It was a lead pass intended for me and my momentum carried me deep in their zone. When the whistle blew, I turned in the corner (I didn't fall), glided toward the sideboards and skated back up ice.

Bridgman was covering me down the wing, but had let me go once the icing occurred. As I skated back for the face-off in our zone, Bridgman stopped near the Flyer bench and stood in my path. I was 20 feet away when I spotted him. He saw me, too. And he wouldn't move.

I had come to the crossroads, with only a split-second to think: Do I sidestep him and make him think he got the best of me? Do I nudge him to send a message? Do I run over him and risk waking up in the doctor's room with two black eyes?

I stood my ground and ran over him. I sent him flying. I didn't hit him that hard, but I caught him completely by surprise. With Bob Dailey and Moose Dupont standing there menacingly, with Bridgman looking at me with those piercing eyes and his mustache drooping halfway down his face, with their entire bench cursing at me, I was scared to death. I prayed that some of my teammates would get here real quick, just in case a couple of them decided to make mincemeat out of me.

But nothing happened. I did what I said I would do. I stood my ground when a Flyer shoved me, I steered clear of the usual pushing, shoving and milling around, I kept my gloves on and I kept myself in the game. And that was that. No harm, no foul.

I felt proud of myself. At that moment I knew I would never have to drop my gloves to prove anything again. That was the day I had earned the NHL's respect.

We won the game, 4–3, on Denny's power-play goal at 4:07 of overtime.

We got blown out in Game 2, 8–3, but nobody sensed trouble. We knew it was going to be a long series and we were satisfied to leave the Spectrum with a split. Losing big didn't matter to us, because we were going home for Games 3 and 4.

We swept the Flyers at the Coliseum, 6–2 and 5–2. Our power play was awesome. Smitty was awesome. We were playing like a team. We were up three games to one, just one victory from the Stanley Cup. We had reached the point we were supposed to reach a year and two years ago.

Now we had to finish the job.

In Game 5 we were blown out 8–3.

I wasn't worried, but I felt that we'd better win Game 6 at home or we were in major trouble. I didn't like our chances in a seventh game at Philadelphia. Nobody on our team did.

We wanted to win it at home, in front of our loyal fans. May 24, 1980, was a Saturday afternoon. Game 6 was televised nationally in the States on CBS. Each one of us walked into the locker room that morning saying to himself, "we'd better do it this time."

Believe it or not, I don't remember much about the game. I remember our fourth goal was two feet offsides and shouldn't have counted, but Leon Stickle, an excellent linesman, made a blatant mistake.

We led 4–2 after the second period. In those 15 minutes before the third, I felt more pressure than in any other game I'd ever played. When they made it 4–3, I shuddered. When they tied it, I was scared to death.

And then overtime.

As I sat silently before overtime, a part of me prayed I wouldn't make the mistake that led to their goal, but another part of me wanted to be the hero. And one thought kept creeping into my mind: If we lose this, we have to go there for Game 7.

As I worried about having to go back to Philly if we lost, I remembered that we had won five overtime games already in these playoffs. We were 5–1 in overtime. We had developed a great over-time record and we knew it. Most of the overtime goals had come from guys who weren't expected to score them, guys like Morrow and Nystrom.

As we grabbed our sticks and headed out for the most important period of our lives, we reminded ourselves that we were the guys who kept scoring the big overtime goals. We believed it because it was true.

I played scared in overtime. I had one long shot from high in the slot that their goalie, Pete Peeters, stopped. Although I was the guy most likely to score, I wasn't thinking that I was going to get it. I was just praying that the guy who was going to get it was wearing white.

Seven minutes into the extra period, an innocent play at the red line suddenly turned into a dangerous play at their blue line, Tonelli and Ny on a two-on-one. Tonelli made a pass to Ny and from the bench I could tell that it was going to leave Bobby in an awkward spot. It wasn't a pass that he could one-time before Peeters could set, but it wasn't a pass that he could backhand, either.

What was Ny going to do?

He just jabbed at J.T.'s pass. He redirected it over Peeters, who didn't know then that he was going to be beaten by us many times in the playoffs.

Nystrom scored at 7:11.

Pandemonium.

I can't tell you where on the bench I was, who I hugged first, or what I did. I just leaped over the boards, jumped on the ice, threw my gloves in the air and started screaming with joy. I must've carried the Cup around after Denny accepted it from President John Ziegler, but I don't remember. I do remember drinking the most vile liquid — it was some $2 champagne — I ever tasted out of the Cup in a circus of a dressing room.

It felt like there were a thousand people in the room: wives, family, friends, the press. Television cameras were everywhere, champagne was everywhere, beer was everywhere. It was incredibly exciting, more exciting than I could have ever imagined. All my emotions bubbled over with the euphoria of trying and trying and finally winning a Stanley Cup. It was an afternoon game, remember, which meant very few of us had any food in our systems. It didn't take very long once we started celebrating for us to become drunk out of our minds.

I was blasted half-an-hour after the game. I had scored four goals and 11 points in the series for ten goals and 23 points in the playoffs. Trots set an NHL record (since broken) with 29 points and won the Conn Smythe Trophy as the most valuable player in the playoffs.

Bill invited us to his house that night, but Lucie was so drunk from the locker-room celebration that I had to go alone. I left Lucie sleeping on the sofa, drove Josiane's baby-sitter home and headed over for Bill's. I'm ashamed to admit this now, but I hopped into my car with a blood alcohol level undoubtedly over New York State's legal limit. There were dozens of people at Bill's house that night, which meant drunk driving must have been legal on Long Island that day.

A few days later we brought Josiane to the Coliseum to be photographed with the Cup. Her bottom fit neatly into the goblet. We headed from the photograph session to the kick-off site of our parade up Hempstead Turnpike. The parade started off orderly enough, with fans cheering behind barricades and the players riding in antique convertible automobiles. But the closer to the Coliseum we got, the more fans there were. And the more fans there were, the more pushing and shoving went on behind the barricades and the less orderly the parade became.

By the time we pulled into the Coliseum parking lot, it was bedlam. Cops on horses were trying to keep fans away from the cars. Appreciative fans who wanted us to join their celebration pitched cans of beer to us. With Josiane on my lap, it was scary. Instead of coasting pleasantly at five and ten miles per hour while we waved, we sped 30 miles per hour through the parking lot and down the service ramp into the Coliseum, where the cars were parked while we prepared for a grand entrance onto a stage erected adjacent to the building.

The fans became too rowdy. When they broke through the barricades and stormed the foot of the stage, the ceremony outside the Coliseum had to be called off.

Four days later, Lucie, Josiane and I drove home to spend the greatest summer of my life with my family and friends. I smiled that whole summer. No matter how good my first two seasons were personally, being a Montreal boy with my name on the Stanley Cup was the greatest. I could only think of one thing better.

Another Cup.

Chapter

10

50 in 50

$\mathbf{M}$y brother-in-law Bob was the first to know.

We were sitting in his house late one night in the summer of 1980 talking about the Islanders, the Stanley Cup and my three straight 50-goal seasons. It must have been three or four in the morning because Lucie's sister Carol, Bob, Lucie and I had grown tired of Yahtzee, the dice game we played for hours and hours almost every night.

I told Bob that scoring 50 goals was a thrill, but next year it wasn't going to be enough. I needed a greater challenge.

"I'm going for 50 in 50," I declared. "That hasn't been done in 30 years."

Thirty-six, to be exact. Maurice "Rocket" Richard scored 50 goals for the Canadiens in the 50-game 1944–45 season. Although Phil Esposito set the NHL record when he scored 76 in the 78-game 1970–71 season, nobody since The Rocket had averaged a goal a game. I never thought about Espo, 80 in 80, or anything else. Rocket's 50 in 50 had become legendary. It hadn't been approached in nearly four decades.

I wanted it.

My desire stemmed from the 1980 finals. After standing up to Bridgman, shedding my fear of fighting, having a great series against

Philadelphia and winning the Cup, my confidence level was at an all-time high. There was nothing I thought I couldn't do.

Bob loved the idea. He believed I could do anything. I could have said I wanted to score 100 goals in 50 games and he would have said, "Yeah, you can do that."

We kept 50 in 50 a secret until training camp, when I quietly told Trots. Long after I scored my 50th, he told me he thought I was being unrealistic. But that day he said it was a great idea. Added motivation for him, added motivation for me.

Our first training camp as Stanley Cup champions wasn't easy, but it was the most relaxed of the four Islander camps I had skated through. That September, we weren't feeling the pressure to repeat, only the joy of success. There were no black clouds wearing Toronto blue and white or Ranger red, white and blue over our heads.

And then the season began. I scored five goals in ten games and we went 3–4–3. It was embarrassing, but there was no panic, no sense of urgency. The Islanders had 70 games to go. I had 40. And so I got rolling.

I scored a hat trick in Game 11 against Montreal; a hat trick in Game 15 against Chicago; four goals in Game 16 against Minnesota. I scored 14 goals in Games 11 through 16, the best streak in my career.

Nineteen in 16.

Oh, was I hot. The game in the Coliseum against Minny, a wild 6–6 tie filled with great goals, funny bounces and virtually no defense, typified the luck I was having. Long slappers were squeezing between goalies' pads; tip-ins were tucking inside posts; rebounds were obediently reporting to my poised stick.

Hat tricks became special to me because they were considered special by the fans. The number itself, three goals, holds no special significance; but I loved watching the different kinds of hats float down from the Coliseum stands after I'd scored that third goal. I still have about 20 of the colorful sombreros regularly thrown to the ice by one Islander fan (I think his name is Tye) who usually sat behind the net we shot at twice.

Although I was three games (or three goals, depending upon how you want to look at it) ahead of the pace after 16 games by the middle of November, I didn't see my quest becoming any easier. The fear of failure drove me from one game to the next, one week to the next, one season to the next — even after three 50-goal years.

I was blanked in Games 17 through 19, but I notched a hat trick in Game 20 at St. Louis. We erased our sluggish start by going 8–1–1 in our second ten-game stretch and that helped me tremendously. When we were winning, there was less pressure on my line to score, which made it easier for Clarkie, Trots and I to score. Call it hockey's Catch-22.

Twenty-two in 20.

It was interesting to hear and read how players around the league perceived my scoring ability. After I scored my 24th and 25th goals in Game 23 against Winnipeg, Jude Drouin was quoted as saying: "It was unbelievable. [Goalie Pierre] Hamel told me he had the angle covered and Mike put it in sideways."

I didn't know what Drouin was talking about. I can't deliberately shoot a puck so that it flips onto its end and propels itself toward the net vertically. No shooter can. If Drouin saw that goal correctly, the puck must have hit a bump on the ice and flipped over. I had nothing to do with that.

Chico, who was traded to Colorado later this season, was the same way. I played four years with the guy and I must have taken ten thousand practice shots at him. But two years ago, when Chico was in goal for the New Jersey Devils, I won a game at Meadowlands Arena in overtime with a slapper from the right circle. It was a hard, low shot that I tried to put on net because only 1:30 remained in the five-minute overtime. I was hoping that if the shot didn't go in, Chico might leave a rebound for Trots or J.T.

I scored. Simple slap shot, simple goal. Or so I thought. About 20 minutes after the game, a bunch of the regular reporters asked me to explain how I learned to put spin on the puck and curve it so precisely.

Huh?

Chico, the reporters told me, had just finished explaining to the media how I was able to slap a puck in such a way that it headed toward a goalie's leg pad or skate with enough spin to curve past his kick. Chico said I'd been doing that for years, that he'd watched me do it in so many practices.

I didn't know what Chico was talking about any more than I knew what Drouin was talking about. But I never discouraged such speculation because I would have a huge psychological advantage over any goalie who worried about me squeezing the puck on its end or curving a slap shot.

The point was, I had goalies thinking too much, especially this season. With 25 goals in 23 games, my scoring became the story in every city we visited, even before my attack on Rocket's 50 in 50 became known. People wanted me to share my goal-scoring secrets.

When I insisted there were none, they created their own ridiculous hypotheses. Drouin couldn't have seen me shooting the puck on end because I never did. Chico couldn't have faced my curveball (curve-puck?) because I didn't have one.

I was halfway there with 25 in 23, but I still kept 50 in 50 a secret. I didn't want any more pressure than was already self-imposed. I knew that as I got closer, some reporter would ask me about it. I decided to wait until the story came to me.

Then I slowed down. I had 26 in 25, then 27 in 27. That goal was the 200th of my career in my 255th game. At the time it was the fastest anyone had scored 200 NHL goals (Gretzky broke that record with 200 in his first 242 games), but that round number didn't feel special because I saw it only as a stepping stone to the next round number.

Our record improved to 17–5–5 after a 13–0–2 run. I had scored 18 goals in November, the most in a month since Esposito scored 19 in March 1971. Not only was I on pace for 50 in 50, but I was on target to break Espo's NHL record 76 goals.

And I didn't think I was playing well. Seriously. I was scoring, but I wanted to be doing more. As I reflect, I was more pumped up than ever before and I asked myself for more than I ever had before because I was convinced I had more to give.

We embarked on a six-game road trip. I failed to score in Colorado (when our 15-game unbeaten streak was snapped) and in Los Angeles. I scored once in Vancouver, then twice in a 3–2 win at Edmonton on December 10.

Thirty in 31.

Clarkie never understood why teams left me alone in front of the net to check him. I scored my 30th goal with 31 seconds left against Edmonton to break a 2–2 tie. Trots had the puck and was looking for Clarkie, but when two defenders collapsed on Clarkie near the net, Trots hit me low in the right circle and I snapped a quick shot past goalie Ron Low.

"Two of them came to me," Gillies said. "I can't figure out why they always take me out and leave Boss open."

It wasn't that I was left open, but I always moved in the slot to keep from being taken out. What often happened is that while I moved, Clarkie anchored himself in one spot near the net and became an easier target to cover. I crossed in front of Clarkie a lot of times, sometimes unconsciously grabbing passes that were intended for him.

I failed to score in Game 32 at Calgary, then climbed back on pace, 33 in 33, with my fourth hat trick of the season. It was a 5–4 win at

Winnipeg. Hamel was the goalie, but I didn't shoot any pucks on end. I scored once short-handed, once off a three-on-one, and once from the slot off a great pass from Clarkie. It's hard for any goalie to defend against plays like those.

I was blanked in Game 34 against Winnipeg, then scored Number 34 in Game 35 against Quebec. Christmas was approaching. Rocket's record was growing more real. And on December 21, I scored my sixth hat trick of the season and we walloped the Blackhawks, 9–0, in Chicago.

Thirty-seven in 36. It was time the hockey world learned what I was up to. Mike Perricone, a *Chicago Sun-Times* sportswriter who was stringing for *Newsday*, Long Island's newspaper, asked me after the game if I was thinking about Espo's NHL record.

"I'm not really thinking of the 76," I replied. "What I have on my mind now is 50 goals in 50 games. I know I have 37, and I know I need 13 in the next 14 games. The team is going well, my linemates are going great, and that just makes it easier."

There, I had done it. Now everybody knew. With Trots and my brother-in-law no longer sworn to secrecy, I promptly went into my only prolonged slump. I scored my 38th goal in my 38th game, went two games without a goal, scored 39 and 40 in Game 41 against Hartford at home, then failed to score against Toronto on January 6, at Pittsburgh on January 7, or against Boston on January 10.

With 40 in 44, it looked bad. I refused to be discouraged, but the press had all but forgotten about it. Trots and I didn't talk much about it. Neither did Bob and I. Was it out of reach?

Saturday, January 10 was a normal day. I awoke early, drove to the Coliseum for our morning skate and drove home for lunch and a nap before the game with the Bruins.

We lost, 3–2. I scored an apparent goal late in the game that was disallowed. We pulled Smitty, but we failed to score with six attackers and dejectedly marched into our dressing room. It was our second straight loss after a 9–1–3 run and we were unhappy.

Before our Coliseum dressing room was refurbished four or five years ago, we had a little stick room adjacent to the dressing room. I called it the Bad News Room because Bill and Al often pulled guys in there for a spur-of-the-moment chewing out. That's where Harry and Lewie were told they were traded.

As soon as I sat down to unlace my skates, Bill stuck his head out of the Bad News room and called me in. I had no idea why he wanted to see me, but I was too scared to look at Trots or anybody else. The only thing I had time to think of in the few seconds it took me to walk in was: "Omigod, I've been traded." I know it was absurd for a player who had 40 goals in 44 games to think he was being shipped out, but that was all I imagined in the few seconds it took me to walk in and close the door.

I was immediately affected by the look on Bill's and Al's faces. I had grown accustomed to seeing their postgame losing expressions, but this was ridiculous. They looked like somebody had died.

Close.

"I guess I'd better tell you this straight out," Bill said nervously. "Someone called the Coliseum today and said they were going to get you."

"Get me?" I asked.

"Yeah," Bill replied. "Someone said they were going to kill you tonight."

I turned white. I felt the blood drain to my toes. Bill told me that someone called the Coliseum's security office that afternoon and made the death threat. Bill said he didn't tell me before the game because he didn't want to make me any more nervous. The caller obviously didn't identify himself. He made no reference to Richard, the record or anything else. But they immediately suspected that the caller was from Quebec, or was a Montreal fan.

I was very confused. I wanted to get home to Lucie, who had stayed home from the game to be with Josiane. Before I left the Coliseum, a Nassau County detective asked me if I had gotten any strange phone calls at home during the day, if anything unusual had happened around the house, or if I had noticed anything strange during the game. I told him I hadn't.

Lucie spotted the car that followed me home, but she had no idea that it was a detective in an unmarked police car. And I didn't tell her. I said it was somebody who needed directions. I had decided on the drive home not to tell Lucie about the threat because nothing had happened and there was no sense worrying her.

But I was still very, very worried.

We bussed the next morning to Philly and I scored my 41st goal in Game 45, a 4–2 win. It was one of my best goals of the 50, and it came after I drew a penalty on defenseman Glen Cochrane for cross-checking me into Peeters' net. Six seconds after the face-off following the penalty, Clarkie set me up for a blast from the inner edge of the right circle that sailed in and out of the net before Peeters moved. It was one my hardest shots ever.

The detectives insisted on continuing their steady patrol around our home, but I had stopped worrying. We bussed home from Philly after the game, got a good night's sleep and reported to practice on Monday morning. The Cantiague Park rink manager intercepted me on the way to the dressing room, pulled me aside and whispered, "Mike, someone called this morning and said that you 'won't make it home from practice.'"

Now it was serious. I practiced, but I was barely able to stand up.

Although Saturday's initial threat was reported in the paper on Monday morning, Lucie hadn't heard about it when I walked into the apartment that afternoon. Now that it had happened again, I couldn't keep it from her any longer. I asked the detective who needed to interview us together to wait outside for a moment.

"Lu, there's something I have to tell you," I said as I walked through the door. "I got a death threat after the game on Saturday and I just got another one this morning."

Lucie was shocked. The detective entered and the policework began.

"Do you owe anybody money?" We didn't.

"Does anybody owe you money?" No.

"Do you know anybody who hates you." Not that we knew.

I told the detective about a 14- or 15-year-old girl, a groupie who hung around Cantiague Park and liked to meet me at the dressing room door after practice. She told me that she had a boyfriend and she liked to tell me how things were going with him. Not long before the first threat she told me she was having problems with her schoolwork and her boyfriend. She said her mother was mad at her. Trying to be helpful, I suggested that perhaps she should break up with her boyfriend.

It was the only scrap of information I could provide the detective, but he didn't think it was too strong a lead. When I asked Lucie if anybody had called the house while I was at practice she said, "Yes, someone did call. He told me he didn't want to leave a message, but he asked what time I was coming home."

And Lucie told him.

The detective stayed with us until late that afternoon. By the time he left, we were so spooked we could barely speak. We decided to release a bit of the stress by treating Josiane, who was nearly 16 months old, to an early dinner at a nearby Ground Round. In the middle of our meal, which we barely ate, someone accidentally opened an emergency exit door and tripped the alarm. Lucie and I nearly hit the ceiling, we were so on edge, so afraid.

We didn't sleep that night. Even Josiane sensed something because she cried all night, something she rarely did. We were acting crazy. Every time a car or a person passed our home we wanted to check to see if somebody had planted a bomb. Detectives patrolled through the night, shining their lights everywhere.

I was determined to play in our next game, Tuesday against Pittsburgh at the Coliseum. It's funny, but when I got on the ice, I forgot all about the threats. Lucie went to the game but left Josiane with a friend of ours instead of at home alone with a baby-sitter.

I scored four goals, giving me 45 in 46. The police kept detectives around Lucie and stationed plain-clothesmen elsewhere in the stands. Each time I scored, they stood rigidly on guard just in case. If a sniper was going to "get me," they figured he'd try while the crowd was cheering and everyone was on their feet.

I kept the cops on edge all game.

"You didn't make it easy for us," a detective joked as he escorted us to our car after the game.

And that was the end of it. They assumed that the prankster was a disgruntled fan of Richard's who figured that nothing was going to stop me, not even his death threats.

At least that's what I hoped. I was so happy that the trouble had blown over that I never got mad at Bill for withholding word of the first threat from me until after the Boston game. Didn't he think that if I was going to get killed I had a right to know about it? I didn't think of that until the whole thing ended. I'm not sure I would have wanted to play in that game if I knew I might be assassinated.

My four goals against Pittsburgh, my second four-goal game in two months, turned the chase into a full-fledged media event. Now I was the NHL's biggest story. Now I was on everybody's mind. My fourth goal came after the Penguins pulled goalie Greg Millen. Trots had the puck with nobody between him and the empty net, but he ignored it and passed to me.

"I know he's going for 50 in 50," Trots told the press. "I want to help him."

"If there's any record I'd like to own, that's the one," I said. "I'm going to do my best to reach it. No matter how much I try to tell myself that I shouldn't think about it, I'm sure it will be on my mind for the next four games."

From that moment, 50 in 50 was all I could think about. Because Rocket's achievement wasn't an official NHL record, reporters began to wonder how I would beat it. Would I need to score my 50th in my 49th game? Would I need to score 51 in 50? All I wanted was 50 in 50. After that, I didn't care.

Game 47 was at home against Washington on Saturday, January 17. Trots was a machine, feeding me pucks every shift. He had a fabulous game. I took ten shots, nine at Rollie Boutin and one at an empty net. Three went in: Bossy from Trots at 19:36 of the second; Bossy from Trots at 8:35 of the third; Bossy into the empty net from Trots at 18:52 of the third. We won, 6–4, our third straight victory.

Forty-eight in 47.

"We're still worried about winning games, most of all," Al told a press corps that was growing by the goal. "But when Mike got that third goal, even I got excited."

Without a game until Tuesday, I went a little stir-crazy. Practice on Sunday and Monday was a mess because reporters were everywhere looking for a new angle to my chase. There was one: Los Angeles Kings left wing Charlie Simmer had 44 goals in 46 games. He wanted no part of the circus, though. He wished me luck, told the press that he admired how I put the pressure on myself, and said he would be much happier once this whole story went away.

Game 48 was against Calgary at the Coliseum on Tuesday, January 20, two days before my 24th birthday. There were camera crews on hand from the six local television stations, Cable News Network and *Hockey Night in Canada*. In addition to the pack of New York radio and print reporters who covered us each game, I recognized reporters from *The Toronto Star, The Globe and Mail, The Montreal Gazette* and *La Presse* of Montreal.

The attention by the press was almost overwhelming, but since I was scoring, the pressure hadn't gotten to me. I did agree, however, with one of Simmer's points: I wanted to get the whole thing over with as soon as possible.

The Calgary game was awful. Eric Vail, a physical defensive left wing who had a dislocated finger, wasn't supposed to play. But coach Al McNeil put him in the lineup and used him against me because Vail volunteered to check me. He shadowed me all game.

"You're going to get a lot of ice time," I said to him after one of my first shifts. He just nodded.

I took four shots at goalie Rejean Lemelin in our 5–0 win, but I didn't have one good scoring chance. The Flames were more interested in stopping me than winning the game. When I was on the ice they didn't give two hoots about scoring. Vail guarded me fairly cleanly, but he hooked and held me, got in my way, dumped me, did all the little things that a guy does when he's assigned to shadow a scorer.

"The only reason I'm tired," I said afterwards, "is from picking myself up all night."

I didn't feel that badly. We scored all five of our goals in the third period, two by Trots and one by Clarkie without any assists from me. And I still had two games to score two goals.

With 48 in 48, we flew to Detroit for a game on my birthday at Joe Louis Arena. The Red Wings had a left wing who usually checked me closer than Vail ever did. Paul Woods was twice as fast as Vail and more of a defensive specialist, so I knew it was going to be a tough night.

We won, 3–0, but Woods didn't let me breathe. The ice was terrible and I felt like I was standing still. Goalie Larry Lozinski stopped my four shots, two in a flurry in front of the net and another from ten feet away that I shot right into his pads. It was 2–0 with 1:30 to go when they pulled Lozinski. Twice I had the puck just over the red line in the final 90 seconds, with Dale McCourt tugging at my arms each time; I shot wide right once and wide left once. I was sick. Clarkie scored into the open net, almost apologetically, with four seconds left. He looked and looked and looked for me, but I couldn't get open. He finally had no choice but to score.

The pressure I felt after that game was unreal. I was escorted into a special area adjacent to the visitor's dressing room for a press conference. For the second game in a row I had to explain why I didn't score, explain how much Richard's record meant to me and explain how it felt to have an opponent shadowing me every step.

I was a little peeved at Detroit defenseman Jean Hamel for one play. With the score 1–0 in the second period, I fed Clarkie the puck early on a two-on-one, fully expecting Hamel to react to the pass. I was hoping that Clarkie would return the puck to me when Hamel challenged him, but Hamel never did. He followed me to the boards, leaving Clarkie the room and time to skate in alone on Lozinski and score, which he did.

"I think if I had stopped, turned around, and gone to the bench, Hamel would have followed me there, too," I said angrily.

I was frustrated and embarrassed. I still felt I was going to get two goals in Game 50 that Saturday night at home against Quebec, but the media kept asking me how I'd feel if I didn't.

My teammates were very supportive throughout the hectic last two weeks, but the Calgary and Detroit games frustrated them, too. We had won 5–0 and 3–0, but the press spent almost all of their time with me. It didn't matter to them that we had posted back-to-back shutouts or that we were 31–10–8.

Lane tried to lift the tension in Detroit. He had scored his first goal of the season early in the game and demanded to know why nobody was talking to him. "Just think," Lane said. "If I score 49 goals the next game, I can tie the record, too."

We didn't skate on the morning of Game 50, so I slept late. I decided not to take my pregame nap because Los Angeles was playing at Boston that afternoon, the game was on television, and Simmer had 46 goals in 49 games.

I thought there was no way he could score four goals, but I had to watch anyway. What a fool I'd feel like if I failed to get 50 in 50 and Simmer did.

I was a nervous wreck. I wasn't rooting against him, but I wasn't rooting for him. I didn't feel that threatened until he scored Number 47 ... and then Number 48 ... and then Number 49 in the final seconds. His empty-netter gave the Kings a 6–4 lead, but the Bruins didn't put their goalie back in the net for the final face-off. That's when I stopped breathing and my heart started racing.

He didn't score. That left it for me.

For two periods that night against the Nordiques, I was awful. Terrible. I couldn't do a thing. I felt like I had a ball and chain hanging from each skate and cement blocks in my gloves. I felt worthless. We were tied 3–3 going into the third period, no thanks to me.

Nobody had a chance to offer me any encouragement during the second 15-minute intermission because as soon as I got into the room, I dropped my stick and ran to the bathroom. I spent the break hiding in a toilet stall, smoking like a chimney. I was panicking. The pressure had gotten to me and for the first time, I felt I wasn't going to do it. That's when I started crying. I started thinking about what I was going to say at my press conference when I had to explain why I didn't get it.

Al was panicking for me, too, because he gave me an incredible amount of ice time. A forward skates about 15 shifts of 60–90 seconds each in an average game, but I took 21 shifts that game, one of which was clocked at 3 minutes, 13 seconds.

Every time I got on the ice, every time I touched the puck in the third period, the crowd screamed. BOSS-SEE! BOSS-SEE! Adrenaline raced through my veins, but oh, was I tired. I skated the entire third period in a desperate state that I can compare only to the final ten minutes of Game 6 against the Rangers in the 1979 playoffs.

The Nordiques, coached by Michel Bergeron, didn't shadow me even though they had a left wing named Alain Cote who checked me throughout my junior career. Quebec tried to win the game. But with 6:04 left, Michel Goulet took a penalty and Al put me out for the power play. The penalty was almost over when Trots fed Persson at the left point. Stef saw me heading for the net, so he shot it in front. A defenseman stopped the shot, but the rebound came to me and I stuffed a backhand between goalie Ron Grahame's pads.

Bossy 49 (Persson, Trottier) 15:50.

The Coliseum went nuts. Our bench went nuts. For an instant, I felt relieved that I had tied Simmer. Then I started trembling again. With a 5–4 lead, I knew that in three minutes Bergeron would pull Grahame for a sixth attacker. First I worried about how scoring my 50th into an empty net would look. Then I flashed back to Detroit, when I twice missed the empty net.

I was a basket case.

"C'mon, Boss," my teammates screamed over the roar of the crowd. "We know you'll get it." Trots didn't say a word. He didn't have to.

With around 1:40 left in the game and 15,008 people deliriously waiting for Quebec to pull Grahame, Trots and I jumped on the ice. Clarkie was waiting for Tonelli to come off so he could complete the line change, but the puck was dumped into their left corner and J.T. went deep to forecheck. I went down the left side while J.T. forced them to the right.

A Nordique tried to dump the puck out of the zone, but J.T. grazed the puck. He slowed it down enough for Trots (third guy high) to stop it before it crossed the blue line in front of Quebec's bench. When I saw Trots control it, I skated from the left wing boards toward the middle. Trots spotted me.

He whipped a perfect pass to me near the inner rim of the left circle, but when the puck hit my blade it bounced a few inches off the ice. Instead of waiting until it settled flat, I whacked at it just before it hit the ice. Defenseman Dave Pichette lunged with his stick in an attempt to block my shot, but it whizzed past his blade and toward the net, a few inches off the ice.

Grahame wasn't screened, but he didn't have his stick on the ice. My shot whipped under his stick, between his skates, and...IN!!

Bossy 50 (Trottier, Tonelli) 18:31.
BEDLAM.
I threw my arms in the air. J.T. fetched the historic puck. My teammates violated an NHL rule by tumbling off the bench to smother me. Chico came racing out of the goal to join the jubilant pile. Sirens rang, fans screamed, I jumped up and down like a lunatic. I emerged from the pile and started jumping up and down again, throwing my fists into the air. I looked like a jerk, but I didn't care.

Fifty in 50.

Nineteen seconds later, Trots and I skated down two-on-one. Without considering 51 in 50, I passed him the puck for the goal that sealed our 7–4 win. It was the least I could do. After the game, I raced into the room yelling to myself "I did it! I did it! I did it!" I shouted out: "Thanks guys" a couple of times. Trots whispered, "Calm down, calm down."

I was greeted in the dressing room by a telegram from Richard, who congratulated me for tying his record. The Islanders had offered to fly Rocket in for the game, but he politely declined due to a prior commitment. I read the telegram to the press and then joked, "I know what he's going to say when I see him. He'll claim he still holds the record because I scored my 50th in the last minute and he scored his with two minutes to go."

OK, OK, my math was off. I scored mine with 1:29 left. I knew one thing. I wanted no part of Espo's record then. When a reporter asked me if that was my next quest, I told him I wouldn't even think about it. "If I get close, you can ask me then," I said.

My nerves deserved a rest.

Fifty in 50 drained me and the team, because after we beat Quebec for our sixth straight win we went 2–6–2 in our next ten games and I scored only five goals.

I scored 18 goals in the final 30 games, although I missed one game with the flu. I never got close enough to Espo to make a legitimate run. I had 67 goals with seven games to play, but scored only once in those seven games.

Bill geared for the playoffs with two significant personnel moves. In late February, he recalled center Billy Carroll and right wing Hector Marini from our new Central Hockey League farm team in Indianapolis, Indiana. And on March 10, the one-year anniversary of the Goring trade, he dealt Chico and Tambellini to Colorado for

McEwen, who played for the Rangers in 1979, and minor-league goalie Jari Kaarela. McEwen was the offensive defenseman and power-play specialist we needed. But it saddened me to have to say good-bye to Chico.

Chico was a classic, a wonderfully funny man who has had more to say than any other human being in the history of the world. You didn't say good morning to Chico if you had an appointment in an hour, because you were afraid of being late. Chico's ten-minute chats lasted two hours.

He got his nickname because he looked like Freddy Prinze's character in the TV show *Chico and the Man*. Chico always made me feel good because of the way he used magic to describe my goal-scoring skills.

Chico showed up last for buses, planes, practices, everything. He would get to practice, sit in the parking lot reading the newspaper, bolt into the room ten minutes before we were due on the ice and jump into his goalie equipment in five minutes. Chico was the reason Al made a rule that we report to the dressing room 30 minutes before practice.

If he wasn't reading, Chico was talking. To teammates, fans, strangers. We'd be sitting in the airport and there he'd be, off to the side discussing something with somebody he had never before met. I was in Atlanta once for some NHL-affiliated event and the promoter told me Chico had been there and said hello.

"Does he always talk that much?" the guy wanted to know.

Chico has one of the largest hockey memorabilia collections in North America. He always asked Pick to save pucks for him. I scored a goal one time and I spotted the referee scooping up the puck and handing it to Pick, who tucked it away. I had no idea why.

"It's for Chico," Pick said.

I knew we'd miss him, but we could afford to trade him. Although it never mattered to me who was in goal, Smitty had proven to the organization that he deserved to be Number 1 come playoff time. And rookie Rollie Melanson was a capable backup.

We said good-bye to Chico and finished first overall in the NHL with a 48–18–14 record. I finished fourth in the scoring race (behind Dionne, Gretzky and Calgary's Kent Nilsson) with 119 points. I tied Esposito's NHL record with 28 power-play goals, became the first player in NHL history to score 50 or more goals in his first four seasons, notched an NHL-record nine hat tricks and was named the first-team all-star right wing.

We opened the defense of our Stanley Cup against Toronto. The Leafs, who had traded Tiger Williams in 1980, weren't the same team that upset us in the '78 playoffs. Neither were we. We blew them out three straight, 9–2, 5–1, 6–1. I scored four goals and had six assists.

Our quarterfinal opponent was the Edmonton Oilers. This young, talented team had opened our eyes by upsetting Montreal three straight in the first round. They didn't open our eyes too much, though, because we routed them 8–2 in Game 1.

I had heard about Gretzky. The first time I saw him was in 1979–80. He was a skinny 19-year-old who made the bigger guys look foolish. He was obviously talented. He tied Dionne for the scoring championship in his first NHL season.

We knew about Gretzky, but we didn't know much about Glenn Anderson, Jari Kurri, Mark Messier, Paul Coffey and Kevin Lowe. Anderson and Messier were skilled players, but they showed no respect for me whatsoever in that series. If those guys could have injured me on a particular play, without a doubt they would have.

Those guys were too young and undisciplined. At one point in Game 2, which we won 6–3 at the Coliseum, a few of our guys heard them singing on their bench: "Here we go, Oilers, here we go. Here we go Oilers, here we go." That got Bournie mad.

They beat us 5–2 in Game 3 at Edmonton, but Mr. OT, Morrow, scored in sudden death to win Game 4, 5–4. They came to the Coliseum and beat us 4–3 in Game 5, but we took the series in Edmonton, 5–2, in Game 6. Although we beat the Oilers soundly, we felt challenged in that series. With the young talent they had, I knew that we would have to reckon with them down the road. But not this year.

After Edmonton came the Rangers, who eliminated Los Angeles and St. Louis in the first two rounds. The Rangers had finished fourth in the Patrick Division, 36 points behind us. We had nothing to fear, but something to avenge. I hadn't forgotten 1979, and I still haven't, not even after winning four Cups. Visits to the Garden conjured memories of my poorest performance ever. I was uptight.

But in the easiest series we ever played against the Rangers, we bombed them four straight: 5–2, 7–3, 5–1, 5–2. I led the team with five goals.

We were roaring. We were 11–2 in the playoffs going into the finals against Minnesota, the dark horse that finished ninth overall with 87 points and reached the finals by eliminating Boston, Buffalo and Calgary.

The question wasn't "Could we win our second straight Cup?" It was "How many games would it take?"

It took five. We won three straight, lost Game 4 at the Met Center and returned home to treat Long Island to a second victory dance with a 5–1 win.

Throughout the playoffs, I thought about winning the Conn Smythe Trophy as playoff MVP. I had 13 goals and 27 points going into the finals and I scored four more goals and four more assists in the five games against the North Stars. If I wasn't the Most Valuable Player of the playoffs, who was?

Sure Smitty had been playing well, Trots had been playing well, Denny had been playing well. But not only had my 17 goals and 35 points led all playoff scorers, it was an NHL record for points in a Stanley Cup tournament, easily breaking Trots' 1979 mark of 29.

The writers voted for Goring.

The Conn Smythe is supposed to go to the MVP of the entire playoffs, but the writers often select the guy who had the best final. Mine was great. Butchie's was, too. He scored five goals and seven points, including a hat trick in Game 3. I felt I deserved the award and I was shocked when I didn't get it. Shocked, angry and hurt.

The announcement, which came while we skated around the ice with the Cup, initially dampened my pleasure. Eventually, though, I shrugged it off.

And then Dad died, two days after Game 5. We had just finished the parade and were on the ice taking pictures with the Cup just like the year before when Potsy told me there was a message from my Uncle George.

"He probably wants a hockey stick," I said.

"No," Potsy said. "You'd better go and call him right away."

There was a telephone in the Bad News Room, so I jumped in there not knowing what my uncle wanted. The team must have known, because Bill, Al, Trots and Clarkie were there when I called my uncle and got the news. Dad, who was in great health, had suffered a heart attack.

Mom, Dad and my youngest brother, Gordie, had been living in the house they were building in St. Lazarre. They had been there for about a year and the house was almost finished. Dad woke up that morning feeling like he had indigestion, so he and Gordie drove to the hospital.

Dad, who was driving because Gordie was 16 and a year too young for his license, went into cardiac arrest behind the wheel. Gordie ran to the nearest house for help, but it was too late.

Mom, who suffered from high blood pressure, went into shock and, for a while, we were pretty worried about her, too. Lucie, Josiane and I drove home immediately. His death and the fact that at the funeral I saw my nine brothers and sisters together for the first time in years, struck a nerve. It made me feel the importance of family like I never had before.

Dad and I rarely had deep discussions, but he was always with me. He never visited Long Island to see me play because after his stint as a navigator in World War II he wouldn't fly. I understood. Dad lived to see me realize our dream. He wanted me to become a National Leaguer as much as I did, more than I did when I was young. Once I turned pro, became an all-star and won a Cup, his dream was complete. He didn't need to fly to Long Island to watch me play. Turning on the TV, picking up the newspaper or watching me play in the Forum was enough.

All I thought about that summer was how much I'd miss Borden Bossy. Two straight Cups didn't mean as much. Neither did 50 goals in 50 games, not winning the Conn Smythe, and picking up the new Mercedes that was waiting for me in Laval.

That was a bittersweet Cup.

Chapter

11

MVP

My family had to go on. Although Mom was going to be alone in the house that Dad built, she never considered selling it. Dad plowed too much of his life into that land for us to sell it on account of his death. Mom slowly came to terms with Dad's passing. And so did I.

I had to get back in touch with reality: the 1981 Canada Cup and new contract talks. For the third time in five years, Bill and Pierre prepared to negotiate. Both sides wanted this contract to be my last. I was excited because I was on the verge of major money. The dollar signs that I had envisioned through junior were finally coming into focus.

Pierre and Bill sat down in Montreal at the amateur draft in June. "You know us by now," Pierre said. "Put something in writing, make an offer and we'll start from there."

We received Bill's offer in early July. It was $2.5 million for six years, only $500,000 more than the package he proposed two years ago.

Pierre and Denis prepared a negotiations strategy schedule. We decided to sit on Bill's offer until early August. August 10 was the latest Bill could make an offer and September 10 was the day we had to sign papers if I intended to play out my option. We wanted to press the deadline and see how the new NHL-NHLPA collective bargaining agreement would treat free agency.

We acknowledged receipt of Bill's first offer and although I thought it was incredibly low, I asked Pierre for his opinion. He sat me down and gave me a quick lesson on the NHL's financial structure.

"Look at what's happened over the last three years," Pierre began. "From what we've heard, Guy Lafleur, the league's top player, was making $150,000. Then the Rangers signed the two Swedes from Winnipeg of the WHA, Ulf Nilsson and Anders Hedberg, and we were told they were each making $300,000 per year.

"And now this year, Marcel Dionne signed a multi-year contract with the L.A. Kings worth around $600,000 per year. If, in the last 36 months, salaries of all-star players had doubled every year for the last three years, where do the increases end?"

I smiled. That was the way I wanted Pierre to look at it.

"If you sign a long-term contract," Pierre warned me, "you're going to sign a long-term contract and you're not going to call me back in two years and say you've been screwed."

Pierre was saying that he wasn't going to allow me to renegotiate. Whatever I signed, I was going to stick with. That's why we wanted to make sure that the long-term deal we were going to propose was going to protect me five years down the road if salaries continued to escalate.

"We're going to act inflexible," Pierre said. "Our demand will be very high. You have to expect that you might play your option year at $250,000 even though you're still scoring 50 or 60 goals and winning Stanley Cups. If the Islanders balk, you're going to feel underpaid. You're not going to like $250,000 while the Swedes with the Rangers, who are doing much less than you, are making over $300,000 and Dionne's getting $600,000. Think about that."

I wasn't thinking that seriously of free agency. I was extremely happy playing for the Islanders, living on Long Island, playing with Trots and winning Stanley Cups. Deep down my insecurity made me feel hesitant about playing out my option. Would I be able to handle the pressure? Would I be as good in my option year as I was the year before?

Then why gamble? Pierre and I believed that I deserved the money we decided to request: $5 million for six years, and not one penny less. That was more money than anybody, even Gretzky, was making.

I knew Bill was going to think we were crazy. Frankly, when I first heard it out loud I thought it was a little crazy, too. I feared that a demand like that would force Bill to break off negotiations, and then I'd have no choice but to play out my option.

"Relax," Pierre said.

Team Canada opened its Canada Cup training camp at Montreal in early August. Our first head-to-head session with Bill was a few days later at the Château Champlain following a morning practice. Pierre started the meeting by presenting the $5 million request.

"Bill, here's the story," Pierre recited. "Thirty-six months ago Guy Lafleur was making $150,000. He went on strike to get more dollars when the Swedish guys signed with New York in 1978, and he got $300,000. And Marcel Dionne just signed, we were told, for $600,000."

"That's just speculation," Bill replied. "You didn't see the numbers."

"I have my information," Pierre said. "What we want to do is create a situation where Mike will retire after this contract. But we don't want an unhappy player and you don't want an unhappy player. The situation is obvious. Salaries have doubled every year for the past three years."

"But $5 million U.S., Pierre? Are you serious."

"Yep. And there will be no negotiation. How you pay it to Mike we don't care. You want a balloon payment, deferred payments, structure it any way you want. We want $5 million for six years, $5 million by July 1, 1987. Take the month of August to decide how to do it. We've got time. We'll be around."

"We're not even close."

"I know. But then there'll be no contract. Mike will play out his option. He's willing."

Bill turned to me. "Mike, do you think you should play out your option for $250,000 instead of the offer I made you?"

"Yeah, Bill. I'm willing to play out my option, I'm sorry. I'm very happy with you, but like Pierre says, I don't want to feel embarrassed a year from now and reopen the contract. I want to finish my career with the Islanders. Pierre gave you our proposal and I want you to understand there will be no renegotiation if we sign the long-term contract. The way the business has gone over the last three years, I have to agree with Pierre. I'm going to play out my option and see what the market is for me."

Although we didn't seriously consider testing the free-agent waters, Pierre had talked informally with other teams. He couldn't officially fish around because I was under contract and nobody wanted to risk tampering charges. We didn't have to. I had scored 53, 69, 51 and 68 goals in my first four seasons. Of course there would be interest at any price.

As Pierre kept drilling into my head: "How many players have your bargaining leverage? How many have played four years, averaged 60 goals a year and won two consecutive Stanley Cups?"

The Canada Cup opened in September. The option deadline was approaching. On the seventh or eighth, Bill called Pierre and said, "We have to sit down before the tenth. Can we do it tomorrow?" We agreed. We met informally, Bill, Pierre and I, at the Forum after practice.

"I can't reach your figure at all," Bill said. "It makes no sense to sit down."

"That's OK," Pierre said. "We'll play out the option, that's all. No bad feelings, don't worry."

We had to file a letter with the NHL's Central Registry by September 10 stating that I had received an offer from the Islanders by August 10, but had elected to play out my option. Pierre sent a copy to NHL executive vice president Brian O'Neill and he sent a copy to Bill.

Maybe that's when Bill realized we were serious.

Six years, $5 million.

I was comfortable with our decision. I trusted Pierre's judgment enough to believe that if I played the 1981–82 season for $250,000, far less than I deserved, I would make the money back down the road. I began concentrating on the Canada Cup.

Bill called Pierre when he got our letter. He wanted to meet again. On September 10, three days before the Canada Cup final against the Soviets, Pierre asked me if I minded sitting down with Bill after practice. He was afraid another round of negotiations would distract me, but I said it wouldn't be a problem.

That afternoon we met in Bill's suite at the Château Champlain. He said, "I don't know where to start. We can't reach $5 million. You've got to help us out."

"We won't move at all," Pierre said.

We went back and forth a few times, getting nowhere, until Bill said, "Let me make a call."

He went into another room and called Bill Skehan, the team's alternate governor. They must have been on the phone for an hour while we waited. When Bill came back into the room, he made his first significant counter-offer.

"We can't afford to pay $5 million on a six-year deal, but give us another 12 months," he said. "We need an extra year to pay the

$5 million. We can pay it out over the seven years, $400,000, $500,000 per year. But we need to have over $1 million payable at the end, seven years from now."

Bill explained that Skehan was working with the Islanders' financial people, trying to project the team's cash flow and costs. They felt the only way they could consider a contract that size was if they were able to defer more than $1 million, without interest but guaranteed, until the end of the contract.

We called time, left the room and caught our breath.

Pierre asked me how firm my plan was to retire at 30. The extra year meant I'd be playing 11 years, until I was 31. I wanted one day to think about it.

"Bill, Mike wants to think it over," Pierre reported. "He strongly believes he wants to retire at 30. In his mind he's confused about whether he'll be in position to play until he's 31. He's trying to imagine how he'll feel in five years. Give him a day...or two."

"OK," Bill replied. "I'll wait for your call."

I did want to retire at 30 after ten NHL seasons, but $5 million was too great a financial package to turn my back on. Bill was being reasonable. I was willing to bend.

"I'll play the extra year. Let's sit down with Bill as soon as we can," I told Pierre.

When Bill asked us to add another year to the life of the contract, he never said "We agree to this." Instead he said, "I presume we could agree to this." I guess he needed to think about the ramifications of such a monstrous financial package, too. So, when Pierre told Bill we were willing, Bill wanted until the following morning to agree to terms.

We scheduled a meeting for September 13 at the Château Champlain, the morning of the Canada Cup final, and Pierre went to work. He prepared a confirmation letter with blank spots for salaries, bonuses and the deferred payment. We agreed to the $5 million over seven years, bonuses of $25,000 each year the Islanders finished first overall in the NHL and $25,000 each year the Islanders won the Stanley Cup. I didn't mind that I no longer had any 50-goal bonuses. For the money the Islanders were paying me, they deserved 50 goals each year.

Everybody's hands were sweating the day Bill and Pierre inked all those zeros onto the worksheet. I was shaking. I think Bill was, too. We signed the agreement, shook hands, and locked the door behind us. I still have the key to that hotel room.

That contract, which officially expired on June 30, 1988, ended up being worth $5.075 million, because I collected $25,000 bonuses for our first overall finish in 1981–82 and our Stanley Cups in '82 and '83. I felt bad about being unable to play that seventh season, but when you stop to consider that it was because of my bad back, I was paid $5.075 million for playing six seasons until I was 30.

The contract talks never interfered with my first Canada Cup training camp. Trots, Clarkie, Denny, Smitty, Butchie and I all were selected to play for Team Canada. Lucie and I invited Trots and Nickie to move into our house in Laval during the tournament. Trots and I had a ball.

The team jogged through the streets of Montreal as part of off-ice training. Al McNeil, one of the team's assistant coaches, happened to be jogging alongside Trots and me, tiring as we passed our first half-mile. The more we jogged, the more tired he got, and the more Trots and I peppered him with questions. They were inane questions designed only to make him gasp even more. He was too winded to pick up on our troublemaking.

Lucie got me in trouble with coach Scotty Bowman one morning by cooking a delicious veal parmigiana dinner the night before. In those days, I never had a problem maintaining my weight; I usually weighed in at 185 or 186. Trots in fact, considered me a sickly looking, skinny kid. So I didn't think twice about stuffing my face with two helpings of veal and rice and salad.

Team Canada kept us on a rigid conditioning program. We weighed in when camp began, had our body fat measured, and were instructed to weigh in before every practice. I was on the ice waiting for practice to begin the morning after Lucie's delicious dinner when Bowman called us over and started lecturing us about ideal weight and body fat. You could tell he was building to something.

"I don't want to get on everybody's backs," Bowman bellowed, "but I can't believe that someone could gain five pounds from one day to the next. Mike Bossy, what the hell's with you?"

I couldn't believe it. There was Pittsburgh defenseman Randy Carlyle, who had to be 20 pounds overweight with a ridiculously high body-fat count, on the ice; and Denny, who always was considered chunky. And Bowman's yelling at *me* about *my* weight? Trots cracked up. A lot of guys did, guys who were happy Bowman wasn't talking to them.

I promised that I'd get the weight off. The veal was out of my system by that afternoon, if you know what I mean. I never explained to Scotty why I had gone from 186 to 191 in 24 hours, but I was back down to 185 in two days.

A few days later, while we were stretching on the ice, Trots and I were giggling again. Assistant coach Red Berenson, then coach of the St. Louis Blues, skated over.

"Aren't you guys ever serious?" he said angrily.

We found out later that Berenson called Al later that day. Berenson thought we weren't taking the tournament seriously enough and wanted to know from Al if we were always like that. Al told Red not to worry.

Trots and I were giddy, but Smitty was grumbling. He, Don Edwards, Mario Lessard and Mike Liut were the four goalies in camp. Although Smitty accepted the invitation on behalf of his country, he really didn't want to be here. He was having a new house built on Long Island and he wanted no part of hockey in August, especially since we were hardly getting paid anything. Smitty is the most generous guy I know when it comes to buying you a drink, but when he's asked to stop pucks, he expects to be paid well for it. He does nothing for nothing.

We were practicing in Winnipeg before a pre-tournament exhibition game one day when I wound up for a half-slap, half-snap shot from just inside the blue line (Smitty insists it was a full slap shot from between the circles. Trots says it was a three-quarters slap shot from between the blue line and the circles). The puck flipped on end when I shot, but instead of trying to glove it, Smitty stuck his blocker hand in front of it. The puck smashed one of his fingers against his goalie stick, cracking a bone.

Smitty growled at me, then headed to the hospital for X-rays. When he came back, he was smiling. The finger was slightly fractured. He couldn't play. He was free to go home.

Bowman played Clarkie, Trots and I together, but we combined for only one goal in our first big win of the tournament, a 7-3 rout of the Soviets at the Forum. That win assured us of a spot in the semifinals. We beat the U.S. and the Soviets beat the Czechs to set up our one-game final on September 13.

We got whomped, 8-1, in front of 17,003 angry Forum patrons. I know Clarkie scored from Trots and I to tie it 1-1 in the second period and I know Liut gave up five third-period goals on eight shots. The rest of the game is a blur.

Losing to the Russians mattered, but it didn't have a backbreaking effect on me. I was too elated by my contract, too excited about trying to win a third straight Stanley Cup. With eight goals and 11 points, I finished second to Gretzky in scoring and was named Team Canada's MVP.

Trots, Clarkie and I were given a week off before reporting to the Islanders' training camp. When I arrived, I was a little on edge because of my new contract. I wanted to prove I was worth the money they'd be paying me, so I put a little more pressure on myself. I didn't set my sights on anything like 50 in 50, but I wanted to end a four-year pattern that had seen me have a good year (53 goals), an excellent year (69), a good one (51) and an excellent one (68).

We were extremely confident without being arrogant as we prepared to defend our back-to-back titles. We were cocky in a very quiet way. Behind the dressing room doors we bragged, but we were extremely careful of how we carried ourselves in public, especially on the ice. We were respected as champions because we never flaunted our success. And we relished the respect.

Bill kept strengthening the team. The lone rookie on our season-opening roster was Tomas Jonsson, a fleet skating Swedish defenseman with good moves. On January 7, Bill promoted center Brent Sutter, our first-round draft pick in 1980, from the Western League. And a week before the season began, he traded defenseman Bob Lorimer and center Dave Cameron to the Colorado Rockies for the Rockies' first pick in the 1983 draft.

Jonsson and Sutter made Lorimer and Cameron expendable. But who knew then that Bill had pulled off one of the all-time steals, that Colorado's draft pick would be used to select Pat LaFontaine?

I scored a career-high 147 points this season and finished second in scoring, 65 points behind Gretzky's 212. I had a shot at the scoring title ... at least through Opening Day. I had ten goals after nine games, but 50 in 50 became moot. Gretzky scored 50 goals in his first 39 games.

I always felt in competition with the guy who was leading. I wanted to be the leading goal-scorer and point-scorer. By this time I realized, though, that it was going to be extremely difficult for me to win the scoring championship, because we played four lines and because I was very rarely double-shifted. I had come to understand and accept it. Deep down I wanted to win a scoring championship, but there was no way I was going to say or do anything to disrupt the balance that we had on a team that had won two Stanley Cups in a row. Trots used to double-shift at times. I was never jealous of the fact that he double-shifted, but at times I got mad that I wasn't the one double-shifting.

My 83 assists broke Lafleur's record for most assists by a right wing, an NHL record that still stands. My 64 goals gave me 50 or more for the fifth straight season and my third 60-plus year. I was the first-team all-star right wing for the second straight season, and I actually outpolled Gretzky. I received 309 points out of a possible 315 at right wing; he received 305 at center.

What an awesome season we had: first overall with a 54–16–10 record. Second overall behind Edmonton with 385 goals for, second overall behind Montreal with 250 goals against, first overall with a 28.2 percent power play, fourth overall with an 80.4 penalty-killing unit. We used only 20 skaters and two goalies all season, except for one-game cameo appearances by rookies Greg Gilbert, Paul Boutilier and Neil Hawryliw.

And we broke a 52-year-old NHL record by winning 15 straight games. From January 21 to February 20, we did not lose: 6–1, 6–1, 9–2, 6–3, 4–2, 7–6, 5–2, 6–2, 7–3, 8–2, 8–2, 9–1, 6–2. Those were the first 13.

The All-Star break wedged between our ninth and tenth wins and divided the streak. After I was selected to the Wales Conference team for the game at Capital Centre, Lucie promised she'd learn to drive if I won the car as MVP. I have to admit it was a great motivator. I was a little tired of driving her to the grocery store, to the doctor, to everywhere.

Starting with the Volkswagen Rabbit Smitty won in the 1977–78 game, the Islanders on the All-Star team had a standing agreement that if one guy won the car, all would share. Smitty kept the car that year and gave us each a nice cash prize.

You should have seen the joy on Trots' and J.T.'s faces when it was announced that I won a $16,000 Pontiac Firebird for scoring two goals to break a 2–2 tie and leading the Wales over the Campbells, 4–2. They wanted the money. I was ecstatic, too. I wanted to see Lucie get her license. That was no $16,000 car, though. Not when I sold it. After taxes and immediate depreciation for resale, each of us ended up with $1,500. It was worth it, though. Lucie learned to drive.

When the team bussed to Philly a week later for the game that would tie the 1929–30 Boston Bruins' 14-game winning streak, we were nervous. This was as important to us as a playoff game. We fell behind, 4–2, in the second period, but I scored at 17:09 and Brent scored at 18:31 to make it 4–4 after two. I set up J.T. for the tiebreaking goal at 7:08 of the third, and Ny and J.T. added empty-netters in the final minute.

"We were just scared to lose," I told the press. "But we channeled that fear toward going at them. Sure we were tense. But we were tense in the right way. We never panicked."

We went for the record-setting 15th at home two nights later, against Colorado and Chico. He was unbelievable in goal. He tested us and tested us, stopping great scoring chance after great scoring chance. But with the score tied 2–2 and one minute left Al sent J.T., Trots and I over the boards. Trots and J.T. skated in two-on-two and criss-crossed over the blue line. At the top of the left circle, Trots left the puck for J.T., who snapped a hard, low shot between Chico's legs.

We erupted. The guys spilled off the bench and mobbed J.T., Trots and I, who were already celebrating. After the game, a few of us wondered if Al would have risked the tie (there was no five-minute overtime in the regular season in those years) by pulling Smitty for a sixth attacker. Moments before J.T. scored, in fact, Smitty had looked over to the bench for instructions.

"No way," Al insisted.

"We'll never know, will we?" Bill teased.

We lost our next game, 4–3, in Pittsburgh the next night. Obviously we had let down. None of us expected to play the rest of the year without losing, but we almost did. We went 15–0–0; lost 4–3 at Pittsburgh; went 7–0–2; lost 3–0 in L.A.; went 7–0–2 again; and then lost the season finale at Pittsburgh, 7–2.

Game 79, a 6–3 win over the Flyers at home, was a thrill because Trots scored the only 50th goal of his career. What a struggle that was. Trots had scored his 49th in Game 70, then couldn't score for ten games. At first we weren't worried, but with five, four, three games to go, J.T. and I got desperate. We kept trying to feed and feed Trots, who kept missing great chances. It got nervewracking.

Finally, with five periods left in the season, Trots scored on Peeters. We were on a second-period power play when I passed to McEwen at the point. Peeters stopped Q-Ball's low slapper, but Trots swatted at the rebound and it trickled between Peeters' legs.

Trottier 50 (McEwen, Bossy) 0:36.

I was so happy that I got an assist. After all the key goals he had assisted me on, I badly wanted to be a part of his big goal.

Game 80, our 7–2 loss to the Penguins should have been a playoff tuneup, a light skate for both teams. But that's the game I sprained the ligaments in my left knee. I was skating toward the crease from the side of the net when Pat Price hit me just as I caught my skate in a rut.

That was on Sunday. On Monday morning, two days before our best-of-five series with the Penguins began, Dr. Minkoff examined me in his Manhattan office and sent me to have a derotation brace fitted at Lenox Hill Hospital. At first, we thought the ligaments were only sprained. But they were partially torn.

My knee was too swollen for me to skate Monday or Tuesday, but I tried skating with the brace on Wednesday morning. When the medical staff told me I couldn't do any more damage to the ligaments, I told Al I wanted to play. He agreed. I guess he thought having me on the bench for power plays was better than not having me at all.

Games 1 and 2 at the Coliseum were almost identical for me. I scored the first goal of each game on a power play, barely played again, and left the game before it ended. In Game 1, an 8–1 rout, I undressed after we took a 6–1 lead out of the second period. In Game 2, which we won 7–2, I got out of my uniform after we took a 4–0 lead after the first.

Pittsburgh owner Ed DeBartolo added some flavor to what looked like a three-and-out disaster for the Penguins by declining to attend Games 3 and 4 in Pittsburgh and offering a refund to any fan who was as embarrassed by his team's performance in the first two games as he was. That must have fired up the Penguins, because they beat us in Game 3, 2–1, on Rick Kehoe's overtime goal and whipped us in Game 4, 5–2. I played very little in the third game. My knee started to feel better in Game 4, when I took a semiregular shift.

Still, I was worried. My knee wasn't 100 percent and I wasn't skating like I knew I could. I was hardly helping the team. By blowing a two-game lead, we faced elimination for the first time since the Rangers beat us in 1979. We were tense. We blamed this predicament on ourselves. There was no way a team that had a 31–36–13 record during the season should have been in a position to steal a series.

But in Game 5, there we were, down 3–1 going into the third period. The Coliseum was stunned. So were we. Although very little was said, I sensed panic in the dressing room before the third period. "What are we going to say after the game if we lose?" I asked myself. "What's the reason for us losing?"

It was 3–1 with 18 minutes left...with 15 minutes left...with 10. I couldn't help but peek at the clock time and again. We were desperate and afraid. But we refused to lose. With 5:30 left, I took a shot on a power play that Clarkie deflected into goalie Michel Dion. Q-Ball swooped in for the rebound and lifted it into the net with 5:27 left to make it 3–2.

With 2:21 left, Gord Lane dumped the puck into the corner to Dion's left. The puck skipped over Randy Carlyle's stick and landed on J.T.'s. His quick shot surprised Dion. It was 3–3.

In the dressing room before overtime I knew that we had nothing to gain, but everything to lose. We were supposed to win this series easily. We had to win it. And then I remembered: overtime is our time. Always was, always will be.

The Penguins had the first great chance just 90 seconds into sudden death. I was one of the frantic backcheckers when Kehoe and Mike Bullard skated in two-on-one. Kehoe's cross-ice pass was perfect. My heart stopped as I saw Bullard with the puck and half the net open. He shot. Smitty sprawled across the crease and made a fabulous save.

And then came J.T. He had tied and won our 15th straight victory. He had tied this game. And he kept our drive alive by poking a loose puck behind Dion at 6:19 of overtime.

He was the man of the moment.

Johnny and I played together a lot, but we were never close. He was a very intense player, one of the most intense I've ever seen. He worked his ass off in practice like he did in games. He was the Islanders' first and only holdout. Prior to the 1985–86 season, when he was going into his option year and negotiating a new contract, he refused to report to training camp because he was insulted that Bill had offered him a two-way contract.

Although I live by the principle that if I sign a contract, I honor the contract, I didn't care that J.T. held out. He took a stand for something he believed in and I respected that. As long as he wasn't hurting the team, which he wasn't because it was the exhibition season, what he did was fine with me. If he would have come back out of shape and I had to play with him that would have been another thing. But I knew he was working out by himself and he always was in great shape.

He reported the week before the season began and he eventually signed a contract worth about $400,000 a year for four years (*with* the two-way minor-league clause that got him so upset in the first place). It was a heck of a lot, but I was happy as hell that he got it.

Johnny was a dedicated team man, although he got a little distracted in 1983–84 when he began building a house in Brookville; he was the contractor and he supervised the entire construction. He came to practice at the last minute almost every day in muddy work clothes and then left as soon as he could, wearing a suit, trying not to be late for a business meeting. We hardly saw him until Christmas, but that didn't bother any of us. It didn't bother me because I was usually in and out of the dressing room in a hurry, too. But Al hated it.

Everybody loved J.T. after the Pittsburgh series. It was a relief to still be playing for the Stanley Cup. After the Penguins came the Rangers and another three visits to the zoo.

I always felt discouraged playing at Madison Square Garden. The atmosphere in that building took away the good feeling I had about being a human being. Although the abusive fans were a minority, they were such a vocal minority that the whole place felt like a jungle. I don't think I looked up into the seats once after my first year. Making eye contact with any of the crazies who liked to lean over the glass during warmup and scream the most vile things gave them the impression that you were acknowledging them. And that was their signal to act worse.

One incident stands out, though. It happened a few years ago, and I'm sure if the guy reads this he'll know who he is. He used to hang out near the penalty boxes during warmup screaming profanity after profanity at me. I recognized his voice every time. I don't know what prompted me to do this, but one time, as I skated by, I mimicked him. He had gotten to me. I stooped to his level.

The guy went crazy. Absolutely nuts. He did everything but jump on the ice. He screamed; he banged on the glass with his fists. I laughed and laughed, which only got him angrier. And I skated away.

The media and the Garden fans made the rivalry between our teams more emotional than it actually was. When you play 80 games a season and then play the playoffs, a game is a game is a game. I will admit, though, that since the '79 series I got more psyched up for the Rangers because I felt I had something to prove. The 1979 semis no longer haunted me, but it stayed etched in the back of my mind.

We lost Game 1 at home, but we won the series easily, four games to two, sweeping the three games at the Garden. Clinching the series there and extending the Rangers' Stanley Cup drought to 42 years in front of their lovely fans was sweet.

We swept Quebec in the semis. I expected a tough series, but it was surprisingly easy: 4–1, 5–2, 5–4 (on Wayne Merrick's overtime goal), 4–2. I scored four goals in the four games. My knee was starting to feel better. A third straight Cup seemed inevitable.

While we waited for Chicago and Vancouver to complete their Campbell Conference championship, I thought about how easy this final should be. The Blackhawks were 15th overall with a 30–38–12 record. The Canucks were 11th overall with a 30–33–17 record.

The Canucks won in five. "Uh, oh," I warned myself. "Here we go again."

Tiger Williams was now a Canuck. I knew Tiger would be trying to kill me again and I was right. Tiger was Tiger. He taunted me, threw elbows at me, hooked, cross-checked, punched me. This time I was not afraid. I was determined to make him look foolish by ignoring him and scoring goals. I kept thinking about that first Toronto series in '78, when Tiger said that Trots and Gillies could take the abuse, but the rest of us couldn't. Although he never named me, I knew he was talking about me. I wanted to shut him up.

I also wanted the Conn Smythe.

My assault for the playoff MVP began in Game 1, when I scored my second Stanley Cup hat trick. My second goal tied the game, 5–5, with 4:46. J.T. raced after a loose puck that was sliding toward goalie Richard Brodeur. The puck came loose. There was a Canuck player chasing the rebound (I don't know who it was, but it wasn't Tiger), so I knocked him down, got to the puck, and flipped it behind Brodeur.

I wonder if Tiger was proud of me.

If he was pissed at me for tying it, he probably wanted to slit my throat for winning it. With five seconds left in the first overtime, defenseman Harold Snepsts tried to pass the puck up the middle from the left of his net. Why he didn't just freeze the puck in the corner I'll never know.

At the time I didn't care. I intercepted his pass in the right circle and from between the circles snapped the winner over Brodeur's shoulder.

Overtime was our time, remember?

I scored once in Game 2 and we won, 6–4. Tiger was yapping, only nobody was listening.

We won Game 3 in Vancouver, 3–0, and I scored the goal that's my second-favorite, after my 50th in 50. It was my most spectacular goal. I have it on tape and I watch it from time to time. I have no idea how I scored.

We were leading 1–0 in the second period when I took two shots from the slot that Brodeur stopped. Save-rebound-save. My momentum from the follow-through of my second shot carried me to the inner rim of the left circle, where I was dumped by defenseman Lars Lindgren just as Brodeur kicked my second shot back to me. I was parallel to the ice, in the air about to land on my stomach and face from the force of Lindgren's hit, when the puck reached me.

Instinctively, I cradled it with my blade and managed to flick a backhander toward the net. Defenseman Colin Campbell slid behind Brodeur to block it, but the puck flipped Brodeur, past Campbell, off the post and into the net.

I was amazed. I still am. I'm so proud of that goal. Henry Saraceno used to say that in pee-wee and junior I had scored goals standing on my head, and this one came close. The only part of me touching the ice when I shot was the blade of my stick.

Going into Game 4, I knew we were going to sweep them. Tiger was frustrated by the fact that he wasn't frustrating me. Their whole team knew they couldn't play with us. We knew we were too strong to be beaten. We completed the sweep, 3–1. I scored two power-play goals to break a 1–1 tie. The goals were my 16th and 17th of the playoffs, my sixth and seventh of the finals, which matched a record for goals in a Stanley Cup final that Montreal's Jean Beliveau had set in 1956.

With 1:37 left and the outcome obvious, Tiger hit me with a sucker-punch, a swat with his stick in his clenched glove. "I wanted to cut his head off the first shift on the ice," Tiger had told one reporter. The Canucks pulled Brodeur a few seconds later and I thought I'd have a shot at breaking Beliveau's record, but Al took me off the ice. There was no need for me to mess with Tiger any longer.

The third Cup was ours. Once we escaped Pittsburgh, it was the easiest Cup of the three. We dominated. As we celebrated on the ice at Pacific Coliseum, I heard the announcement; I had won the Conn Smythe. MVP of the Canada Cup, MVP of the All-Star Game and now MVP of the playoffs. I was thrilled.

In the champagne-filled locker room, the media began uttering the magic word — dynasty. Were we a dynasty? Did we have to match the four straight won by the 1976–79 Montreal Canadiens? Could we win as many as five, as the 1955–60 Canadiens did?

I never liked the word dynasty. We were three-time champions of the NHL. We eased through the Rangers, Quebec and Vancouver. There seemed no stopping us. But in the back of my mind, I knew that our reign was about to be challenged.

I knew we were going to see Edmonton soon.

Chapter

12

The Drive for Five

I found out what it was like taking care of a newborn baby when Tanya was born on July 12, 1982. I wasn't at training camp like I was nearly three years earlier, when Josiane was born. Tanya taught me how to get up at all hours of the night, how to sleep with one ear open, how to feed, diaper and dress an infant. I didn't mind at all. Lucie delivered both Josiane and Tanya by Caesarean section. Although we considered building a larger family (Lucie wanted a third child more than I did), we stopped after two.

When I did get to training camp that summer Tanya was born, I suffered from epidytomitis, just before the season opener. That's the clinical way of saying I got whacked between my legs. A few of us were scrambling for the puck along the boards during a scrimmage when somebody's stick inadvertently struck me in the groin. I was wearing my protective cup, but it didn't matter. My testicle swelled to the point where I could barely sit down without intense pain. The guys thought my "groin injury" (that's how we described it to the press) was hilarious.

It wasn't. It hurt like hell.

"Ah, you'd do anything to get out of practice," Trots said.

I was well enough to start the season, which was the strangest of our reign as champions. It was a six-month roller coaster ride. We started

11–2–0, then went 8–14–7. Not long after Bill embarrassed Trots and I in front of the team after practice one day in early January, we sizzled through a 10–1–2 stretch. Then we went 3–5–3, before finishing this dizzying season 10–4–0.

"Is this what every year is like?" asked Paul Boutilier, one of three rookies on the team.

Thankfully, no. It's just that after enjoying so much success, it was difficult to get excited about the 80-game season. Subconsciously, we often waited until we were in trouble, in particular games and in stretches of the season, before we flicked the switch and started pounding our opponents. It got to the point where we felt we could turn it on at any time and win any game in the third period. For two years, we had. But in this, our fourth year on top, it began getting harder.

We were getting older.

Boutilier, who joined us in January, and left wings Greg Gilbert and Mats Hallin were the only additions since our third straight Cup. Smitty, who was one of the few guys to publicly admit he was having trouble caring about the regular season, had the veterans howling one day during the winter when he approached the rookies with an offer.

This happened not too long after Smitty moved into his new house in Huntington that has this long and winding driveway. Long Island was hit by a snowstorm the night before, so most of us were still wiping slush from our shoes when Smitty shouted, "You should see all the snow I have in my driveway. Do any of you rookies want to shovel my driveway and get in my good eye?"

Smitty had such a mean streak that we tried never to laugh at him, but this time we roared. The man had a knack of saying the funniest things while trying to be serious, which he was trying to be with the rookies. He meant to say "my good graces," of course, but neither Hallin, Gibby nor Boots chose to get into Smitty's "good eye."

Trots and I climbed into Bill's bad eye one day in early January after a 4–6–2 stretch in December. Bill walked into the room after practice one day at Cantiague and, in front of everybody, chewed Trots and I out for being the last guys on the ice for practice and the first guys off.

I was a little embarrassed, but how could I be mad at Bill? It was true.

I got off to an excellent start that season with 20 goals in 26 games, but I didn't score a goal in seven games from November 30 through December 14, the longest drought of my NHL career. I wasn't worried, but I was frustrated and disappointed because I was one of the reasons we weren't dominating the league like we did the two years before. The writers apparently thought I wasn't having a great year, because they elected Quebec's Marian Stastny to the Wales Conference first-team All-Star team for the All-Star Game at Washington. Stastny won the vote, 126–114, and I was annoyed because I had 29 goals to his 27 and 62 points to his 61. I thought I deserved a little more respect from the media, the same media that voted Lafleur to the first-team postseason all-star team in 1978–79 even though I had scored 17 more goals. I accepted losing to Lafleur because he was a veteran and I was a second-year pro. This time Stastny was the sophomore and I was the veteran.

I took my anger out on the L.A. Kings. A few hours after the vote was announced, I scored my second hat trick of the season.

The media was very critical of me all season and their comments fired up my pride. Perhaps it was the kick in the butt I needed, because I scored 27 goals in my last 25 games to finish with 60. We won 10 of last 14 games to finish 42–26–12, second in the division behind Philly and sixth overall.

I finished fourth in the scoring race with 118 points after my third straight 60-goal season and sixth straight 50. I was named to the first-team All-Star team for the third straight season and I won the first of my three Lady Byng Trophies as the league's most gentlemanly player. I was happy to get the Lady Byng, but I didn't understand what I did this particular year that I hadn't done in years past. I guess it was just my turn.

Our third Stanley Cup defense began with a message from Bill taped to the dressing room wall, above where we kept our sticks. It was an old black-and-white photograph of Montreal coach Toe Blake celebrating his team's fourth straight Stanley Cup in 1959. Blake's left hand was caressing the Cup. His right hand was thrust in the air, four fingers waving.

Underneath the picture, Bill scribbled, "History is yours for the making.... Let's put "Radar" in the same picture — Good Luck." "Radar" was Al, who got the nickname because he wore big, black horn-rimmed glasses his entire career.

Very few people expected us to win a fourth straight Cup. Smitty had won only 18 games during the regular season. Clarkie, Butchie, Bournie and Ny, the veterans, all had had subpar seasons and Clarkie was out for at least the first two rounds with a sprained knee. I knew it wasn't going to be easy, but I couldn't understand why we were being written off so early.

After beating Washington, 5-2, in Game 1 of our best-of-five first round series, I quickly learned I wasn't the only one who felt his pride was being tested.

"This is the playoffs," said Ny, when asked by one reporter why the team played with so much more enthusiasm than it had during the season. "This is different."

"Maybe this proves we didn't have our foot in our mouths all season," Butchie told the press. "Maybe it shows we were right when we said when it came to the playoffs we'd be ready."

Butchie was right. We eliminated the Capitals rather easily, three games to one. In the Patrick Division finals we bounced the Rangers (who had shocked the Flyers three straight in the opening round), four games to two. I scored my only three goals of the first round in Game 4, my third playoff hat trick, and added three goals against the Rangers.

Bournie, the most critical Islander when it came to the behavior of the fans at the Garden, had a tremendous series playing with the Sutter Brothers. Duane's and Brent's energy seemed to inject Bournie with young blood and he scored two goals and 12 points in the six games. He also scored the prettiest goal of the series, an end-to-end rush in which he split the defense and sealed our 7-2 win at the Coliseum in Game 5.

I had a lot of close moments with Bournie in my career, more than with any teammate besides Trots. Bournie and I were able to communicate on a personal level. We discussed family and life, matters that had nothing to with hockey. The media loved Bournie because he was friendly, interesting, quotable and honest. I found him to be the same way. He said he admired me because I looked like I knew exactly what I wanted and where I was going all the time, but that air of confidence annoyed him at times, too.

"You always think your way is right," he'd yell.

Usually, I did. But in the first two rounds, I wasn't happy with the way I played. I felt out of synch. Was it my own ineffectiveness, or the fact that I played without Trots, who had sprained his knee in Game 1 against the Rangers and missed Games 2 through 4? I'm not sure. But Trots and I scored a goal each in Game 5 and I had eight shots in Game 6. Eddie Mio stopped me eight times, but Butchie won it for us with two goals and an assist.

We weren't supposed to beat Boston in the semifinals. The Bruins won the regular-season championship with 110 points. They allowed

228 goals, only two more than we did in helping Smitty and Melanson win the Jennings Trophy for fewest goals against. They had Peeters, the Vezina Trophy winner as the NHL's most valuable goalie, who had given up only three goals against us in three games during the regular season.

I bombed Peeters single-handedly. I tied a record for most goals in one playoff series with nine. I scored all four of our game-winners. I had a hat trick in Game 4 and four goals in our series-clinching Game 6.

My slump was over. We blasted the Bruins in six.

A French-Canadian left winger from Chicoutimi, Quebec, named Luc Dufour covered me that series. He shadowed me in Game 5 after my first hat trick. He wasn't dirty, but he wasn't subtle either. In the first period he could have been called for interference every time he was on the ice. There were no Tiger Williams tactics, just clean interference, if you call interference clean.

When it was obvious that we were going to win that final game, I heard a Boston fan in the Coliseum screaming that we didn't deserve to be here because of our lousy regular season. We had finished sixth overall with 96 points, but everyone thought we were lousy. Well, we wanted to make up for it.

We wanted that fourth Cup. We wanted to win it by beating Edmonton, already regarded as the NHL's next great team. We were the three-time Stanley Cup champions, they were the team with Gretzky. We were old and confident, they were young and cocky.

It was the series North America wanted.

Game 1 at Northlands Coliseum was one of the greatest hockey games I've ever seen. The goaltending by Smitty and Andy Moog was unbelievable. The skating was smooth, the hitting ferocious, the tempo wildly fast. I had a great view of all 60 minutes, from my hotel bed, because I came down with tonsillitis the day before our thrilling 2–0 win.

I felt fine the morning of our charter flight. We practiced at Cantiague before we bussed to the airport, but I didn't start feeling dizzy and nauseous until we were in the air. When my throat started to ache I knew exactly what was wrong because I contracted tonsillitis about once a year. Trots and I checked into our hotel room and I collapsed immediately, totally sapped of strength. The Islanders took no chances. They moved Trots into another room.

I slept through dinner, through the night, and through the morning skate before Dr. Minkoff examined me again. My head hurt, my glands were enormous, every part of my body ached. But when it was time to leave for the rink, I boarded the bus. I knew I wasn't well enough to play, but I wanted so badly to be a part of this series that I hoped and prayed that Al would let me dress. No chance. Al took one look at me when I hopped out of the bus, had Dr. Minkoff examine me again, and sent me back to the hotel in a cab.

The Islanders hid my illness from the media and the Oilers until just before gametime, when the lineups were announced. Everyone figured my absence would deflate us and give Edmonton a lift, but it worked the other way around. Duane scored in the first period, Smitty nursed the 1–0 lead throughout the second and third, and Morrow scored into an empty net in the final seconds.

After the game and at practice the next day, my condition was a big part of the series' story. "Apparently it's a very severe case," said my self-appointed hospital spokesman, Dr. Bourne, who, last I looked, was a few credits short of his medical degree. "But Mike is an incredible person. He might make it."

I have no idea why I never had a tonsillectomy. Dr. Minkoff told me when he examined me that if my problems persisted, he'd remove them after the series. I haven't had a problem since. (Remember the bone spur that hasn't bothered me in ten years? I guess I'm so afraid of surgery that I will myself to heal.) I spent the day between games in bed and started to feel better late that afternoon. Even if I didn't, I told myself there was no way I was going to miss Game 2.

In Game 1, Smitty slashed Glenn Anderson in the knee as Anderson tried to circle in front from behind the net with the puck. It was a slash, but not one of Smitty's blatant chops. Before Game 2, Edmonton coach Glen Sather made the mistake of trying to paint Smitty as the villain. Public Enemy Number One, one Edmonton paper called him. But Smitty loved playing the villain.

"Smith clubbed him with his stick viciously," Sather said. "It was a deliberate attempt to injure.

Anderson didn't practice the day before Game 2, but he played, a fact Smitty found amusing. "Wasn't Anderson hurting?" Smitty asked after the game. "I thought his funeral was today."

We won again, 6–3. I scored a goal, but Smitty the swashbuckler was the story again. This time he got Gretzky with a slash when Gretzky tried to skate in front from behind the net. Smitty tapped Gretz in the left leg with the blade of his stick, but from the way Gretz collapsed you'd have thought Smitty used an axe. It was some dive. Gretzky got up, skated right to Smitty with the blade of his stick pointed at Smitty, and started screaming. I wasn't on the ice, so I didn't hear what he said.

Smitty coolly lifted his goal stick to eye level, a few feet from Gretz's face. Referee Wally Harris handed Smitty a five-minute slashing major, but Dave Lumley evened that up in the final minute by spearing Smitty in the throat. The Stanley Cup finals between the National Hockey League's two proudest teams had become a gang war.

Smitty was all the gang we needed.

"I hit him in the pants," he told a horde of media that relished this confrontation. "You see guys slashed in the arm and they don't go down like that."

Said Gretzky, with a sarcastic smirk, when the reporters asked for his version: "I had the puck at the left side of the net and cut around to the other side and was coming out when Smith accidentally slashed me. What I say now means nothing, so I'd rather let it die and say it was an accident."

Smitty was not to be stopped. When he wasn't stopping shots and hacking Oilers near his crease, he was yelling at them, taunting them. Smitty was as intimidating a goalie as any I saw, until Philly's Ron Hextall. The more the Oilers screamed, the better Smitty played and the more frustrated they got. Games 3 and 4 at the Coliseum belonged to Smitty, too.

We won Game 3 with four goals in the third period, 5–1, and we won Game 4 with three goals in the first period, 4–2. I scored the third goal, the game winner, my second straight Cup winner. The Cup-winning goal this year was deceptive. Once we handed Smitty the 3–0 lead, there was no way he was going to lose it.

Four straight. We weren't too old.

To Sather's and Anderson's and Lumley's frustration, Smitty was the overwhelming choice for the Conn Smythe, our fourth different playoff MVP in four straight Cups. It was our finest moment. Not only weren't we supposed to sweep Edmonton, we weren't supposed to beat them. They scored 424 goals in 80 regular-season games, but Smitty and our defense held them to six, none by Gretzky.

And leave it to Smitty to throw a parting shot.

It was during the nationally televised Conn Smythe presentation. President John Ziegler made some kind remarks, handed the trophy to Smitty, and cringed when Smitty decided to discuss his play of the game. It happened at 8:26 of the third period, with Edmonton on a power play and the score 3–2. Anderson skated in front of the net and grazed Smitty's facemask with his stick. Smitty, doing his best Gretzky imitation, toppled to the ice. Referee Andy van Hellemond slapped Anderson with a five-minute high-sticking major.

On national TV, with the Conn Smythe Trophy beside him, Smitty admitted he faked being hurt.

"I did the same thing to Anderson as Gretzky did to me," he said as Ziegler turned a shade of red. "I threw myself on my back on the ice and squirmed around. I want the world and all of Canada to know that two can play at that game."

That was the talk of the team in the days following our fourth Cup and fourth parade in four years. Smitty was, well, being Smitty. And he thought his speech was the greatest.

The nonsense aside, this was a terrific Stanley Cup final, the most satisfying moment of my career. Although we swept them, every game in this series was fabulous hockey. Up-and-down, run-and-gun, hard hitting, great goaltending. We were the veteran champions who knew what it took to win. They were still young and needed to mature. I didn't know it at the time, but this series was to Edmonton what the Ranger series in 1979 was to us.

It was my sweetest Cup of all.

That summer I accepted an invitation with Bill, Al, Trots, Denny, Smitty and J.T. to meet President Ronald Reagan at a White House reception in the Rose Garden. I had been to the White House once before, during the 1982 All-Star Game at Washington, and I ate lunch at the same table as Vice President George Bush. I was happy for the chance to return, because I didn't get a picture with the President the first time. Some were taken, but the photographer told me none came out.

Our Stanley Cup visit was a thrill, but the ceremony was so fast it was comical. President Reagan shook our hands as cameras popped, Smitty presented him with a stick (without slashing him), Reagan said a few words, we posed for more photos. It couldn't have been more than a minute before ABC-TV White House correspondent Sam Donaldson interrupted our moment by asking Reagan a question about MX missiles. And then a dozen other reporters shouted political questions.

End of ceremony. End of interview. We were ushered out of the Rose Garden and back to the airport. And a few weeks later I was told for the second time that the White House didn't have a picture of Reagan and me. Check out the cover of the Islanders' 1983–84 media guide. There's Reagan shaking hands with Denny. There's J.T., Trots, Smitty...and the Stanley Cup.

I was there, honest. I met the President twice, even if I can't prove it. The summer of 1983 was otherwise uneventful. I sold my Mercedes because I had driven it only 6,000 miles in more than two years, I played a lot of golf, I basked in the glory of four straight Stanley Cups, and I contemplated our Drive for Five.

Everybody began making the comparisons between us and the only team to win five straight Cups, the 1956–60 Montreal Canadiens: I was Rocket Richard, Trots was Jean Beliveau, Denny was Doug Harvey, Smitty was Jacques Plante. It was fun to hear hockey's experts, GMs like Emile Francis and Scotty Bowman who had been around forever, discussing who was better, who would win a best-of-seven, who would finish first in a regular season.

It didn't matter to me. I had four Cup rings.

Although I won my second straight Lady Byng (eight penalty minutes) and was a first-team all-star again, the 1983–84 season was physically and statistically a disappointment. I scored only 51 goals, my lowest total since 1979–80. I missed six games in October with a pulled right thigh muscle and six in February with a sprained right knee. I never grew weary of scoring goals, but my body at age 27 wasn't responding like it did at age 22.

In early November, *Newsday* columnist Steve Jacobson asked me after my thigh injury if the regular season seemed too long. "I don't mind it," I said. "Except there are times I get up in the morning and have trouble putting my socks on, my back hurts so much."

Little did I know what a hurt back really felt like.

On December 1 at Calgary, during one of those long western road trips I disliked, Paul Baxter high-sticked me in the face. He cut open my nose for three stitches, and as I sat there in a pool of my blood, I heard bells ringing in my head for the first time in my life. I actually heard church bells.

We were 26–12–2 halfway through the season, first in the division and second overall, but we were unhappy because after an 8–0–1 run, we were 2–2 in our last four games. This is how demanding we had become:

Trots: "There's been a lack of concentration lately."

Smitty: "We haven't been sharp in our own end and it's costing us."

Bournie:"I look at some of the games we've blown and it makes me wonder."

Me: "There's a lot of pressure on all of us now. We react quicker because of it. We know if we go through more bad periods, some of us will be threatened with trades."

I had 30 goals in 40 games, 38 in 52 when Detroit's Dwight Foster and I collided, leaving me with a Grade 1 sprain of the medial collateral ligament in my right knee. I couldn't have gotten hurt at a more opportune time. The All-Star Game was coming up and although it was the Jersey Meadowlands, I needed and wanted a break.

But because I was worried about returning to the lineup in time to have a reasonable shot at 50, I didn't get my break. I spent all my free time rehabilitating my knee so I wouldn't miss too many games. I got back into the lineup with 22 games to go, needing 12 for my seventh straight 50.

I almost didn't get it. I scored seven goals in my first 12 games back, but then failed to score in four straight games. Trots and I, who played most of the season with Gilbert, were playing terribly.

With six games left in the regular season, Bill called me into Al's office at Cantiague for a 40-minute chat. He knew I was discouraged. I had no zip, no confidence. I had no shots on goal in Game 72 and two feeble shots in Game 73. Trots and I didn't have to talk about it. We knew how to count. Bill suggested I not shoulder so much responsibility to score. When he said that, I started to accept the possibility of not getting 50.

And so I got 50.

I scored my 46th and 47th at Boston in Game 75, my 48th at home against Minnesota in Game 76, my 49th against Montreal in Game 78 and my 50th and 51st in Game 79, the 3–1 win over Washington that clinched our fifth Patrick Division title in seven years. Seven 50-goal seasons broke a tie with Lafleur and Dionne and gave me the NHL record. Seven straight 50s was the record I liked even better.

Our 50–26–4 record was forged by a 5–0–2 finish due in part to the arrival of our two Olympic Pats, Flatley and LaFontaine. Patrick Flatley was our first-round pick in the 1982 draft, a physical right wing from the Canadian Olympic Team. Pat LaFontaine was a roadrunner center, a stickhandling speed demon with a great touch.

We needed them to make a difference in our Drive for Five because, for the first time in our championship reign, we were hurting. We hurt mentally and physically all playoff long:

Before our first-round series with the Rangers, Langevin's father died. Bammer went home to Minnesota for the funeral, but returned in time for Game 1.

Bobby Ny missed Games 1 and 2 with a sprained wrist.

Kenny Morrow missed Game 2 with a stomach virus.

In the second round against Washington, Bournie separated his shoulder in Game 1 and didn't return until Game 5.

J.T. separated his shoulder in Game 2 and didn't return until the semis.

Brent missed Game 2 with a bruised knee.

Bammer separated his shoulder in Game 2 and didn't return until the finals.

Denny missed Game 5 to return to Ottawa for the funeral of his father.

In the semifinals against Montreal, LaFontaine missed the first five games with a sprained ankle.

Ny bruised a knee in Game 5 and missed Game 6 and the first three games of the finals.

Persson separated a shoulder in Game 2 and was out until Game 2 of the finals.

Bournie injured a knee in Game 2 and missed the remainder of the playoffs.

It was incredible. No wonder we had so much trouble getting to the finals.

Our best-of-five series with the Rangers was the fifth Battle for New York in six years. Although we had won the last three, I couldn't forget 1979, the last series we lost before our Cup run. That series still worried me. If the Rangers were able to upset us once, they were able to do it again. I suspected that the Rangers drew from 1979 just as we drew from 1980, 1981, 1982 and 1983.

We won Game 1 on April 4, but by April 7 we were facing Stanley Cup elimination. It was incredibly quick. We lost Game 2, 3-0, at home and Game 3, 7-2, at the Garden. Four days into the playoffs and our Drive for Five was stuck in neutral. I was stuck in park, with only one assist in the first three games.

We went into Game 4 at the Garden facing elimination for the first time since 1982, when we were tied 2-2 with the Penguins in the first round. But this was different. That game against Pittsburgh was sudden death for both teams. This time, we had to beat the Rangers in a game they didn't have to win.

We fell behind 1-0 after two. "Oh, no," I whispered to myself before the third period. "Not again."

No, not again. We silenced the Garden in the third. J.T. tied it at 0:49 and Brent broke the 1-1 tie ten minutes later after Flats separated Barry Beck's shoulder with a titanic hit in the corner. Smitty made the key saves and Clarkie and Trots iced it in the final minutes. That 4-1 win was fantastic, but New York, New York, hadn't seen anything yet.

I don't remember that much about Game 5, but so many New Yorkers over the years have told me that it was one of the greatest games they ever saw, that I recently made a point of watching it on tape. Everybody was right. It was a classic.

I do remember the dressing room before Game 5, because it was no different than normal. I wasn't one of our rah-rah guys. Whenever I said something before a game, I tried to make it mean something. I didn't like talking for the sake of talking. Duane was our yapper. Half of what he said before a game or between periods was worthwhile and the other half was gibberish. It was noise, but that's how he got himself psyched.

We had different idiosyncrasies. Trots and I chatted normally. J.T. sat silently in his stall with a towel over his head for 10 or 15 minutes. Smitty, who didn't like to be talked to before a game, never said a word. Ny was either working on his sticks or his skates, always keeping busy in the back room to burn off nervous energy.

We were nervous for Game 5. We fell behind 1-0 on a Ron Greschner goal, but I tied it 1-1 with 11 seconds left in the first period when I stole the puck from Tom Laidlaw and slipped a short shot between Glen Hanlon's pads.

Neither team scored in the second period. Tomas Jonsson gave us a 2-1 lead with 12:04 left in the third, but Don Maloney tied it with 39 seconds left in regulation and Hanlon off for an extra attacker. Maloney batted a shoulder-high rebound behind Smitty, a goal that Smitty argued should not have counted. The replay was inconclusive, which proved that referee Dave Newell made the right call by allowing the goal.

Overtime was phenomenal. Smitty made seven saves, I hit a goalpost and Morrow (who else?) won it with a slapper from the top of the right circle at 8:56.

Whew!!

We always teased Kenny about his overtime touch. "C'mon, Wolfie, end it quickly," somebody shouted before every overtime period the last few years. His overtime goals amazed me because he's not a typical goal scorer. Flukes happen, but three overtime goals in one career is no fluke. I'm proud to be tied with him in Stanley Cup history.

Despite losing Bourne, Tonelli and Langevin, we knocked off Washington four games to one in the second round. Flats scored five goals in the five games. I had three and three assists. That brought us to Montreal, which finished fourth in the Adams Division with a 35–40–5 during the regular season, but upset Boston and Quebec to reach the semifinals. It was fate that decided we couldn't win five straight Cups without eliminating the Canadiens, who were determined to protect the honor of their 1956–60 brethren.

Although we finished the regular season with 104 points to their 75, the series started in the Forum because for the first time, the Board of Governors predetermined home-ice advantage and gave it to the Adams Division winner. We lost Games 1 and 2. We were intimidated by the crowd, by the building and by the Canadiens' tradition. We were hurt and against the ropes, but I didn't feel like we were in danger. I wasn't frustrated either, although I had only scored one goal (into an empty net against Washington) in the last five games.

For Game 3, Al sensed that Trots and I were getting stale so he split us up and we won, 5–2. I scored a goal playing with Gibby and Brent, and Trots had an assist playing with Clarkie and Flats. In Game 4, Smitty preserved a 1–1 tie by stopping Mats Naslund on a penalty shot and I scored at 16:40 of the second. We won, 3–1.

Al put Trots and I back together for Game 5 at the Forum. Trots scored on a power play four minutes into the game and we won again, 3–1.

And we won our 19th consecutive playoff series two nights later in Game 6 at the Coliseum, 4–1. I notched my third game-winning goal of the series when I scored the first of my two goals early in the first period to give us a 2–0 lead.

Four straight wins after two losses. Bring on Edmonton. I was psyched up. So were our fans, who chanted "We Want Gretzky" when I scored late in the game to put Montreal away for good.

The Oilers wanted to stop our Drive for Five in the worst way. Before the series I said, "What worries me is that we haven't lost to the Oilers. They tell me it's been ten straight. They've only beaten us three times since they came into the NHL. I don't like that. They're too good a team for that to continue."

Unfortunately, I was right.

Game 1 of the 1984 finals was the one-year anniversary of Game 1 of the 1983 finals, when I was in bed with tonsillitis and Smitty blanked the Oilers in Edmonton. The only difference between the two games was that goalie Grant Fuhr did to us at the Coliseum what Smitty did to the Oilers 12 months earlier. Kevin McClelland scored in the third period and we lost, 1–0.

We were tired and banged up, but I was worried for only one reason. This was the year we got screwed because the NHL changed the finals schedule. In past years, home ice was divided 2–2–1–1–1. This year, the Board of Governors changed it to 2–3–2 to save the finalists money by knocking out two extra flights. Although I knew the Wales Conference winner got the extra home game, I didn't like that we had to play the middle three games in Edmonton. After falling behind one game to none, I liked it even less.

We evened the series in Game 2. Clarkie, who scored only 12 goals in the regular season but scored 12 more in a great postseason performance, got a hat trick and we blew them out, 6–1. We held Gretzky without a point for the second straight game; we held the potent Oiler offense to two goals in two games; and we gave up only one goal for the fifth straight game.

We were going back to Edmonton for Games 3, 4 and 5. I was confident that if we won one, we'd finish them off at home.

But we never got them back home. Game 3 was the first sign of the changing of the guard. Our time had come and gone. Edmonton's was beginning.

It actually began in the second period. We were winning 2–1 until they scored three goals in 11 minutes of the second: the first on a great solo dash by Messier and the last two 17 seconds apart in the final 48 seconds of the period, by Anderson and Coffey.

When Messier and McClelland scored 20 seconds apart early in the third period, I sensed that we were done. We were worn out, tired, hurt and discouraged. They were gaining confidence with every shift. The more I tried, the less I did.

They clobbered us again in Game 4, 7–2, with Moog in goal. Fuhr was injured in Game 3 when LaFontaine, going in to forecheck, was rammed by Pat Hughes into Fuhr and the three of them slammed into the boards behind the net. This game was especially discouraging because Gretzky made it 1–0 just 1:53 into the game, his first playoff goal against us in two years. That's all we needed, a fired-up Edmonton team and Gretzky about to break out.

Game 5: Gretzky at 12:08 of the first; Gretzky at 17:26 of the first. It was 4–0 after two. LaFontaine scored at 0:13 and 0:45 of the third period, but we could do nothing. I could do nothing. I had a cold and a sinus infection and I finished the series without a goal.

We failed. I failed. And it hurt.

When I lined up for the ceremonial post-series handshakes, I looked into the eyes of every Oiler and recognized the joy. I've never forgotten what it was like to win for the first time. They looked like we did in 1980. They didn't steal anything from us, they beat us fair and square.

The word *dynasty* never meant anything to me, so on the flight home I didn't consider this the end of our dynasty. I still don't. We had a great hockey team that had a great run. I knew it wouldn't last forever. We all did.

Who was better, the Islanders from 1980–84 (four straight Cups, one loss in the finals) or the Oilers from 1984–88 (two Cups, one loss in the quarterfinals, two more Cups)? Hmm, let's see . . . .

Goal, Smitty vs. Fuhr: If I had to play a whole season and the playoffs, I'd take Fuhr. If I had to play just the playoffs, I'd take Smitty.

Center, Trots vs. Gretzky: Trots. He was in total command of the game. Defensively, Gretz doesn't match up to Trots anywhere inside the blue line. Gretzky knows that. I hope he knows that, anyway.

Right Wing, Bossy vs. Kurri: I'm a little prejudiced, I admit, but I always felt I could do more than Kurri could. I'd give him the nod defensively because he, throughout his career, has had to play more defense because of Gretz. I think his concentration level on defense was higher than mine was. As far as his shot, he's slightly more accurate than I was. I was a better puckhandler and playmaker than he was, though.

Left Wing, Tonelli vs. Anderson (who also played right wing with Messier): Even. They're very similar, except that J.T. was the most tireless worker along the boards that I've ever seen. Anderson was a much better skater than J.T. As playmakers, they're even. J.T.'s shot was more dangerous because he could take the goalie's head off. Goalies were intimidated by J.T.'s shot because nobody, not even J.T., ever knew where it was going.

Defense, Denny vs. Coffey: Defensively, Denny was much better than Coffey. Skating, Coffey had it hands down over Denny. If I'm trying to win a Cup and I've taken Smitty, Trots and me, I'd have to take Denny as a stabilizing force behind the blue line. Passing, they were equal. Denny had a better shot. Puck handling, Coffey was better.

Second center, Goring or Brent Sutter vs. Messier: Messier, easily. It makes more sense to compare Messier to Trots, because Messier now is almost as good as Trots was when Trots was at his best. Messier is a quicker skater than Trots was, although Trots will deny it. They're both bulls. Trots was a much better puckhandler and playmaker. And Messier wasn't much meaner. Trots was mean, boy. Trots never meant to be dirty, but at times he was. He was so strong that he did things he didn't mean to do. He'd push guys into the boards and he'd push them too hard. He'd lean on someone and end up creaming the guy. Trots wasn't a stickman, though. Messier early in his career was dangerous with the stick. I could personally vouch for that.

Defense corp, Morrow–Persson–Langevin vs. Huddy–Lowe–Gregg: They're so similar. The only guy who stands out as being superior in a particular category is Langevin, who could put a guy out of the game with a bodycheck at any time. Morrow is similar to Gregg and Persson and Huddy are alike. Defensively, Lowe was better with the puck than Langevin.

Since we weren't at our peaks at the same time, I don't think our four-game sweep in '83 or their five-game triumph in '84 was a true test of who was better. It's too bad. The 1980–84 Islanders vs. the 1984–88 Oilers would have been the NHL's best show. It would have gone seven games, two or three of which would have probably gone into overtime. Smitty and Fuhr would have played dueling acrobats.

Who would win? I'll take us in seven.

Chapter 13

One Awful Canada Cup

I quit smoking on July 29, 1984, several days before I reported to Team Canada's training camp in Montreal for my second Canada Cup. I wanted to stop smoking. I didn't want to start playing hockey. I was mentally and physically drained from losing to the Oilers in the finals and from playing into May for five consecutive years. Counting the regular season and playoffs, I played 91 games in 1980, 97 in 1981, 99 in 1982, 98 in 1983 and 88 in 1984.

But I felt obligated to accept Team Canada's invitation. The Canada Cup, which became Alan Eagleson's favorite toy when the international tournament was introduced in 1976, had become a show of patriotism. Players who declined invitations were labeled selfish and ungrateful because the tournament was officially a players' association event. I didn't want to subject myself to that nationwide criticism.

Although I scored the winning overtime goal in one of the greatest international games every played, our 3–2 triumph over the Russians in the sudden-death semifinals, I made a mistake by going. I bickered with GM-coach Glen Sather, I got hurt, I bickered with Trots, I called the Canada Cup an Eagleson ego trip, and I pissed off a few of the Oilers with my comments to the press.

Although I had a good time with Michel Goulet and Ray Bourque, let's just say I didn't enjoy that Canada Cup.

Why did I want to quit smoking? I'd been thinking about it for a while. I was 27 years old, I hadn't had a good Stanley Cup playoff and it was getting tougher and tougher for me to stay in shape during the off-season. I started smoking when I was 18 with my teammate in junior, Jeff Meier. Laval had a rule against smoking, but away from the rink it was easy to avoid getting caught. We used to hide in the back of the bus during road trips and blow the smoke out the windows so our coaches wouldn't smell the tobacco.

Lucie, Carol and Bob were smokers, so I guess I picked it up from them. I'm not sure why I started. I don't know if the Islanders knew I was a smoker when they drafted me. They never asked. I don't remember the first time I smoked in front of Al, but when I did I bet he had a cigarette in his mouth, too, because Al was a very heavy smoker. Denny, Clarkie, Ny and I were the Islanders' smokers. The Isles had a rule against smoking in the dressing room, so before, after and between periods of games the four of us hung out in the back changing area or the toilet stalls, puffing away. I was smoking half-a-pack a day when I turned pro and at my heaviest, in the late '70s, I was up to a pack a day.

Smoking never affected me when I played, but I did try to stop twice before. I got hypnotized on Long Island before our fourth Cup, walked out of the place, and didn't feel like smoking anymore. The only problem was, I told myself that I was stopping for hockey and I promised myself I wouldn't smoke until after the season. During the wild celebration in our dressing room after we beat the Oilers for our fourth straight, I pulled somebody aside, asked for a cigarette, and lit up.

I stopped again the following winter, in Calgary. Trots was out with his relatives and I was in our hotel room. I laid on my bed and tried to hypnotize myself. I woke up the next morning and didn't feel like smoking. My next cigarette was in Edmonton, after we lost Game 5 of the finals.

This time I was serious about quitting for good. Bob gave me the incentive because he quit three or four days earlier. July 29 was a Sunday. Carol, Bob, Lucie and I were having dinner at my mother-in-law's home, as we did almost every summer Sunday. All day long Bob moaned for a cigarette. I tried to help.

"If you don't have a cigarette the rest of the night, Bob, I'll quit smoking with you," I said in a show of support.

I got home a few minutes before midnight and called Bob. He swore that he hadn't had a cigarette since we left Lucie's mother's house. So I officially quit. Two days later, Bob confessed that he had been sneaking cigarettes all week. But I held firm. I haven't had a cigarette since. Not even a puff. I can't say I'll never have another cigarette because never is a long time, but I don't intend to smoke again.

Quitting smoking was only one of my conscious attempts to prepare for the Canada Cup team I didn't want to join. For one of the first times in my life, I tried getting into shape before training camp by jogging through the streets of Laval. The day before training camp opened, however, my left foot swelled and my right knee ached. I reported for physicals at McGill University hardly able to walk. The doctors told this novice jogger that I had worn improper running shoes. That's what caused the inflammation in my foot and aggravated my knee, the one with the floating kneecap that I've had since I was 12.

That was the least of my problems.

I had heard through the grapevine that Trots, a North American Indian, had accepted an invitation to play for Team U.S.A. North American Indians hold special cards that allow them unlimited access between Canada and the U.S., dual residency, and allow them to work and pay taxes in both countries without special permission. All Trots needed to qualify for Team U.S.A. was a U.S. passport, which his Indian card allowed him to get within a matter of weeks.

To me, this was a dumb old hockey tournament, so I pouted when Trots made his decision official. I was angry that my only source of motivation was gone. I expected to spend two or three weeks with him, have him move in with Lucie and I, and make the best of what I considered a bad situation.

Selfishly, I questioned Trots' decision when I came to camp without him. I questioned it publicly. I told the press that I didn't think he was wrong, but I didn't understand why he did what he did. Trots and I hadn't spoken, so I didn't know that he had made a conscious decision to embrace the United States, where his wife and two children were born and where he plans to spend the rest of his life. Trots became a U.S. citizen because the United States was where he worked, lived and built a family. Playing for Team U.S.A. was his way of giving something back to his adopted country.

I realize now it was wrong of me to question what was a major decision in Trots' life. I knew Trots well enough to know that he didn't do things without a great deal of thought. I should have respected his decision from the start, even if I didn't know why he did what he did.

The reporters made the situation ugly. They painted a feud between friends. I answered difficult questions frankly, but only the negative half of my answers were written. The articles that appeared across Canada made me seem angrier and more critical of Trots than I was.

Coincidentally, Trots and I got a chance to talk about it on a plane from New York to Halifax, Nova Scotia, during the tournament's exhibition games. I was in New York to have Dr. Minkoff examine my knee. Trots was in New York because his daughter Lindsy had gotten hurt. I told him that the reports had been blown out of proportion, that I recognized there was no reason for me to question his decision. He explained why he did what he did and I told him I was just sad that we were missing a chance to spend a few good weeks together.

We played against each other on September 3, when Team Canada played Team U.S.A. to a 4–4 tie in the Forum. It was so strange to see Trots in another uniform. We didn't match up against each other much that game, but we did collide once at the blue line. He had the puck and I went to take him out of the play. He made a move to avoid me, so I stuck my knee out and tripped him. I didn't get a penalty, but he went for a spill and the crowd went crazy. Remember, Trots wasn't too popular in Canada once he opted for U.S. citizenship.

"You lazy bastard," Trots later told me he mumbled to himself as he climbed to his skates. "You little rat."

Trots got even. Late in that shift, he skated behind me as I rushed up ice without the puck, wedged his stick between my skates, gave a little yank, dumped me and skated innocently away.

Fair enough.

The media covering the tournament exaggerated a Trottier vs. Bossy conflict and they exaggerated an Islanders vs. Oilers rift. Team Canada was heavily flavored with Edmonton guys, from GM-coach Sather, his assistant coaches and trainers, to Gretzky, Messier, Fuhr, Anderson, Coffey, Huddy, Lowe and Gregg. We were represented by Smitty, Bournie, J.T., Brent and me. Because we had had two volatile Stanley Cup final series the last two years, the media looked for personal wars. There weren't any, but the hype kept everybody uncomfortable and on their toes. I didn't help matters by limping into camp with a bad foot and staying out of practice the first few days.

Late that first week, things got worse. Sather called me into his office after practice and asked, "Are you staying at home?"

I said, "Yeah, I am.

He said, "Everyone else is staying at the hotel and I think you should, too."

That caught me by surprise because I thought Bill had worked this out with Slats in advance. I had had enough grief for one week.

"Slats, if you want me to stay at the hotel, you might as well kick me off the team. I worked this out with Bill. He knew I was staying home." I wasn't being arrogant and I wasn't trying to show Slats up. But there was no way I was going to stay at the Château Champlain when I lived 20 minutes away in Laval.

Slats dropped that subject and floored me with his next remark. "We're thinking of making you and Gretzky captains," he said. "What do you think?"

I said, "Sure. Fine."

He knew I wasn't happy to be there and I think he figured that the captaincy would give me a little more responsibility and make me a little more enthusiastic. But he didn't name me one of the captains. He named Gretzky and Larry Robinson instead.

The tournament never got better. We spent a week in Banff during training camp and, before we left Montreal, I asked to be assigned my own hotel room. They ignored my request and roomed me with Denis Savard, who turned out to be a great roommate. We returned to Montreal and opened the tournament on September 1 at the Forum by beating West Germany, 7–2. Two nights later, we tied the U.S. Our next game was on September 6 against Sweden at Vancouver.

We lost, 4–2. We were 1–1–1. After the game, a reporter asked me if things would be different if Al was coaching instead of Sather. If I was smart, I would have said what a great job Slats was doing and that he and Al are the greatest coaches I ever played for, blah ... blah ... blah.

Instead, I did what I always do. I told the cold truth.

"Yes, they'd be different. I don't know if they'd be better or if they'd be worse, but they'd be different," I said, meaning that the two men had different coaching styles. Was mine a controversial answer or an obvious response to a shit-disturbing question? I didn't give the question another thought until I picked up the paper the next morning and was quoted as saying, "Things would be different if Arbour was here."

I was furious. The writer made me sound like I was inferring that Al would be doing a better job and that was not what I said or meant. I couldn't tell that to Slats and the Oiler players, though, they were so mad. Now they had a reason to be pissed at me.

In that same interview I called the Canada Cup Eagleson's ego trip. That comment made headlines, but at least I was quoted accurately. I felt that way then. I still do.

"For the last 12 years it's been the chance for someone to flex his muscles," I said. "It seems to be a psychological high for only one person (Eagleson). He stages the show and it's his tournament."

Eagleson, one of the most powerful player agents and the longtime executive director of the NHL Players' Association, created the Canada Cup as we know it today when he organized the 1972 SuperSeries, the eight-game series between the Soviets and Team Canada. He has since become one of Canada's key negotiators in virtually every international tournament.

The Eagle was never my favorite person. From the first day I met him when I was in junior looking for an agent and he was soliciting his services, I saw how cocky the guy was. He thought he was going to do me a favor by taking me on as a client? I was turned off immediately.

I will say that the guy has never done anything bad to me, never said a bad word about me in the press. Even when I blasted him for turning the tournament into his ego trip, he never said anything bad in response. He even came over to me the next day and joked about it.

Obviously he's been great for international competition. My only gripe about international competition is it's always the same guys who play. The best players are asked to volunteer their free time for a few thousand dollars. The NHLPA's pension fund benefits from proceeds of the Canada Cup, so I feel I should do my share. But after so many years it got to be too much. From the day the first guy who declined to play for whatever reason was belittled in the papers, it was play or be ridiculed. That's what happened to Gretzky and Mario Lemieux before the 1987 Canada Cup, when they considered not playing. I'm glad Lemieux chose to play because it was his first Canada Cup and it was his turn to participate.

I'm glad Gretzky played, too. But I would have fully understood if he declined the invitation because he deserved a rest.

Eagleson is why I never became active in the Players' Association. Trots, who became president when Tony Esposito retired in 1984, tried and tried to get me involved, but each time I told Trots that it was no use. There were too many guys in the association, especially out of the 21 player representatives, who always agreed with the way Eagleson did things. I didn't want to waste my time trying to break his powerful clique.

Eagleson's conflict of interest bothers me. He's so friendly with most of the teams' owners that I can't understand how he can negotiate a collective bargaining agreement objectively. At this stage of my career, though, it doesn't matter what I think about Alan Eagleson. It's up to the players who plan to be in this league another five or ten years to decide if his leadership is in their best interests.

And then came the rest of the tournament. My knee was killing me, but I played. I played in every game. We went from Vancouver to Calgary and on September 8 beat the Czechs, 7–2. Slats put me on a line with J.T. and Brent. We clicked. Considering the talent on the team, though, we were disappointed with a 2–1–1 record. It got worse two nights later, when the Soviets completed a 5–0–0 preliminary round by whipping us at Edmonton, 6–3. By finishing fourth in the round-robin portion of the tourney, we drew the Soviets in the sudden-death semifinals on September 13 at Calgary's Olympic Saddledome. It was one of the greatest and most exciting games I've ever played in, and not because I scored the winning goal in overtime.

Both teams were sky high. Both teams skated beautifully. The tempo was unreal. After a scoreless first period, J.T. gave us a 1–0 lead on assists from Coffey and Larry Robinson, but the Russians went ahead 2–1 on third-period goals by Sergei Svetlov at 5:19 and Sergei Makarov at 7:08.

We tied it 2–2 with 6:01 left when Doug Wilson, on assists from Gretz and Bournie, put one past goalie Vladimir Myshkin.

Just before we scored in overtime, Coffey made a great defensive play by intercepting Vladimir Kovin's pass for Mikhail Varnakov from his knees on a two-on-one. Coffey then hopped to his skates and led a rush back into their zone. Coffey lost control of the puck, but some incredible work by J.T. helped keep the puck in their end. Brent and J.T. started the play that led to the goal with some strong mucking in the corners. J.T. was behind the net fighting for the puck and I went in there trying to help. I got knocked down and the puck squirted into the right wing corner, so I got up and headed to the front of the net.

As I stumbled to the right wing side of the net with Kovin on my back, I ran into Myshkin's stick and knocked it out of his hand. Kovin and I fell down again. I got up just as J.T. at the right wing boards shoveled a pass to Coffey behind the right circle. I saw Coffey's shot coming, so I placed my stick stomach-high, where I thought the shot would be.

I didn't deliberately redirect the puck, I just got my stick in the way and redirected the puck into the left wing corner of the net. Bossy from Coffey and Tonelli at 12:29. The Saddledome shook. Coffey danced to center ice and slid to his knees as the team streamed off the bench to congratulate him. Only Brent and Wilson knew that I had tipped Coffey's shot, but it didn't matter. Referee Mike Noeth and the official scorer knew it was mine.

I met Igor Larionov, the Soviet Union's best center, in a bar after the semifinals. Most of Team Canada was celebrating our great victory when Phil Scheuer of the NHL's Montreal office came in with Larionov and introduced us. Larionov, who's smaller than me, was drinking straight vodka out of a huge tumbler like it was beer. He spoke a little English, so I jokingly asked him, "Why don't you come and play in the NHL? I know we could certainly use you."

He smiled and said, "I can't."

The best-of-three finals against Sweden were anti-climactic. We beat them 5–2 at Calgary and 6–5 at Edmonton for the championship. J.T. was named Team Canada's tournament MVP. Against my better judgment, I played in both games. I wanted to sit out and let my knee rest because I wanted to be ready for the NHL season, and I knew I needed at least a few weeks of rehabilitation.

Before Team Canada split, each of us were presented with a picture album of the tournament and a personal note. Mine read:

> **Mike**
> **Thanks for your efforts with Team Canada.**
> **It was a great victory for Canada (and of course for my ego)**
> **Sincere best regards,**
> **Alan Eagleson**

One awful Canada Cup ended, but not without one parting shot from Coffey. He told the press I was a complainer. That hurt. We were together for nearly six weeks. Why didn't he say that to my face?

I missed the Islanders' entire exhibition season while I rested my knee, but I came back in time for the opener and got off to the best start of my career: 17 goals in ten games. Trots, who injured his adductor muscle during the Canada Cup, missed 12 of our first 15 games. Al left J.T., Brent and I together and we were immediately dubbed The Canada Cup Line. Although I missed playing with Trots, I loved playing with Brent because it put an end to the widely held belief that Trots was the secret to my success. I was the NHL Player of the Month for October. On November 3, I led Gretzky in the scoring race, 33–31. I finished sixth with 117 points. He won with 208.

Trots had a tough year. That leg muscle injury never went away and he finished with 59 points, by far the lowest total of his career. Instead of taking all the time he needed to heal it, Trots did what he always does, he tried to play through his injury after missing those 12 games early in the season. Unfortunately, he couldn't.

Athletes shouldn't feel obligated to play hurt because they're paid generously. Most professional sports teams pay close attention to their players' physical needs, but there's always been an underlying feeling that if a player can possibly play, he should. I think any team that pressures an athlete to "heal faster" is making a big mistake. There's no sense in somebody risking a permanent injury or playing when he's unable to give a decent performance. We're human beings. In Trots' case, though, he didn't want to let down his teammates. Nobody would have questioned Trots sitting out because for nine seasons he proved himself nearly indestructible. But Trots couldn't keep himself off the ice.

As a team, we couldn't keep ourselves much over .500 all season. We scored tons of goals, but gave up tons of goals. Bill made a major move on November 19 when he traded Rollie Melanson to Minnesota for a first-round draft pick and handed the Number Two goalie's job behind Smitty to Kelly Hrudey.

Hrudey, Gibby, Boots, Patty and Flats were forming the new generation of Islanders. Clarkie, Bournie, Smitty, J.T., Denny, Trots and I were the old guard. The generation gap grew as the season wore on. It's not that we didn't get along; we did. It's just that we weren't a finely tuned machine anymore. The older guys were having trouble playing like they did in the past and the younger guys were having trouble trying to help us find our old Stanley Cup form.

Morrow missed the first 61 games following major knee surgery. Ny was plagued by injuries all season. Butchie was waived in January and claimed by Boston. Bournie missed 44 games after a skate sliced his left hand. I pulled a muscle in my ribcage in mid-January and missed three games.

We were third in the division behind Philly and Washington, only a few games over .500, when Bill said we were deteriorating mentally, not physically. He said the hunger was missing. Despite the injuries, he was right.

"If guys don't have the incentive and they aren't as hungry, then I wish they would leave," I said to the press. My comments didn't help, though. We didn't win more than four straight all season and finished 10–12–3 for a 40–34–6 record, the worst of my NHL career.

The All-Star Game on February 12, 1985, at Calgary was the worst of my career, too. My skates felt dull during the morning skate, so I asked Boston trainer Dan Canney, who was chosen to the Wales Conference staff, if he'd sharpen them after practice.

"Sure, Mike," he said.

They still didn't feel right after warmup, so I asked Dan to sharpen them again. It was 15 minutes before gametime. I got the skates back, quickly put them on, and nearly fell when I was introduced during the pregame ceremony.

"What's the matter?" Trots said as we stood under the spotlights at the blue line.

"I can't understand it," I said. "I can't stand up. These are the worst my skates have ever felt."

Bourque, standing near Trots and I, overheard us. "Who sharpened them?" he asked.

"Canney," I said. And Bourque, the Bruins' best player, gave me this look that said, "Well, you asked for it." Bourque knew what I didn't, that Canney was not the team's skate sharpener. He barely knew how to operate the machine.

On my first shift of the game, I veered into the corner to control a puck that had been shot around the boards and nearly killed myself. I lost my edge and rammed into the boards. Canney sharpened them a third time, after the first period, but he made more of a mess. I don't know why I didn't think of this earlier, but finally in the second period I looked over to Bearcat Murray, the Calgary trainer who was working for the Campbell Conference, and I asked him to sharpen my skates.

Other than my sticks, which have to be perfect, I'm not picky about my equipment, although I like my skates sharpened before every game. Jim Pickard has been the Islanders' equipment manager since their inception and he's a fabulous skate sharpener. "Pick" and my cousin Eddy Palchak with Montreal are the best skate sharpeners in the league. That's not just my opinion, but the opinion of a lot of players who have worked with them at All-Star games and international tournaments.

I scored 13 goals in my final 25 games to finish with 58, my eighth straight 50-plus season. Kurri scored 71 goals to break my NHL record for right wings and drop me to the second-team all-star team. I was satisfied with my season, but we weren't satisfied with ours. We finished ninth overall with 86 points.

The Islander mystique carried us past the Capitals in the opening round of the playoffs, though. After losing the first two games in our best-of-five series (both in overtime), we became the first NHL team to rally from an 0–2 deficit by winning the last three. But the thrill was brief. We lost in five to Philly in the Patrick Division finals.

The biggest surprise of the 1985–86 season came before training camp opened when Al announced that he'd be back as coach. I had a feeling he was going to retire after we lost in the '84 finals. When he didn't and we were knocked out in the second round in '85, I was sure he had had enough.

But there he was for the start of my ninth camp, barking the same orders, answering to "Radar" and maintaining the respect of every player, although he was unintentionally one of the easiest men to laugh at. He once told Trots and I that he walked off the roof of his house in Sudbury, Ontario, when he went to get a hammer without thinking where he was.

Al wasn't very good in cars, either. He jumped out of his station wagon one day in front of his house without putting the transmission in park. When he walked behind the car, it nearly ran him over before it rammed into a tree on his property. Another time he told us how he was driving to practice one morning with a cup of coffee in one hand, a cigarette in the other and his hands somehow on the steering wheel. Something happened on the road in front of him and he ended up in a ditch with his pants on fire and his body burning from the coffee.

The wildest story involving Al, his car and that mischievous automatic transmission occurred during the 1980 playoffs, when we chartered from Buffalo or Philadelphia and landed at Republic Airport, a small airport on Long Island. Al got off the plane and walked to his car, which was parked in a lot near the runway. Al had to pick someone or something up at the plane, so he tried to drive the car onto the airstrip. There was a gate that had to be lifted manually, so Al got out of the car and pulled the gate open.

Yes, he left the car in drive.

The car crept toward a few two-seat prop planes that were parked near the team's plane and held sturdy on the airstrip by guide wires. Al ran after his car, didn't see the guide wires, and tripped over one. It was a nasty spill that separated his shoulder. As Al looked up from the tarmac, he saw his car smash into the body of one of those small planes, totaling it. That mishap cost Al a lot of money in insurance premiums.

By 1985–86, the humorous stories and special memories of Stanley Cups past were all that was left. Al and Bill continued to insist we were Stanley Cup contenders, but their hopeful optimism obscured the obvious. We needed a major overhaul. Trots was coming off a bad year; Smitty, Ny, Clarkie, Bournie, Denny and I were aging; Morrow's knees were crumbling; and very few of my teammates were as motivated as they once were.

When I first came into the league I wanted everybody to be like I was, easily and consistently motivated by the need to succeed and the fear of failure. As I went through my career, though, I realized not everybody was. I scored 61 goals and 123 points that year, my highest goal and point total since 1981–82. Al reunited me with a healthy Trots, who rebounded remarkably well from his injury-plagued 59-point season to collect 96. I won my third Lady Byng Trophy, was fifth in the scoring race, and earned my fifth NHL first-team all-star berth.

I scored my 500th goal into an empty net on January 2, 1986, and my 1,000th point three weeks later. In the All-Star Game at Hartford, I fed Trots on a two-on-one for the winning goal in overtime. On March 11, Bill's overhaul began. He traded J.T. to Calgary for left wing Richard Kromm and defenseman Steve Konroyd. The press speculated that this was Bill retaliating for J.T.'s training camp hold-out, but I disagreed. If Bill wanted to get back at J.T., he wouldn't have given him the generous four-year contract J.T. got and he would have gotten rid of him sooner. I think Bill just got two young players he thought could help us.

On January 5, while playing a post-practice game called Keepaway, in which players try to steal the puck from one another, Gerald Diduck accidentally poked Ny in the left eye with his stick. Ny needed surgery on his retina. His career was over.

Almost over. The game before the injury was his 899th. On April 5, in our home finale, Al put Ny in the lineup and started him alongside Trots and Rich Kromm in my place on right wing. The puck was dropped, it came to Ny, he batted it forward and skated off to a wild ovation. He had played in his 900th and last NHL game thanks to the class of the Islanders, Bill Torrey and Al Arbour.

Ny was quite a player, one of the proudest Islanders. He and Smitty were originals, the last two members of the 1972–73 expansion team. I don't know if there was anybody more dedicated to the game than Ny. He was quite a fighter, too. As much as I disliked fighting, I admired Ny because he never picked a fight with anybody who didn't want to fight him. And of course, he scored the biggest goal in all of our careers, on May 24, 1980, at 7:11 of overtime, the goal that brought the first Stanley Cup to Long Island.

The less said about the playoffs the better. Peeters and Washington held us to four goals in three games and swept us, 3–1, 5–2, 3–1. It was the Islanders' quickest post-season exit ever. I scored my 83rd playoff goal to move past Rocket Richard and become the all-time leading Stanley Cup goal scorer, but that was little consolation. I was terrible, the team was terrible.

Now there was no question about it. An era had ended.

Chapter

14

What's Wrong With My Back?

Al resigned to become our vice president of player development. Ny retired. Terry Simpson, a successful Western Hockey League coach from Saskatchewan who built the Prince Albert Raiders into a WHL power and led the 1985 Canadian Junior National Team to a gold medal in Helsinki, Finland, was hired as head coach. Ny was named his assistant.

Not only did I want to make a good impression on the new coaching staff, but I was also eager to make up for an unfulfilling spring. I trained during the off-season harder than I had ever trained before. I actually watched my diet, ran regularly, exercised on the stationary bike, and skated before training camp began. A bunch of us practiced informally at Cantiague for three days before the rookies reported. I felt exactly how I expected to feel: my feet ached slightly and my legs felt tight. But I was excited about a new coach and a new season. We weren't one of the NHL's elite anymore. We were starting over.

Ny ran the first official practice while Terry, who had never seen most of us play, watched from the stands. Ny's second-to-last drill was basic figure-eights around the rink, a drill I had done a thousand times before. We started behind one net and skated figure-eights to the other end, slowing down at the blue line. After the drill ended, I bent at the waist and rested my stick on the tops of my knee pads. After a few gulps of air, I straightened up ... and felt a sharp, burning pain in the lower left side of my back.

That scared me. I had felt sharper and more intense pain, like when I broke my kneecap, but I had never felt anything like that. The burning sensation started in the middle and radiated to the left. Before the last skating drill I twisted, turned and bent at the waist to see if my back was all right. Ny saw me.

"Are you OK?" he asked.

"I think I hurt my back, but it feels OK now," I told him.

I got back into line and finished practice without a problem. When we were dismissed, I threw my gloves and stick into my stall and headed for the training room.

"I think I hurt my back," I said to Craig Smith, who became our trainer in 1984. "I felt this really sharp pain across the left side when I was skating, but I don't feel anything anymore. Now it feels OK."

And Craig said, "Why don't you stay in and skip the scrimmage?"

I didn't feel like being teased by the guys and I didn't want Terry to think I begged off the ice whenever I felt a little ache or pain. So I said to Craig, "No, no, no, no. I'll go out and see how it is."

My back stiffened midway through the afternoon scrimmage, but without the sharp pain. I skated through the entire practice and bathed in a pool of ice. Craig again asked me how I felt and I told him it wasn't bothering me much. Just a tight muscle, I figured.

When the pain continued throughout that first week of camp, Craig and Dr. Minkoff suggested I take a few days off. I missed the first exhibition game. Dr. Minkoff examined me that night. I told him that my back hurt most when I skated. I also complained that my right knee was aching, but we both knew that the grinding of my kneecap was the result of arthritic changes that dated to my boyhood injury. I linked my back problem to my knee problems. I wondered out loud if the pain in my right knee was causing me to compensate with the left part of my back.

Ask Dr. Boss.

Craig and Dr. Minkoff didn't think so. They said they thought I had pulled a muscle in my back that needed to be stretched and rested. As for my knee, they recommended extensive rehabilitation for my entire right leg, especially the quadriceps, to compensate for the weakness around my kneecap.

Training camp continued without me.

On October 2, the city of Laval named a new rink after me: Mike Bossy Arena. I was honored in the afternoon and that night we played an exhibition game against the Canadiens at Laval Sports Centre. It was great seeing the faces from my junior career: the same Zamboni driver, many of the same fans, the familiar warm ovation. I was touched. My back was killing me, though. I had been off skates for about a week during training camp and this was my first exhibition game. If not for the dedication that afternoon, I wouldn't have played. I shouldn't have played, and I didn't play the following night at Quebec.

We said good-bye to Bournie and Clarkie a few days later, just before our season opener in Chicago. Bill left them unprotected in the waiver draft. Bournie was taken by Los Angeles, Clarkie by Buffalo. We lost two of the nicest people, and it sadly reminded me that our Stanley Cups had long passed. But the rebuilding was inevitable.

We flew to Chicago the day before Terry's NHL coaching debut. Since Ny had been around us for nine years and was now a member of the management team, we assumed that Trots and I would be rooming together. But we weren't. Terry had paired me with Brent and Trots with Pat LaFontaine.

Trots and I didn't say anything before the game, but the morning after our 3–2 loss to the Blackhawks, when Terry and Ny met with the captain (Denny) and the two alternates (Trots and Brent), Trots told Terry that we'd roomed together for nine years and wanted to continue rooming together. Terry said he didn't know it was that important to us. He said he'd change the list when we got to Los Angeles for the second stop of our season-opening trip.

The L.A. rooming list wasn't different from the Chicago list, so Trots and I made the switch ourselves. We picked up our room keys and asked Brent and Patty if they minded rooming together. They didn't, so we exchanged keys. I thought nothing of it until I found out that Terry and Ny were angry at us. They wanted to take care of our request and they felt we had usurped their authority.

To be honest, Trots and I thought it was ridiculous that we were broken up in the first place. It was too silly a problem for me to get upset over. My back still bothered me. I couldn't get loose in Chicago, so I spent the game fighting the occasional sharp pains and making sure I stayed away from a direct hit. The more I skated, the worse I felt. I took four shots in the first period playing with Trots and rookie Brad Lauer (a left wing who took Clarkie's spot on the roster), but did nothing afterward.

We practiced the next day in Chicago before we flew to Los Angeles, and I began to feel a pinching pain every time I bent over. When teams practice the power play there's a lot of standing around. I couldn't stand the pain, so after five minutes I had to get off the ice. Craig examined me again but offered no new answers. I was scared and confused. I flew to L.A. in severe discomfort. When I got off the plane, the right side of my lower back was hurting. I hardly slept. I finally threw a pillow and blanket on the floor and spent the night squirming and stretching, trying to stretch the pain out of my muscles.

I felt slightly better after the morning skate, but the game was a waste of time. I couldn't skate or shoot without pain. My contribution was staying out of everybody's way. I was frustrated by my inability to do anything, embarrassed by my performance, and angry at the injury. I didn't sit on the bench between shifts because it hurt less to stand. By the end of the game, which we lost 5–4, I couldn't turn my torso from my waist. It hurt too much.

I headed directly into the trainer's room, where Terry and Bill stood somberly. We were 0–2, so neither man was in a very good mood. I walked over to Craig, laid down on the medical table and said, "Craig, that's it. I can't play anymore. I'm going to have to see some kind of back doctor."

Craig looked at me with eyes that said, "I didn't realize it was that bad." I stared back silently with eyes that said, "It is that bad."

The team flew home on October 12. Two days later my medical odyssey began when I visited Dr. Patrick O'Leary, a back surgeon in Manhattan. After a radiologist took X-rays, Dr. O'Leary examined me. His first question was, "Do you have any pain down your leg?"

When I said no, he looked at me as if to say, "Then what are you coming to see me for?" He didn't say that, but that's how I interpreted the expression on his face. He examined my X-rays and explained that people go through minor arthritic changes in the course of their lives. He used some technical terms I didn't understand, then offered an opinion I understood perfectly.

He said, "You could be out a couple of weeks, you could be out a couple of months, you could be out a couple of years."

My immediate thought, "Two weeks." Dr. O'Leary didn't say I had a broken back, or a slipped disc or anything that sounded serious, so I didn't consider my problem serious. He said that minor arthritic changes occurred in all people and that I hadn't done anything to worsen my condition. In a letter written to Craig that day, Dr. O'Leary diagnosed problems with two of the lower discs in my back.

I'll skip the medical jargon, which I never understood anyway.

I told Craig that the doctor said it could be a couple of weeks and we outlined a basic rehabilitation program to keep me in decent shape while my back rested. I didn't worry about aggravating my back riding the stationary bike or lifting light weights because my back only got worse when I skated. I missed our home opener and three other games. I stayed off skates for seven days, then skated alone on October 19 at the Coliseum. I pushed myself hard. Al, who heard me on the ice, walked over and asked me how I felt.

"It feels good," I said happily. "No pain."

Dr. O'Leary was right, I said to myself in the shower. I waited two weeks and I let my back heal. Thank God this is over with. We played the Devils on October 21, but since our next game wasn't until the 25th we decided to play it safe and give my back another full week's rest. I returned on the 25th and scored my first goal as we beat L.A., 4–3.

Terry ticked me off in our next game. We were ahead of Philly at home, 2–1, when the Flyers pulled Ron Hextall out of the net for a sixth attacker. With a face-off in our end, Terry replaced me with Duane on right wing with Trots and Kromm. I couldn't believe it. I didn't want to say anything, but after steaming through practice the next day, I decided to say something the following morning, the day of a game at New Jersey.

"We have to talk," I said after the morning skate. "I don't understand why you pulled me off the ice at the end of the game the other night."

"Don't read into it," he said. "I just want to see every player in every kind of situation."

I wasn't satisfied with his answer. "Listen," I said, growing angrier. "I've been good enough to play in those situations the last seven or eight years, and if you don't think I'm good enough to play in them anymore, then there's no place for me to play here anymore. I paid my dues at the beginning of my career. I've proven myself in those situations."

He had no reaction. I didn't expect one. I just walked out as annoyed at him as when I walked in. I didn't need this aggravation. My back had just gotten better, I was in my second-to-last year, and I didn't have to prove myself to Terry Simpson after eight seasons and more than 500 goals. "If that's the way it's going to be, then I can't worry about him," I told myself as I walked out of his office. "I'll just try and forget about the whole thing."

I tried to accept Terry from the first day of camp, I really did, but I missed Al. Al was the only NHL coach I had ever played for and he was a large reason why I developed into a complete player. When I walked out of Terry's office after that conversation, I knew that things would never be the same.

November was more like old times. Although I was aware of the pain gradually returning to my back, it didn't hinder me all month. I scored two goals two games in a row, got shut out twice, then reeled off 12 in ten games, giving me 18 in 23. I passed Stan Mikita for seventh place on the all-time goal-scoring list on November 9 in Buffalo and Richard for sixth place on November 16 in Winnipeg. I scored my 550th goal on November 26 in Pittsburgh and three days later, at home against the Flyers, I notched my 38th career hat trick.

Then we went West. We tied Calgary on December 2 and got bombed 7–1 by Edmonton the next night. We practiced in Edmonton the following day, before our flight to Vancouver. We were practicing line rushes. I took a pass out of the zone and saw that I was going to collide with Denny. I made a quick turn to try and avoid him, but we clipped each other's sides, my left into his left. When we collided, I felt a twinge. It wasn't the pain I felt during training camp, but one thing was certain: November was only a cruel tease.

From the moment Denny and I collided, my back got progressively worse. What was I going to do? Bill and Terry left it up to me. I decided to play until it became too painful to play for two reasons: first, I wanted to get my 50 goals; second, because I had played well in November, I thought I could continue to help the team.

Craig tried everything to lessen my discomfort: heat, elastic wraps, ice, balm, ultrasound, muscle stimulator. Nothing felt good. I scored in three straight games two weeks before Christmas to tie Johnny Bucyk for fifth place on the all-time list with 556 goals, but I didn't pass Bucyk until four games later.

On January 17 we started a two-night, home-and-home series against Philadelphia at the Coliseum. I boarded the bus for the two-hour ride to Philadelphia immediately after our 4–2 loss feeling my usual stiffness. I thought nothing of it when I checked into the hotel and went right to sleep. We didn't skate the next morning, but we met for our pregame meal. I was talking to Trots, eating, when all of a sudden my lower back went into a spasm. It was an excruciating pain I hadn't felt before, but I didn't say anything to anybody except Trots. He helped me creep back to our room and laid me down on the floor.

"Why don't your try a hot bath?" he suggested. "That'll do you good."

For a half-hour I soaked myself in that scalding water. It did no good. I tried to sleep, but when I awoke after an uncomfortable few minutes I couldn't even walk upright. I was scratched from the lineup. Three days later, I was in Huntington for my first MRI exam.

MRI stands for magnetic resonancy imaging, a process that searches for imperfections through the use of pictures much more precise than an X-ray. I don't completely understand how it works, but I can assure you of one thing: it's hell. I can only compare an MRI machine to a coffin with both ends cut open. I was strapped in this cylinder and told not to move. The polite technician told me the test would take approximately 30 minutes.

An hour later in this oversized drinking straw, I had to go to the bathroom so badly I thought my kidneys were going to burst. A nurse finally approached. Before I could plead for a minute's rest she said, "We'd like to take a few more shots. Can you hold out another ten minutes?"

Not wanting to wimp out, I said, "Sure, no problem." Then I tried to stop breathing, my insides hurt so much. I felt the ends of the MRI machine closing in on me and I thought of Trots, who would never have lasted that long. Well, maybe he would've. He has a lot of stubborn pride, too. Anyway, the ten minutes that felt like ten years ended. I acted cool when they came in and unstrapped me. I sped to the john, got dressed, and went home. It wasn't long before Craig told me that the MRI and the neurological test I took later that week shed no light on my injury.

I sat out from January 18 to 30, six games. I had 29 goals after our team's 51st game. Rendez-Vous '87 was on the horizon. The speculation began. Fans across the continent were voting for the starting NHL all-star team that would face the Soviet National Team in a two-game series at Quebec City on February 11 and 13. I was the leading vote-getter at right wing. I knew that Rendez-Vous was going to be my last international competition. I wanted to play.

I wanted to play, but I wanted to be fair to the Islanders. If I sat out the ten games between the Philly game and the Rendez-Vous break to accept the All-Star invitation, I would have been cheating my teammates. But if I came back too soon, I would have been cheating myself. I played four games before Rendez-Vous because: (1) my back felt a little better; (2) I wanted to see if it was going to hold up for a couple of games; (3) I wanted to get some games in before I went up against the best in the world with the best in the world. If I was going to play with Gretzky, Messier and Lemieux, I didn't want to look silly. I didn't want to get there and then have to sit on the bench because I couldn't keep up.

Our last three games before Rendez-Vous were on the road at Vancouver, Edmonton and Calgary. I don't remember Vancouver. I don't remember Edmonton. Oh, do I remember Calgary. From the start of the game that big and strong Flames team made sure it was my longest game of the season. I can't single out one Flame because they all took shots at me, mostly cross-checks from behind while I tried to establish position in front of the net. That was the first time in my NHL career I felt like giving up. I was in too much pain to compete and too sore and stiff to protect myself by skating out of the way.

I declined my invitation to Rendez-Vous and sent Igor Larionov, my favorite Soviet center, my regards.

I was never one to abandon hope, but when the season resumed on February 14, I knew the chances of me scoring 50 goals were slim. I needed 20 in 26 games, which wouldn't have been easy if I was perfectly healthy. With my back becoming a big story around the league, I was becoming an increasingly easy target. Opponents knew that one first-period cross-check rendered me immobile for the night. And it made sense for teams to key on me because, although I played hurt, I still was our team's leading goal scorer.

By February and March I hardly practiced anymore. While the team drilled between games, I rehabilitated my knee and tried to keep my cardiovascular capacity high by riding the stationary bike. I made three visits to a Long Island acupuncturist. I spent two 45-minute sessions in traction with Steve Wirth, the Islanders' physical therapist. I was willing to do anything to get rid of the pain, anything to improve my chances at 50 goals. With 20 games and 19 goals to go, I refused to let my back get in the way.

But the games became tedious and painful. Scoring goals stopped being fun. Hockey was a job now, a painful and frustrating job. It frustrated Trots, too, who wrote his guest editorial in *The Hockey News* critiquing the officials partly because of the abuse I was taking.

On March 4 in the Garden, I drew 14 minutes in penalties: two for elbowing, two for cross-checking, and my first ten-minute misconduct penalty in years for saying something stupid to referee Kerry Fraser, who had permitted the Rangers' annoying left wing, Jan Erixon, to hook and hold me all game. After the game I ripped Erixon for being nothing more than a checker. "I'd like to have that kind of job," I said foolishly. "You get good pay for standing around, getting in front of people all night."

Now my back was affecting my mind.

From the Garden we flew to Toronto, where we were blasted by the Maple Leafs, 7–2. It left us 0–2–2 in our last four games and 28–28–10 for the season. Second place, which was ours for most of the season, was slipping away.

"What do you want me to say?" I told the reporters who huddled around me after the loss to the Leafs. "That I'm going to get a hat trick tomorrow in Chicago and we're going to win?"

I go into every game hoping I get a hat trick, but in my condition I would have been happy to get one goal and play the entire game without pain. I wasn't making any bold prediction. I wasn't playing prophet. I just made a rhetorical statement to hammer home my point about trying to help the team win and being perplexed by why we weren't playing well.

We flew from Toronto to Chicago, and at Chicago Stadium beat the Blackhawks, 6–5, with five third-period goals; I scored three of them, and assisted on Trots' game-winner with 23 seconds left. Trots and I were patting each other on the back when I remembered Toronto 24 hours earlier.

"Remember what I said to the press last night in Toronto about getting a hat trick?" I asked. We laughed, because we knew that any minute the reporters would be in asking me about my ability to see the future.

And they did.

I spoke confidently in Chicago about my chances of 50, but needing 14 goals in 13 games, it was false confidence. I felt better in Chicago than I did the night before in Toronto, but there wasn't one day that I felt OK. I scored a goal in Pittsburgh to leave me 13 short with 12 to go and I viewed March 13–14, a weekend home-and-home series with Jersey, as my make-it-or-break-it shot at 50. The Devils were out of the playoff race and I figured with a good weekend I'd still have a chance. I figured I could score three of four goals in the two games and close ground.

I scored once. My back was killing me. Devils coach Doug Carpenter assigned left wing Doug Sulliman to be my chaperon, my personal shadow for the weekend. Not only did Sulliman discourage me, but that weekend set me back another 25 percent because with Sulliman all over me, I had to work that much harder to get open.

Sulliman and I took coincidental high-sticking penalties in the second game (we won 7–6 at the Coliseum in overtime) and that little tussle was my fault. I was pretty mean that weekend, but I was mean out of frustration, not out of genuine meanness. Sulliman isn't a dirty player, but he was velcroed to my pants the entire two games and I didn't like it.

After two games with the Devils we flew to Montreal. I wasn't myself anymore. My season was falling apart and my back was unfit for National Hockey League duty. My heart was out of the game. I was desperate for 50, but I was also trying to survive. In the third period of this 3–0 loss in the Forum, I was playing the point on the power play. The puck went down the boards on the right side and Guy Carbonneau, one of the best checkers in the NHL and a guy who spent much of his career holding onto my jersey, ran into me with his stick high and his elbow up. He only grazed me, but I was incensed. We kept the puck in their zone and I circled back to my point. The puck went around the boards again and I skated toward it. Carbonneau zeroed in on me again with his stick up, so I just lifted my left arm and cracked him in the head with my glove, elbow and stick. Referee Bob Hall gave Carbonneau four minutes for high-sticking and me a five-minute high-sticking major, my first major penalty since the Behn Wilson fight eight years earlier.

The Carbonneau incident scared me because I was losing control of my emotions and my temper, two parts of my personality I prided myself on controlling. My mother came to the game and flew back to New York with us on the charter. I didn't even want to talk to her on the trip home, that's how ashamed I was.

I was ashamed that I had stooped that low, to the level of the goons and hack artists. I had always been able to turn my back on the garbage, but now I had let myself get dragged into it. I had become just another bumbling NHL player who used his stick and arms because he wasn't skilled enough to check properly or skate swiftly. Because of my back, I was doing what I regularly criticized the cheap-shots artists of doing.

Playing the game had hurt physically for months. Now it was hurting emotionally too. Paranoia had set in. With less than a month left in the regular season, and with a 50-goal season floating out of my reach, I firmly believed that every player in the NHL salivated when I touched the puck. I expected to get blindsided and I feared getting sticked. I can say now, objectively and rationally, that players viewed me as a target. But when I played those last few games that season I was convinced that every hit was a deliberate attempt to end my career.

After we lost 3–0 in Montreal, we played the Red Wings in Detroit. In the first period, Rick Zombo cross-checked me from behind in front of the net while we were on a power play. A little while later, while I was chasing a loose puck around the boards, Shawn Barr ignored the puck and leveled me before I got to it, a clear case of interference that wasn't called.

My back, my head, everything hurt. Trots blasted referee Don Koharski after that, about two minutes worth. I had tears in my eyes after Burr's hit. I could hardly take it anymore. The hitting, the soreness, not being able to play anywhere close to my capabilities, was just getting to be too much. I felt helpless. I didn't care if any of our guys retaliated against Burr because it wasn't going to make my back feel better and it wasn't going to alleviate the mental agony.

Nothing was going to help and I knew it. I had 38 goals and only seven games to score 12 more.

I played one more game during the regular season, March 21 against the Rangers at the Coliseum. I played terribly again. I couldn't get out of anybody's way. At the end of the game I got the puck and Ron Greschner threw a heavy check that knocked me over. As I was going down, I decided my season was over. If I couldn't get out of the way of Ron Greschner, one of the slowest skaters in the NHL, I had no right playing. Greschner, who could hardly move himself, hit me while my knee was completely extended. I probably came a millimeter from completely tearing my knee up.

It was too much to take. My nerves gave out on me after that game. I cried for 10 or 15 minutes in the dressing room after the game. I saw Bill the next day.

"Bill, that's it. I can't play anymore." I meant until the playoffs.

He looked disappointed, but he didn't look surprised. He accepted my decision, but asked me not to mention to the press that I wasn't playing until after the Washington games. With seven games left in the season, we had two games left with the Caps, whom we led by three points in the race for second place and home-ice advantage in the first round of the playoffs.

I wasn't as worried about second place as I was about my endangered health. I needed a couple of weeks to get ready for the playoffs. My back wasn't going to be fine, but the doctors felt a few weeks would lessen the pain and improve my mobility. After Erixon–Sulliman–Carbonneau–Zombo–Burr–Greschner, I was willing to listen to anything.

Washington beat us out of second place, so we opened a best-of-seven series at Capital Centre. Make that, the Capitals opened the series. We watched. We fell behind 3–0 after 12 minutes of the first period. Duane, who played left wing with us much of the season, Trots and I were on for the second and third goals.

I scored midway through the third period to make it 4–2 and Denny and I assisted on Trots' power-play goal with 1:03 left. We rallied, but we still lost, 4–3.

In the third period of Game 2, I got hurt. I was coming out of the corner with the puck when Lou Franceschetti, one of the Caps' shit disturbers, came at me. I saw him at the last moment, but I wasn't able to get out of the way. He caught my knee with a little bit of his knee. It wasn't intentional.

When I fell to the ice, I looked up at the Cap Centre's ugly black ceiling and shook my head in disbelief. I spent an entire season nursing, icing, heating, protecting and worrying about my back, and two games into the playoffs I injured my left knee. The diagnosis was a sprain. I was out for the series.

After losing second place to the Caps and finishing 35–33–12, we weren't supposed to beat Washington. But Trots broke a 1–1 tie in Game 2 with 2:40 left, added an empty-net goal in the final seconds, and brought the series home tied at one game apiece.

I brought my corroding body home in pieces. I thought my season was over. And to tell you the truth, I wasn't too disappointed. I was ready to relax. I knew the knee would heal in a few weeks, but I needed the spring and summer to rest my back once and for all. But a funny thing happened on the way to the summer. We lost twice at the Coliseum to fall behind three games to one, then won Game 5 on the road, Game 6 at home, and Game 7 in Disneyland.

Perhaps you've heard of that game. The Easter Epic? It was the four-overtime heart-stopper that is the fifth-longest game in NHL history. It was one of the greatest games I've ever seen. It started at 7:35 p.m. on Saturday night, April 18, and ended at 1:58 a.m. on Easter Sunday morning. We won, 3–2, on Patty LaFontaine's goal at 128:47. Two indefatigible teams played 68 minutes, 47 seconds of sudden-death Game 7 hockey after the first 60 minutes ended in a 2–2 tie.

The moment Patty's shot ticked off the post and went in I said to myself, "Oh, boy. Now I've got to start working out again." I hadn't stopped working out, but there's a big difference between working out for working out's sake and working out to play in an NHL playoff game. Until we won Game 7, I didn't think we were going to win the series.

Of course I wanted us to win. I flew down for the game that day and watched all four overtimes from the runway in the corner leading to our dressing room with Denny and Brent, who were also injured.

We played Philly in the division finals and my knee healed in time for Game 4. We lost that game, 6–4, to fall behind three games to one, just as we did against Washington. We won Games 5 and 6, just as we did against the Caps, but the Flyers blew us out of the Spectrum, 5–1, in Game 7.

I don't remember too much of those last four games. My back still hurt and I wore a brace on my left knee. I was a mess. It hurt just to wait for the linesman to drop the puck. I gritted my teeth and did the best I could, although I knew, my teammates knew the media knew and the fans knew I wasn't doing much.

We bussed home from Philly as Saturday night, May 2, 1987, turned into Sunday morning. Terry called a meeting for Monday at 11 a.m. We didn't normally have meetings after our season ended. We usually had parties, even when the Stanley Cup was not on our guest list. The year before, Al's last year, we had a party at a golf club after we congregated at the rink to collect our sticks and pack up our equipment. I didn't know what Terry's meeting was for.

It wasn't a meeting, it was a lecture. I felt like I was sitting in detention while the teacher scolded me. Not just me, all of us. Terry told us that he was happy about the way we came back against Washington, happy about the way we came back against Philadelphia, but those two comebacks shouldn't make us feel good because in the end, we lost.

As I sat there listening to him, I agreed. But I noticed Terry getting very intense. Terry was the type of coach who carried losses in his stomach for days. It became clear that he was going to carry our loss all summer.

"And I hope you all have a horseshit summer because I know I'm going to have one," he said before he left.

Although I knew he was speaking out of frustration, I was astounded. When I left the Coliseum that day, stunned by what Terry had just said, I didn't expect to have a horseshit summer. I expected the months of May, June, July and August to finally cure my back.

Chapter

15

An Off Season

"We're sure that with complete rest this summer you'll be OK."

That's what Craig and Dr. Minkoff assured me in May. They instructed me not to skate, work out, or do anything strenuous. "Don't worry," I told them. All I did for two months was bend. I bent forward from the waist in the morning and I bent forward from the waist at night. When I left the table after breakfast, I bent. When I got tired of sitting, I bent. I must have tested my back 20 times a day for two months, waiting for the pinches and twinges to go away.

Why wasn't my back getting better? Dr. O'Leary said last October to give it two weeks and I gave it two weeks. That didn't work. Dr. Minkoff said to give it two months and I gave it two months. No change. By late June, when Josiane and Tanya were finished in school and we were packing up to spend our first summer at our new home in Rosemere, Quebec, I was frantic. What the hell was going on? Why couldn't anybody help me? Why hadn't the pain gone away?

Nobody knew. Dr. Minkoff couldn't suggest anything other than rest or physical therapy, which left Bill and me feeling helpless. There had to be a cure.

Early in July, Pierre got a call from Dr. Jacques Duranceau, a specialist from the University of Montreal. Dr. Duranceau had heard about my problem and asked to see me. His was one of the hundreds of calls, letters, and suggestions I got since the season began. Most were crackpot ideas (stand on your head; try voo-doo; see a hypnotist; drink some crazy concoction). Some were from friends of friends who knew doctors who once healed somebody's bad back.

Dr. Duranceau seemed sincere, so I made an appointment. No matter how pessimistic I was, I couldn't reject an offer from an expert who volunteered to help. I spent ten minutes telling him the abridged version of my injury, from the figure-eight to the collision with Denny to my last shift in Game 7 of the Philly series, and then undressed for an examination.

"I'm positive you have a disc problem," Dr. Duranceau said, while I tried to keep the tell-me-something-I-don't-know look from spreading across my face. "I'm sure it's not herniated." (So was every other doctor). "Some discomfort might be alleviated through traction."

I told him I had already tried traction and it didn't work. Then he said: "Your condition could go away, but it might be permanent."

Permanent? PERMANENT? After all I had been told about needing a few months of complete rest, after being convinced that my stop-and-start season was why I felt steady pain and soreness all year, I wasn't prepared to believe that there was a chance my pain might not go away by the end of the summer.

Pierre and I met with Bill in Montreal later that month. After we told him that we had solicited the advice of an independent expert who felt my injury was more serious than Dr. Minkoff had led us to believe, Bill floored me by asking if I had any desire to finish my career with Montreal. Although we had said time and again that my current contract was going to be my last, Bill offered me another two years (one plus an option) for $500,000 per year and suggested that he could trade me to the Canadiens.

Take a breath, Boss.

I had fantasized about playing for the Canadiens a number of times throughout my career, mostly during the first three or four years, before Lucie learned to drive and before we cured our occasional homesickness. We considered me playing out my option and trying to sign with the Canadiens as a free agent in 1980 and 1982, but only briefly. The Islanders had been good to us. We were Stanley Cup champions. I had Trots as a centerman and Trots as a friend. And the pressure I put on myself to perform was more than enough. I didn't need the pressure of being the high-priced free agent coming home to play in front of the toughest hockey critics in the world.

Each time Lucie and I or Pierre and I considered Montreal, we came up with the same answer: why rock the boat?

When Bill suggested it, though, I didn't even consider those reasons. I told him I wasn't going to think about anything until my back got better and if it did, I wouldn't consider talking about a new contract until my old one expired.

That was the end of that. I did, however, feel very good about Bill for asking. He did me a favor by asking if I wanted to add a new final page to my NHL career. It was another example of his undying loyalty to the players who had brought him four Stanley Cups and built his organization into one of hockey's best. Bill took a lot of criticism for hanging on to his Stanley Cup veterans long after they lost their value. Although I was one of his critics, I've grown to admire his long-term loyalty. A team does not win on talent alone. Bill bred pride, security and loyalty treating his players well without spoiling them. We were all better players and better men for it.

Would Bill have been loyal enough to grant me permission to play for Canada in the 1988 Olympics? We'll never know. But I considered asking. I had dreamed of playing for Canada in '88 from the moment the IOC deemed NHL pros eligible after the '84 Olympics. I was in awe of the Olympic atmosphere, something I had never considered when I was an amateur. I was willing to offer Bill something in return, like the right to extend my contract another year, for the opportunity to leave the Islanders to compete in Calgary.

By 1986, when I would have had to talk to Bill and the Canadian Amateur Hockey Association, my back had thrown that dream out the window. I never did raise the subject. Would it have bothered me to leave in the middle of a season if we were fighting for first place or a playoff spot? It probably would have, but after giving ten years to the organization I would have done it. Maybe it would have been a little selfish, but it would have been the chance of a lifetime, something I would have been foolish to pass up.

Anyway, I passed up Bill's offer to work a deal with the Canadiens. When we finished that subject, I was told that Dr. Minkoff suggested I visit another specialist, Dr. Peter Fowler, an orthopedic surgeon at the University of Western Ontario. My appointment was for July 29 at the university's hospital in London, Ontario, a short flight from Montreal.

I bumped into Kerry Fraser while I waited for Dr. Fowler. I usually don't hold grudges, but that night in the Garden when Fraser allowed me to get mugged and then hit me with a misconduct for complaining about it was fresh in my mind. I mumbled hello and turned away, but Kerry told me that he, too, had an appointment with the doctor. He offered to give me a lift to the airport after my exam and I said OK.

When the technician informed me that my examination would start with X-rays and an MRI, I thanked her for the warning and headed straight to the bathroom. I didn't stop for a drink of water. I had learned my lesson. After the hour in the coffin, I was escorted to Dr. Fowler's office. He introduced me to yet another specialist, Dr. Stewart Bailey, who, like every back expert before him, asked me to explain the history of my problem.

Figure-eight ... left side ... collision with Denny ... it hurts when I bend forward ... Philly bus ride ... Shawn Burr in Detroit ... sprained knee against Washington ... this is a recording.

Dr. Bailey twisted, turned and examined me for about five minutes and said, "Well, I don't think it's a disc problem because if it was, it would hurt when you bend forward."

Doo-do-doo-do, doo-do-doo-do. Was this *The Twilight Zone*, or what? I had just, and I mean *just*, finished telling and showing him how most of my pain came from bending forward. So then he said, "Well, then it may be a disc problem."

Thanks, Doc.

He suggested I return another day so he could take more tests. "I'll perform the tests and then we can go play some golf," he said. Honestly.

When I saw Dr. Fowler again, I was fuming. "I wasted a whole day here and nobody's told me anything that I haven't heard before," I said. "And what about the results of the MRI?"

"They aren't ready yet," Dr. Fowler replied. "And besides, I don't think they'll show anything."

"I wish you would have said that before I took the test," I replied .

"Did you come here expecting a miracle?" Dr. Fowler asked.

"No," I said angrily. "But I didn't expect this."

I forgot about Fraser and I left. I jumped into a cab, headed for the airport and flew home more disgusted, frustrated and disappointed than ever.

By now the growing team of physicians was pretty certain that my pain was coming from two worn-out discs between the L4–L5 and L5–S1 vertebrae in my lower back, just as Dr. O'Leary had suggested after my first thorough examination ten months earlier. Dr. Minkoff recommended injecting the facet-joint area with novocaine to see if that alleviated the pain. Pierre called former Montreal defenseman Jacques Laperriere, who recommended I visit the Canadiens' team physician, Dr. Eric Lenczner.

I thought I was going to Dr. Lenczner for the facet-joint injection, but first he and an orthopedic surgeon from Montreal General Hospital named K.C. Chan examined me. They suggested a few weeks of physiotherapy with Alain Sheldeman, the trainer of the defunct Canadian Football League Montreal Concordes. Sheldeman made a few visits to my home, but that didn't help. A few days later I checked into Montreal General (more X-rays, of course) for the injection, which didn't help, either.

Craig Smith, who had done a great job playing information coordinator and medical mediator, was growing tired of relaying reports from Dr. Minkoff, to Dr. Lenczner, to me, to Bill and to all the other doctors who were dropping in and out of the picture. Craig sensed tension between me and Dr. Minkoff, who received a letter from Dr. Fowler saying that I called my visit to him a waste of time.

Craig wanted us to share ideas face-to-face. So on August 28, Bill, Craig, Dr. Minkoff, Alain Sheldeman, Pierre and I met in Dr. Lenczner's office. I had grown to trust Dr. Lenczner, but I didn't like his conclusion. He described my bad back as a condition common to thousands of people across the country. He didn't think there was anything we could do.

Dr. Minkoff persisted. He scheduled an appointment for September 22 in New York with Dr. Thomas Errico of the New York University Medical Center. Dr. Errico repeated tests I had taken and scheduled me for tests I never had taken before. By the end of the month I had a myelogram that ruled out the possibility of cancer (just the mention of cancer scared the wits out of me until that test came back negative) and a discogram that confirmed Dr. O'Leary's first diagnosis: I had deterioration of two discs in my lower back, a problem surgery would not repair.

So what was I supposed to do?

On October 5, three days before the start of what was going to my 11th and last season, the Islanders called a press conference and Bill announced that "our plans for the season do not include Mike Bossy. Our concern is to get Michael's health back to that of a normal person walking the street. Only then would we consider any future options regarding Michael's career."

Following the press conference, I met Sherrie Glasser, a Westbury physical therapist who for the next five months became my coach. Sherrie and Dr. Minkoff designed a program consisting of moist heat, electrotherapy, soft tissue stretching and gradual flexibility and strengthening. Except for one week in October, when Lucie and I took Tanya and Josiane to Florida, and the Thanksgiving and Christmas holidays that we spent in Quebec, I reported to Sherrie each Monday, Wednesday and Friday at 8:30 a.m. from October until February.

My body felt stronger. My back felt worse. On March 5, Sherrie wrote Dr. Minkoff a letter that detailed my progress and reported that I still felt "persistent local lumbar pain, left more involved that right . . . . In light of the above, Mike has decided to train at our center for fitness and overall conditioning and to be discharged from physical therapy."

I represented Titan at an international sports forum in Munich, West Germany, from February 23 to 28. On March 1, I agreed to see Dr. Joseph Artusio, a Cornell University Medical Center pain clinic specialist at New York Hospital in Manhattan. I didn't know what a pain clinic was, but since Dr. Artusio was recommended by Dr. George Gilbert, the Islanders' internist, I agreed to see him to find out if there was a form of treatment he could suggest that I hadn't tried yet.

What a fiasco this was.

First of all, I was instructed to bring every relevant X-ray, MRI report, CAT scan, myelogram and diagnosis from all the doctors I had seen. I called Craig and asked where they were.

Craig didn't know.

Dr. Minkoff didn't know.

Nobody knew.

They had been misplaced, somewhere between Montreal, London, Ontario, New York City, Long Island, and Whoknowswhere. While everybody insisted they had forwarded them somewhere else, the only piece of physical evidence I could take to show Dr. Artusio was the report from the first MRI I took in January 1987. I was ready to scream.

I recited my case history to one of the doctor's assistants, who examined me by having me bend a million different ways. Then the doctor walked in and the assistant said. "He has a sore back, he hurt it last year, he doesn't have a herniated disc, there doesn't seem like

there's a problem with the disc, it seems like a muscular problem."
That took her about three seconds.

"I think we should give you an injection," Dr. Artusio said to me.
Injection? "Whoa," I replied. "I was told by Dr. Gilbert that this
was going to be a consultation. What's going on?"

Dr. Artusio explained that my pain could be alleviated by injecting
a form of steroid into my back. When he started explaining how he'd
deaden the nerves, I tuned out. There was no way I was letting this guy
touch me.

I got dressed in ten seconds. "I'll think about it," I said as I ran for
the door. Now maybe I had become too paranoid or too cynical of
these so-called back experts, but how could a doctor who looked at
one MRI report and didn't take an X-ray be confident enough to stick
a needle into a patient he met two minutes earlier?

Dr. Artusio had no information about me. He didn't know who I
was. Before I left, he asked me one more question. "Has this problem
hindered your career?"

March 10, 1988, was Mike Bossy Night at Nassau Coliseum. Bill told
me a month earlier that the Islanders wanted to honor me for all I'd
done for the organization. My first reaction was, "Why now?"

For a few days I thought about it. "Why not now? Nothing was
going to change. They weren't asking me to retire and I wasn't retiring.
Bill said it was simply something he wanted to do. The more I
considered the gesture, the better I felt. My employer wanted to thank
me for the work I had done. I didn't care if it was March 10, 1988, or
March 10, 2000. I was flattered.

The public relations department asked me if I would wear my
uniform for the pregame ceremony, but I declined. I didn't want to
play with the fans' emotions. I wanted to thank them for their support
over the years, their patience last season as I struggled with my health,
and their encouragement and get-well wishes this season. The Islanders were playing the Quebec Nordiques that night, which meant my
friends and family back home would be able to watch on TV.

It was one of the happiest nights of my life. The Islanders introduced Mom, Lucie, Josiane and Tanya. Pierre, Carol, Bob and
Lucie's brother Bernard flew in from Quebec. Bill and Al said some
kind words. I was showered with gifts. the second-best of which was a
trip for Lucie and me to Paris.

As I walked to the microphone with the crowd cheering, Trots
delivered my best gift. He leaped off the bench, skated over to me,

grabbed my hand and whispered, "I'm proud of you, buddy."

I didn't know what to say. I knew it wasn't part of the ceremony, but somehow I sensed that he was going to do it. That's Trots. As close as we've been, we hadn't had many emotional moments. But that was one of them.

Peter Stastny of the Nordiques had me laughing when he presented me with a familiar-looking silver bowl. Quebec didn't have a gift to present me, so one of the Islanders' PR people grabbed the Henry Saraceno Award (the Isles present it to their top training camp rookie each year) out of the office trophy case and had him present it to me. Stastny didn't know what was going on.

"Could you believe this is all we're giving you?" as we smiled for the photographers. Breathe easy, Peter. Your front office sent me a very nice silver tray a month later.

Josiane loved being on the ice in front of so many people, knowing she was in the spotlight and on television. Tanya couldn't have cared less. She wanted the whole production to end so she could get upstairs and attack the pretzels and potato chips. The Islanders gave us the use of their sky box for the game, and while Quebec beat us, 4–3, my friends presented me with a bunch of gag gifts. My favorites were a toy boat and a miniature car from one of our neighbors, Joanne Messina. "See, we told you you'd get a boat and a car tonight," Joanne yelled just after Bill walked in.

Bill laughed. "We didn't get you one, because we knew your friends did."

While everyone had a great time digging into the food, I watched the game. I noticed something incredible. It was 1979 and Trots was the NHL's dominant centerman again. He was hitting like he hadn't hit in years, skating like he was 23 years old again. He scored two first-period goals to give us a 2–1 lead, and when we didn't win, he was crushed.

"You have these chilling moments in your life and this was one of them," he told *The New York Daily News*. "For a high, it's right up there with winning the Stanley Cups. That's how special this night was. I wish Boss was ... it was like I was talking to him all night. Not with words, just the moments we used to have on the ice, when I'd look over and he'd look back and we'd just nod, and we'd know what we're thinking."

Epilogue: The End?

I actually own an appointment book now.

Nobody leaves a neatly typewritten itinerary in my mailbox anymore. There are no monthly schedules on our living room table for me to grab, no message board hanging on the kitchen wall reminding me what time to be at practice, in the dressing room, or on a bus.

I became a civilian again in 1987–88, my off season. For the first time since Dad fitted me with skates and walked me up and down the hallway in our apartment on Meunier St. as a three-year-old, a hockey season started without me. I stayed home to root for my favorite team, the Islanders, and my favorite coach, my brother-in-law Pierre. I rooted against Calgary's Joe Nieuwendyk, who came close to my NHL rookie record of 53 goals and finished with 51. I rooted against Gretzky, whose string of consecutive 50-goal seasons ended at eight and left me with a record that should stand at least seven more years. If Lemieux doesn't tie me at nine straight in 1994–95, the record I cherish most will last until the twenty-first century.

In April and May, I worked as a special color commentator for Quatre Saisons, a French-language television station in Quebec, covering the Stanley Cup playoffs. During the Edmonton–Detroit semifinal series somebody asked me about Gretzky's durability. I said that he rarely absorbed cheap-shots because he rarely leaves himself vulnerable.

Why didn't I play that way? Because I was paranoid. I felt that I had to go into the corners and take abuse in front of the net to be considered a complete player because I didn't fight. I regret that now. If I wouldn't have been so conscious of my image as a pacifist, I might never have heard of Dr. Artusio and his pain clinic, MRIs and lumbar regions, Dr. Fowler and his golfing buddy.

On June 20, I saw another chiropractor, although I didn't tell Bill, Dr. Minkoff or Craig. They'll find out when they get the bill.

Retirement doesn't scare me. From the day I decided that I was only going to play until I was 31, I stopped dreading the final game of my career. From the time I was ten, I was going to be a professional hockey player. If I retire, I'll have to ask myself a question I haven't asked in 21 years: "What next?"

My off season permitted me to consider and experience some options. Karhu, Inc., Titan's parent company, which makes Titan sticks, has offered me a consulting position. Once I retire, whenever that is, after being treated so well by them for the last ten years I'll definitely stay on their staff in some capacity. It could be public relations, endorsements, sales or management. They've been kind enough to give me all the time I want to decide.

And there's television. Quatre Saisons, which first hired me part-time in 1987, has talked to me about becoming one of their full-time color commentators. If I don't play, I'll think seriously about it because I thoroughly enjoyed my brief stints as a member of the media. I loved asking questions instead of answering them. I loved staying close to the game.

Coaching? I don't have any desire to become a junior-league or NHL head coach, but if some GM offered me a job where the circumstances were right, I'd probably be foolish enough to accept it, if I could convince Lucie to let me take it. She's not too keen on the profession these days in light of how the Penguins treated her brother, firing him after one year. I don't think I'd be a good practice coach and I'm not sure I'd be a good strategist, but I'd be able to deal with players. The players are the game, so for that reason I think I could grow into a successful coach.

But I'm not counting on any offers.

I'm not counting on anything. Although my contract expires on June 30, I won't decide to play or retire until just before the start of the

1988–89 season. If I feel well enough in August, I'll skate for the first time since May 2, 1987. If by some fluke my back stops hurting, or some doctor surfaces with some miracle cure, I'll play one more year, the year I lost. But I'm going to have to be almost 100 percent to accept a new contract, because I won't go through the mental and physical pain I endured in 1986–87. I won't put my family through that again, either.

I desperately want to play one more season because I want to leave the NHL on my terms. From the day I was drafted, I designed and played my career exactly the way I wanted. Everything was ending the way I had planned until my back gave out. If I was healthy, I know I would have scored at least 50 goals in 1986–87 and at least another 50 in 1987–88. That's how I wanted to leave the game, with 11 straight 50-plus seasons, with more than 600 career goals, as the only player in NHL history never to score fewer than 50.

But if I can't, if the summer of 1988 isn't enough time for my back to get well enough, then I'll officially retire. And if I do, four Stanley Cups, nine straight 50s and 573 goals will have to be enough.

M.B.

June 24, 1988